T0199220

West Meets East in
Kazakhstan

West Meets East in
Kazakhstan

Life in and Around Almaty, Kazakhstan,
in the 1990's from the Perspective
of an American Expat

THOMAS E. JOHNSON

authorHOUSE®

AuthorHouse™
1663 Liberty Drive
Bloomington, IN 47403
www.authorhouse.com
Phone: 1 (800) 839-8640

Published by AuthorHouse 09/18/2015

ISBN: 978-1-5049-2811-3 (sc)
ISBN: 978-1-5049-2810-6 (e)

Library of Congress Control Number: 2015912802

Print information available on the last page.

CONTENTS

PREFACE

I first arrived in Kazakhstan 22 years ago, late in January 1993. Although I had visited Hungary, Czechoslovakia, Poland and western USSR by car in 1965 and worked on projects in Belgrade, Warsaw and Prague in the 1980s, my previous experience of Iron Curtain countries had not prepared me for the cultural differences I observed in Alma-Ata, as Almaty was then called. It wasn't exactly culture shock that I experienced but, during the course of everyday living in Almaty, I routinely encountered matters that were, to me, remarkable. Eventually, I did remark on some of them not just by letters faxed to friends and relatives but in a then new, but now defunct, English language newspaper, *The Almaty Herald*. I wrote a series of articles that make up much of this book.

My initial idea was to write short notes on legal topics, the sort of informative pieces that are a bit helpful but also remind readers that I am a lawyer, in town, and would like to have clients. Sadly, another expatriate American lawyer, James Varanese, beat me to the punch. Undaunted, I began writing about my perspective on what I was experiencing by living and working in a post-Soviet, recently independent republic that was in the throes of casting off the command economy and adapting to the open market economy.

An age-darkened sample front page of *The Almaty Herald* newspaper before it switched to the broadsheet format.

On November 18, 1996, I wrote to the editor of *The Almaty Herald* to say that I was delighted to see the appearance of the newspaper and that I would like to supports its development. I proposed to write a series of "light reading" articles on topics of interest to foreigners who visit or reside in Almaty. Avoiding politics, economics and the current activities of foreigners, "my objective would be to concentrate each article on some aspect of life and living in Almaty which I have found interesting and which I think will be of interest to foreigners." My offer was quickly accepted, and the first article was published shortly thereafter.

As the years passed while in Kazakhstan my perception dimmed, I am sure, so that I no longer noticed or paid much attention to cultural differences or what had seemed to me to be oddities of local life. Nevertheless, I kept writing articles for *The Almaty Herald* in which I described some of the diversions that we foreigners could enjoy on day trips out of Almaty. Many of my foreign friends and acquaintances felt a bit claustrophobic in Almaty, or suffered from a kind of cabin fever, which made them yearn for a change of scenery. Usually that meant a dash back to Western Europe or perhaps a shopping trip to Moscow. For my part, as an avid skier, I took full advantage of the great outdoors during the winters, mainly at Shymbulak (called Chimbulak in my articles as it was earlier called), and then, in the summer, I explored the surrounding countryside on trips manageable in a single day. Some of those articles are to be found in this book.

I have not reprinted in this book the article on the meaning of the first names of individuals. Local residents have a wide array of first names that fascinated me and were outside my previous experience. Regrettably, I went into print on that article far too soon, and I continued over the years to meet many, many more individuals with, to me, unusual names.

Of course some of the comments in my old writings will now seem archaic, no longer applicable, or out of joint with modern Almaty. For example, my instructions on how to get to Ile-Alatau

National Park from Almaty aren't useful now that a new highway has been constructed.

My articles were spread out over several years with the result that careful readers will note some duplications. For example, I think two or three articles note that some hungry miners or bikers gorged themselves at the Italian Restaurant. I also mention skiing a great deal. It is a love of my life and I had the fantastic opportunity to pursue my sport while in Almaty. Each article stands alone, and I haven't tried to edit out possible overlap.

Most of the articles are faithfully reprinted but I have made some slight changes in a few of them. The name of the country in English initially was "Kazakstan" – without the "h" – and my articles in 1996 and 1997 spelled the name that way. However, when it was discovered that the country had signed the United Nations Charter as "Kazakhstan" in the English version, people quickly fell in step, as I did. To minimize the chance of receiving letters pointing out my typographical errors, this book consistently uses "Kazakhstan."

In addition, in a few cases, I have added some introductory information or concluding paragraphs, in italics, mostly to recognize that there has been much change since the 1990s.

I had fun writing the articles and usually was not wanting for a topic. If you discover that I talk quite a lot about myself in the articles, please recall that many people in the small expatriate community in Almaty in the 1990s knew me personally or of me. And I wasn't writing a scientific analysis of an emerging economy and the local people experiencing it.

You can contact me about anything in this book by sending an email to me at tom.johnson.book@aol.com and I will be sure to reply. If you have an "early expatriate" story to tell, share it with me.

Thomas E. Johnson

7 September 2015

1

HEY, WHERE AM I?

Do you recognize the place I describe below?

We occupy a very large and diverse geographical area buried deep in the heart of a vast continent, just about as far away from a saltwater ocean as you can get. Despite the physical dimensions, we have only an exceedingly small human population. We have a mountainous region with snow-capped peaks that offers mineral wealth and opportunities for the tourist and leisure time industries. The leisure activities include skiing – not great skiing, not Alpine skiing, but at least village-plus skiing. We also have seemingly endless desert areas, some with lunar landscapes, which are basically unoccupied by human beings. In some areas, large herds of wild animals run free. Hunting is not only possible but in fact draws professional and enthusiastic amateur hunters from long distances away during the hunting seasons. We have a large lake that offers both good fishing and recreational opportunities, and the lake is starting to attract tourists, sporty types and vacationers.

Our climate can only be described as harsh, sometimes brutally harsh. Our summers can be very hot, with the sun burning down unremittingly during the long days. As if that wasn't bad enough, the humidity can be very high during this period, draining one of energy. Large, vicious mosquitoes invade the area during the summer to the annoyance of everyone who ventures outside or who has the misfortune of having them buzzing around their bedroom at night.

For some reason, the mosquitoes seem to be more abundant and larger the further north one goes.

Winters can be cruel, at the opposite extreme of summer, with the winds blowing out of the Arctic region at gale force sweeping over our flat plains unopposed by any mountains or other geographical features to the north that might tame them. Snow covers the ground for several months of the year. The days are very short and the nights are long. The temperatures plunge to horrible lows. The ground freezes so deeply that, if someone dies in the depth of winter, the first thing that the survivors do is to build a charcoal fire at the cemetery to permit the grave to be dug in time for the funeral.

The growing oil industry is located mainly out in the Western region, and the flow of oil adds considerably to our economic strength despite the harshness of the climate which makes it a real struggle to reap this wealth. Of course, we also have other subsoil resources, especially gold up in the mountains, but it is unfortunate that we continue to concentrate on raw mineral production and do not have much by way of metal processing and derivative industries such as those that fabricate machines and other things that are made from the metals we produce.

In addition to the oil and mining industries, we are strong in the agricultural sector, being a net exporter of farming produce. In some regions, the farms are enormous in size, and during the growing season you can look out over oceans of grain. But in this industry, as in the oil and mining industries, we mainly export unprocessed grains and other agricultural products for conversion into food and other products elsewhere.

Life in the rural villages and on the farms is difficult, and despite the introduction of television and some of the other ingredients of modern life, many young people and some older people migrate to the cities in search of a better life and a better future. Some people even leave our area entirely, looking for better opportunities and an easier life elsewhere. This migration tends to cast a certain pall over the farming communities, and it also tends to cause some social unrest in the larger cities where the inflow of people from poorer areas must be digested.

We have an indigenous population that has its own language, its own culture, its particular style of clothing, and its own traditions. We also have had so many immigrants from abroad during the last generation or two that they now outnumber the indigenous people. Integration of these two groups and the preservation of the old culture and language are modern-day concerns that probably will remain with us for many years.

So, do you recognize this place? I do. This is the State of South Dakota, U.S.A., my home state in the middle of the United States where we have the Black Hills, the Williston Oil Basin, the Homestake Gold Mine, the Bad Lands, the prairies, the big lake on the Missouri River, the Lakota Indians and the Indian reservations, and the other features of the state where I grew up.

And I thought I had managed to get away from it all!

———⁓———

This article was published on 30 January 1977. Shortly after that, while attending one of the monthly meetings of the Business Roundtable of the U.S. Embassy, a man from Nebraska introduced himself to me, congratulated me on writing articles for The Almaty Herald, and laughingly told me that, when people back home in Nebraska ask him what Kazakhstan is like, he replies, "It's just like Nebraska!"

2

THE CONDOR HAS LANDED!

Lufthansa Airlines led the way in opening up the Republic of Kazakhstan to international air travel late in 1992. During the Soviet era, the Kazakh S.S.R. – with its rocket testing facilities, the spacecraft launching facility at Baikonur, the ICBM silos, and the atomic bomb testing grounds – was pretty much off limits to foreigners, and those few who did manage to get here came primarily by way of Moscow or one of the other rare entry points for international travel to the Soviet Union. Upon achieving independence, the Republic of Kazakhstan suddenly faced the need to operate its own customs and passport control service, and it faced the challenge of opening itself up for the growing number of arriving foreigners.

In fact, however, it was not exactly "Lufthansa" that led the way. "Condor" landed here first, this being the charter flight subsidiary of Lufthansa. Why this was so is not clear. Maybe Lufthansa preferred to use Condor to test out the route, to see what level of traffic would develop, and to permit Lufthansa to withdraw quietly and without adverse publicity in the event that this new and exotic route did not work out. Maybe it was simply a matter of aircraft and crew availability. Anyway, it seems that the new route worked out very well indeed and in not too many months Lufthansa officially took over the route from Condor.

Condor's airplanes are basically laid out as a single class, as one expects on a charter flight, with all the seats being identical with economy class quality. However, for the flight to Almaty, a dividing curtain was installed to segregate the business class up front from the economy class in the rear. Those who sat in front of the curtain were in business class, and those who sat behind the curtain were in economy class. That was useful information to know because, without that curtain, there were very few clues that there was a business class. Nevertheless, despite the lack of significant differences between the two sections, the business class very quickly caught the attention of international business travelers. What a relief it was to be able to skip the horrors of travelling by way of Moscow's airports at that time when the real objective was to come to Almaty. Typically, Condor's business class was entirely filled whereas, in the economy class, one could often stretch out on two or more seats for the long, dark winter flights. On one rare occasion, there were a few vacancies in business class and I, as a frequent traveler, was offered the chance of a free upgrade. I declined. Back in the economy section, three empty seats were available to me each of which was exactly the same size as the seats in the crowded business class.

As a frequent traveler, I observed that on virtually each successive Condor flight on which I travelled the grey dividing curtain had been moved a few notches toward the rear. Little by little, the business class section was threatening to take over the entire airplane. The question passed my mind whether or not there is some rule for international flights that prohibits a commercial airplane operator from converting an entire aircraft to business class. I never did learn the answer from Condor. By the time the dividing curtain was nearing the tail of the plane, Condor was retired from the route and Lufthansa introduced the popular Airbus on which a business class ticket really buys a business class seat with business class service.

Many of the first flights to Almaty stopped as well at Tashkent. I think there was a certain rhythm to these flights, like one time going from Frankfurt to Almaty to Tashkent and then back to Frankfurt while on other days the airplane would fly Frankfurt-Tashkent-Almaty-Frankfurt. Tashkent probably was included on the route because, during those early days of the independence, the Republic of Kazakhstan experienced serious shortages of aviation fuel, and it would have been crucial to pass through the better stocked Uzbekistan. Alternatively, the Tashkent stop might have been part of early testing of the strength of both routes. Those flights, however, were particularly rough on passengers who were going from Tashkent to Frankfurt. They spent hours at the airport in Tashkent awaiting the arrival of the middle-of-the-night flight from Frankfurt. Then, after the one-hour flight to Almaty, they had to deplane while the aircraft was serviced for a couple of hours. At long last, their flight took off for the 7-hour flight to Frankfurt.

Not every flight left Almaty on time, of course, and I can remember at least one flight that was thwarted by bad weather for so long just before Christmas 1993 that everyone returned to their hotels or apartments in Almaty. In a triumph of human endurance over the perils of travel, virtually all of us discovered when the flight was going to leave, and we made it back to the airport in time to board the otherwise unannounced resumption of the flight.

There certainly were some unexpected and even jolting features to those early flights. On one occasion we hit a pothole – that is what the pilot called it – in the runway just as the airplane landed at Almaty. The tires survived but the front wheel mechanism was broken. The pilot tried to steer the plane by using the rudder and by adjusting the thrust of the engines, but to no avail. He simply could not steer the plane on the ground. We sat there for a very long time in the middle of the runway until a suitable tractor was located which towed us to within walking distance of the terminal. Nowadays a tractor is always used to park the arriving aircraft but in 1993-94 the practice was for the arriving aircraft to come as close as it could to the terminal and then swing around quickly in a bravado maneuver so as to prepare the aircraft for departure without the aid of a tractor. There was no need for a passenger bus either - passengers walked the short distance from the airplane to the terminal.

With regard to the broken wheel mechanism, there was naturally no replacement aircraft in Almaty and it was impossible for the outbound passengers to switch to some other carrier. There were none. Nor were there replacement parts in Almaty or experts to install them. I think the outbound flight was cancelled until Lufthansa could specially bring in the parts, the engineers and a replacement flight crew.

As strange as some of these flights seemed in the air, the really weird part was to arrive at the terminal in Almaty. This was at the building destroyed by fire in 1999, not the replacement opened in 2004. (The story at the time – joke? – was that the firemen raced to the Tax-Free Shop before tackling the fire, resulting in loss of the entire building.) In those days, arriving passengers were herded into the same lounge that currently is used only for international departures. The result was that arriving and departing passengers were not entirely segregated, and in the confusion some arriving passengers came precariously close to departing without yet having entirely arrived in the country.

Another noteworthy feature of these early flights was that the luggage was manhandled off the airplane in a labor-intensive and painstakingly slow manner compared to the aluminum containers which now permit bulk transport of the luggage. The items were then handed through a small window, one at a time. Normally there was no one on the inside of the window to accept them, and there certainly was no carousel, so passengers would often initiate a brigade, like a fire-fighting bucket brigade in an old Western movie, and the bags worked their way from the window to the other end of the room.

The procedures at Almaty International Airport have undergone continuous evolution and improvement even if these are rather modest in scope when compared to the changes at Heathrow, JFK and various other major airports which are constantly under construction and never finished. One of the first "improvements" was the installation of an 8-meter long conveyor belt that led away from the window through which the bags were handed. As before, however, no one manned the conveyor belt which simply carried the bags to its end where the bags dropped to the floor and accumulated in a pile. Since most passengers were still tied up in the slow-moving passport queue, the baggage area was entirely littered with bags piled on top of each other. In those days, practically everything conceivable arrived with the passengers. I do not recall ever seeing a kitchen sink but I certainly saw Western mattresses, a lot of computers and many other items of office furniture. You could tell when miners were on the plane because their heavily padlocked trunks which seemed to be filled with very heavy equipment would be among the last items for the unhappy baggage handlers to shove through that window.

Another feature of arriving in the very crowded and small arrivals hall is that most people checked quite a few pieces of luggage, boxes of office supplies and so on. Lone travelers quickly made friends with someone they thought they could trust as they struggled to accumulate their own pile of suitcases, boxes and so on while looking for the last remaining pieces and also peering past the customs officials in anxious search for their drivers.

Lufthansa probably has had a natural advantage over rival airlines so far as Kazakhstan is concerned, and this advantage may explain why Lufthansa was so quick to start the Almaty run. Lufthansa each year carries a large number of the ethnic German immigrants – locally referred to as returnees – who have a right to go back to Germany. It seems that the German government buys the tickets for the returnees and helps to fill up some of those otherwise under-used mid-week flights. Although a large number of ethnic Germans have already left Kazakhstan, one still sees immigrant groups on the airplanes. Not so long ago I was ousted from my favorite seat in the center section of the economy class where I hoped to snooze on four seats for the flight to Frankfurt. Virtually the entire center section was block booked for 50 ethnic Germans "returning" to Germany and a new life in the West.

As I recall, Condor, and then Lufthansa itself, ran the route for quite a long time with a twice-a-week service. Both of them worked in such a way that most people arrived in Almaty at the start of the week and most of them sought to leave on Saturday morning, having finished their week of work. I was aware of this both as a traveler myself and as a lawyer who faced the hordes of new and usually very demanding clients who arrived early in the week without any appointment and wanted their joint venture, company or representative office established before their scheduled Saturday departure. No one considered staying in Almaty for the weekend if it could possibly be avoided.

The Condor flights and the early Lufthansa flights were noted for a sense of adventure and anticipation that could not be suppressed. People wandered up and down the aisles introducing themselves, handing out their business cards, and looking for even the slightest information about what they might encounter when they arrived on the ground in the hope of gaining a slight advantage in this way. Many were pleased when they located one of us who had spent significant time in Almaty. "Oh, have you been there?", someone would say with a mixture of surprise and keen interest, and quickly other passengers would join in the impromptu conversations with their own questions about where to stay, how to cope, and what to do.

While foreigners continue to arrive for their first time in Almaty, they no longer seem to sense that they are entering an unknown part of the world, like stepping out on a strange planet where one simply does not know what to expect. They have missed what was for some of us a unique and interesting time to witness the opening up of a country.

3

THE AMERICAN EMBASSY
BUSINESS ROUNDTABLE

The United States opened its Embassy in Almaty in January 1992. To foster U.S. business interests, the Embassy sponsored what it called the "Business Roundtable" to which representatives of U.S. companies were welcomed each month. This soon became such a popular event that it outgrew the small premises on Furmanova Street. At that point the Embassy hired the amphitheater at Hotel Kazakhstan for meetings. The U.S. Embassy also encouraged the establishment of the American Chamber of Commerce in Kazakhstan which was founded in 1999. After that, the Business Roundtable became subsumed in the activities of the Chamber without the routine presence of Embassy personnel. Typically, AmCham has held a monthly luncheon with a featured guest speaker. While operated by the U.S. Embassy, the Business Roundtable created a quite open forum to exchange information, ideas, and experience of doing business in Kazakhstan. This article was written in December 1996 while the Business Roundtable was still a major event.

The American Embassy's Business Roundtable has become an institutional part of the business life of many U.S. companies with a presence in Almaty. Perhaps the Roundtable lacks some of its previous vitality but then the Almaty of today is not the Alma-Ata of February 5, 1993, when former Ambassador Bill Courtney convened the first session. In those days, the Embassy, which had only recently moved to the Furmanov Street premises, was an obligatory port of first call for almost all American visitors. The Embassy staff had been extending invitations to the Roundtable for several days. However, no one could guess how many people might attend. Only a very few American companies had established a presence in Almaty, and some of them were still in the "brass plate office" category.

Eventually about 20 people came, most being casual visitors who simply happened to be in Alma-Ata at that time. People who wanted to attend simply showed their passports and walked into the virtually unguarded Embassy. The outside gate was open. And there was no electronic gate to pass through on the inside of the Embassy. Indeed, once inside the building, it was possible in those days to stroll the halls, knocking on doors or just peeking into a room to try to locate someone.

The meeting started informally with stand-up drinks of coffee or juice in the Ambassador's own office. A local artist's gift painting of recently-elected Bill Clinton hung on the wall. Most of us were somewhat ill at ease. None of us had previously met each other and most of us did not know how to relate personally to an ambassador. The frontier atmosphere soon cured those problems. Moreover, it was nice to be in a warm and welcoming place because outside the snow was deep, the day was cold and fog hung over the city. After waiting for last-minute stragglers, we moved into the adjoining main conference room of the Embassy. The delegates sat around the tables that were arranged in a large square, with the grand piano shoved aside into one corner.

That first meeting set the pattern for subsequent sessions of the Business Roundtable. All persons present rose in succession to give their names and the name of the company they represented, and they were invited to add a few words that might be of interest to the others in attendance. Maybe someone else kept a complete list of attendees but here are the ones I remember:

William Courtney - U.S. Ambassador

Craig Karp - Commercial and Economic Officer of U.S. Embassy

Thomas E. Johnson - Partner, Faegre & Benson (London, Almaty)

Iliana Haleen - Faegre & Benson (Frankfurt)

Alla Lee - Faegre & Benson (Almaty)

Bernard Bradley - Agland Investment Services, Inc.

Rick Broussard - Pepe International

Anna Pechersky - Pepe International

Stella Aris - Ernst & Young

Britt Allen Shaw - Joint Stock Service Company (Moscow)

Fred and Sarah Haberman - U.S. Asian Enterprises

Catherine Cosman - Free Trade Union Institute

Douglas R. Aden - Coudert Brothers, visiting from New York

Russell Ragsdale - Head Chef at Bastau Restaurant

Sara J. Rhoads - Baker & McKenzie (Moscow)

Dr. Chan Young Bang - Head of Kazakhstan Institute for Management and Economic Research and economic consultant to President Nazarbayev

Most of the attendees were only briefly in Almaty to scout out business prospects -- some never to return -- but one of the delegates, whose identity I have forgotten, stunned all the rest of us when he arose, identified himself, and then announced, incredibly, that "I have been here for one year" and, amid peals of knowing and sympathetic laughter, he added, "and I probably look like it!"

The exchange of calling cards has diminished in importance as a feature of the Business Roundtable but on that first occasion in

February 1993, almost everyone eagerly sought and obtained cards from all others who were present.

The Ambassador gave a summary of recent developments of interest, and Craig Karp discussed economic matters. The featured speaker, Dr. Bang, then spoke on the future economic course of the country that had been set by President Nazarbayev who, Dr. Bang candidly reported, sometimes took his advice on economic matters and sometimes didn't.

During the remainder of 1993 and for many months thereafter, the American Business Roundtable admirably served the purpose of being the main clearing house of useful information, a source of authoritative announcements about new legislation and government policy (U.S. and Kazakhstan), and a welcome opportunity to briefly attain a sense of community among a fairly small band of hardy expatriates who otherwise were pursuing their own business in relative isolation in what could only be described as a challenging, even daunting, environment. Of course, the Business Roundtable continues to serve many of these same functions today -- the U.S. Embassy locally embodies the strong interests of the United States in the Republic of Kazakhstan, and this is reflected in the Business Roundtable. Nevertheless, over the years, other means of achieving some of these objectives inevitably have come into existence and now share the stage with the Business Roundtable.

4

HARD TIMES IN KAZAKHSTAN

The early 1990's were a tough time to be in Kazakhstan for businesses, consumers, visitors and the local inhabitants in general.

Life had already been difficult during Perestroika (beginning in 1987) but the economic infrastructure really crumbled during the early years of Kazakhstan's independence. The breakup of the Soviet Union combined with the collapse of demand for Kazakhstan's heavy industry products resulted in a sharp contraction of the economy starting in 1991. The steepest decline in GDP came in 1994, the year after I arrived in Almaty. Only in 1995-97 did the economy start gathering steam as the pace of the government's program of economic growth and privatization quickened, resulting in substantial shifting of assets into the private sector. The macroeconomic story for Kazakhstan does not disclose the hard times that entrepreneurs were experiencing and that individuals were suffering as they tried to carry on with their lives.

I can't do justice in a brief write-up to the story of how life was lived in those harsh years, but I can provide a few glimpses based on my personal experience of the hardship.

Lights Out – Kazakhstan has an abundance of coal but that didn't prevent Almaty from suffering from electricity shortages in 1993 and 1994. In addition to announced schedules for rolling blackouts when our office was rendered useless on designated days, we suffered from loss of electricity on a number of other occasions due to repairs in the street. With no operational computer, copying machine or fax, we were dead in the water as far as business was concerned. Then the bright idea occurred to bundle up our equipment and decamp to my apartment. As I recall, residences didn't suffer from intentional blackouts. This was not very convenient, of course, but I suppose these occasions contributed to a sense of team building. Which reminds me that our people naturally referred to our office as a "collective," and they easily thought of doing things together outside the office, such as going to the mountains on a weekend day.

Lack of electricity wasn't the only problem with utilities. A huge main water supply pipe was installed near my apartment which left us totally without water for many days. The road was dug up along several blocks to remove the rusted out pipe for replacement. Just think about it. No shave, no shower, no tea, no flush of the toilet, no nothing, and it was the summer time.

The Knock on the Door – One of the banes of running an office in Almaty in the mid-1990s was the frequent appearance of peddlers at our door. An equal bane was the enthusiasm of our staff to let them in so as to inspect their wares and haggle over the price. The worst peddlers were the ladies who came bearing jewellery, perfumes and the like. Our women simply could not resist the call of shopping. I came to understand that the peddlers were offering things for sale that were not found in the shops. How the visitors came to have such items while the shops didn't I never learned.

As the boss, I didn't want this disruption and loss of time but as a human I understood the need of deprived people (who were now earning a respectable salary) to take advantage of the purchasing opportunities presented to them.

In the end, I took my own opportunities with door-to-door sales people. One day a woman came to our office selling alarm clocks. I soon found myself in a buying mood after looking at the polished brass clocks with two bells on top for the hammer to strike. The winning feature for me was the "Made in Kazakhstan" label on it.

Turns out the clocks were made at Almaty's torpedo factory. Torpedo factory? In Almaty? In land-locked Central Asia, at a vast distance from any ocean? Yup. Almaty. The Soviet Union spread the production of all kinds of goods, including military hardware, around the countries and regions that made up the USSR, and Almaty was awarded the torpedo factory. I guess the factory management was scrambling in the early 1990's to find some relevance to the new conditions and came up with clocks, not being too different from some of the internal controls of a torpedo.

As noted below, I also succumbed to buying handmade carpets from a door-to-door peddlers.

Alarm clock manufactured
by the former torpedo
factory in Almaty.

Underfoot – I needed a carpet for my apartment but none could be found in the shops. Then, one day, the aunt of one of our translators phoned the office to announce that a shop on Kurmangazy Street very near to Furmanova Street had just received a supply from the local carpet factory. We were very busy with work for clients so I couldn't immediately dash off to the shop. The next morning, on the way to work, I stopped at the shop. Not a carpet was in sight. Every last one of them had been purchased on the day of delivery.

I did eventually buy not just one carpet but at least seven of them. People in the countryside were desperate for cash and started selling their personal possessions, including carpets, some of which had been dismounted from the walls where they had hung for years. An entrepreneurial man scoured the outlying villages and assembled a collection of handmade carpets. One day he came to our office building calling door-to-door on the different tenants. When I showed interest he and his helper carried in a selection of carpets, some as big as four metres by three metres. They unfolded them on our conference room floor, one on top of the others. I bought a couple of them for as little as US $150 each. That was less than his initial asking price and I probably could have driven him down lower. In due course he returned with more carpets, and I continued buying for my apartment, for my grown-up children in England, and for the wall of our conference room. They are durable, certainly memorable for me, and attractive. Some have the year of production and the name of the creator woven into the design.

Over the years I took all but one of the carpets out of the country as personal luggage on the airplane. First, however, I had to take two photographs of them to the National Museum across from the Presidential Palace for certification that they were not of such historical value as to prevent their export. The carpet that remains in Kazakhstan is on the floor of my apartment waiting to greet me on each return to Almaty.

Once when I went to the National Museum, I asked one of our translators to go with me. I wanted certification for two carpets, and I anticipated that I might be faced with unexpected issues beyond my Russian language capabilities. She gave instructions to our driver, and the first thing I knew was that we were buying a box of chocolates. Sometimes I am a bit slow about things, and I didn't quite see what the chocolates had to do with getting export permission for my carpets. The photos were in order and the carpets were not that unusual. We proceeded to the museum. Well, immediately upon arrival at the desk of the lady in charge, the box of chocolates was presented. Nothing was said. My translator didn't call it a gift. The lady didn't officially accept the box. It just sat on her desk. My business was quickly concluded with no questions asked and we left without the box of chocolates.

Fax machine – I imported our first fax machine as carryon luggage on the airplane. It was a light-weight but sturdy model without some of the more common bells and whistles of fax machines but we worked it until it practically overheated.

Fax machines were almost unheard of in Almaty in 1993. Which reminds me that what seems to have been the first fax machine in Kazakhstan was owned by the Akimat (city administration), having been presented to the Akim (mayor) of Almaty some time before I arrived. It was a gift from the City of Tucson, Arizona. Strange as it may seem, Tucson and Almaty signed "twinning agreements" on 2 June 1989, a couple of years prior to Kazakhstan's independence, and prior to the arrival of practically any foreign investors. The visiting delegation from Tucson brought a fax machine with them as a gift in the expectation that it would facilitate communication between the twinned cities. On a subsequent visit to Almaty, the delegation inquired why it was that they never received replies to their many faxes. They were told that, as the President of Kazakhstan did not have a fax machine, it did not seem proper for the Akim of Almaty to be using one. The machine was kept in a locked cupboard.

Tucson played a prominent role in the difficult years of transition out of the Communist system and economy. An Arizona company joint ventured with the Presidential Administration in the operation of the Dostyk Hotel. This became the hotel of choice for early investors, mainly the big oil companies, assuming their visitors got the nod of approval from the Presidential Administration. The chief chef of the impressive restaurant came from Tucson. The Dostyk Hotel was one of the first places in Almaty to take credit cards in payment of bills, causing a surprise to many people when they later saw their credit card statements. The debt was shown as being to Fair Tradewinds of Tucson. It turned out that all credit card payments were telephoned to Tucson for processing. The twinning committee also persuaded doctors and other medical people to spend time in Almaty in order to help train local healthcare people.

Something on Which to Write Home About - As our work volume picked up and we needed more paper supplies, it soon became apparent that regular white A4 paper was difficult to come by. Indeed, soon it simply was not available. I carried reams with me each time I went to the West but this could not meet our need. We started using the only alternative – light brown paper, in other words paper that had skipped the bleaching process.

The paper mills in Siberia, being the source of paper for Kazakhstan, had apparently run out of bleach and couldn't find a new source as the Soviet Union's economy unravelled. Like others, we learned to live with that paper. However, the system breakdown of the Soviet Union continued and even unbleached paper became difficult to buy. Happily, that aunt of our translator phoned us again one day to report that she know where we could purchase 80 kilos of paper. Wow, were we excited! We could hardly believe our good luck. When our driver returned to the office with the paper, however, the excitement dimmed a bit. The paper was brown as usual but it was longer than A4 in size and not a single corner was cut at a right angle. It was as if someone overtaxed the guillotine which then botched the cuts. Our unfazed translators got out their scissors and re-cut the edges so that the paper would feed in our computer printer and the fax machine.

A bit later, when we established ABN-Amro Bank Kazakhstan, I was so pleased that the bank's representatives who came to Almaty to sign the documents followed our request and brought with them vast supplies of white A4 paper. They didn't just bring a couple of reams of paper, they carried two full cartons which gave us 10 reams. We probably used less than one ream for all the incorporation documents, and the remaining paper carried us through for weeks to come. After having become accustomed to using brown paper for so long, my staff marvelled at how pure white the paper was and how neatly cut the corners were.

Sunday Lunch – In the fall of 1993, on a Sunday, I overheard a strange sound out in the courtyard formed by a number of apartment buildings. It seemed as though someone had run over a cat or perhaps a dog. Curiosity got the better of me and I peered out from my balcony. Lo and behold, there were two men skinning and gutting two sheep.

They had dug a hole near the public clotheslines and had hung the carcasses from one of the sturdy clothesline poles. As I watched, they started to call out "lamb for sale". Soon people descended from their apartments, happy perhaps that Sunday lunch was going to be a meaty meal. The food distribution system had broken down, shops had irregular supplies of everything, and cash-hungry producers or middlemen had stepped in maximize their return with direct supply to consumers. Undoubtedly this was not a feasible (or hygienically acceptable) way to supply meat in the long term, but the demand was there and now, in our courtyard, the supply was there. It was not long before the men probably were wondering why they had brought only two sheep with them.

Milk for Sale – Just as with the direct sale of mutton or lamb, so it was with milk and other dairy products. Early every day outside my apartment building a tanker would arrive and the driver would bellow out that milk was for sale. People would descend from their apartments with jugs or other containers to buy their milk. As with the mutton, the distribution system had broken down but the cows kept producing and the dairy people needed revenue. Bypassing the usual retail outlets, they sent the tankers to concentrations of population for direct sale.

It never occurred to me in going to Almaty that I would one day find myself standing in a queue behind a milk tanker buying what may have been raw, unprocessed milk. But it tasted fine.

The Moveable Gas Stations – Fuel for cars and other vehicles became scarce. Sometimes our office driver would spend much of the day scavenging around the city searching for enough fuel to see us though another day or two. Of course he always carried an extra smelly container in the rear of his car in the hope that he would be permitted to do more than just fill the car's tank. Service stations were closing for lack of supplies. In response to this, tanker trucks began dispensing fuel at laybys on highways and at selected spots within Almaty. Like the milk tankers, they bypassed the previously established distribution structure and went straight for the ultimate consumers. These movable filling stations were potentially dangerous and one never knew for sure what octane or quality fuel one was buying.

Unfair Competition and the Cholera Scare – It had been a hot summer and the heat dragged on into September in 1994. In the middle of that month Almaty experienced a cholera outbreak, or as some might say, a cholera scare or hoax. I remember this clearly because it was at about the same time as France's President Mitterrand visited Almaty (16-17 September).

Schools were closed, fountains and ponds were drained, people bought up all the bottled water they could find, and the city's roads out of town were barricaded to prevent people leaving town or others from entering. In Soviet times, people needed permission to leave the city or town where they were registered and to enter another town. As a result, Almaty had checkpoints at which guards had examined documents of people entering or leaving the city. You can still see the checkpoint structures in some places, such as on the road eventually leading to Charyn Canyon.

But was there any cholera or was this a hoax? The Ambassador from Pakistan was absolutely convinced it was a hoax intended by its perpetrators to persuade the government to refuse to expand the number of charter flights from Pakistan to Almaty, or even to terminate those rights. Up that that point, Pakistan had rights to send a charter fight to Almaty once a week. It was a popular flight and a request had been made to add an extra weekly flight.

An unpleasant feature of life for air travellers at that time was congestion at the airport when airplanes arrived from Pakistan. Those planes were loaded with street vendors and bazaar stall sellers personally bringing in their supplies of inexpensive products. As a frequent air traveller, I was accustomed to seeing people waiting to go through passport control with lots of luggage. There was an occasion when I myself had 14 separate items with me – tied up boxes of office supplies, laptop computer, briefcase, curtain rods and a cordless teapot for my apartment, and other things. But those vendors had enormous rolled up things that they absolutely could not get through the baggage x-ray machines. It was a real curse to arrive in Almaty after a seven or eight hour flight only to discover that people were also clearing customs from a just-arrived plane from Pakistan.

The objection to the charter flights was not the congestion but the goods that were being brought in. Local shops and department stores saw the Pakistani flights as a threat – the goods were going to street vendors or to the Green Bazaar, undercutting the revenues of established businesses. The claim was that established, rent-paying businesses wanted to prevent the doubling of the number of charter flights and perhaps even to get a revocation of the single weekly flights.

Pakistan's ambassador checked the hospitals, the airline, the government and anyone else who could shed light on the claim about cholera. He knew of no cholera in Pakistan at that time, doubted that any infected person was on the flight, and could find no evidence of cholera in Almaty.

The ambassador's story had a ring of plausibility at the time, but to someone like me living in the midst of what might be a cholera outbreak, it didn't give much comfort. A news report on 14 September 1993 said that Kazakh authorities noted a sharp rise in cholera cases on Monday, 12 September. They announced emergency measures in an attempt to prevent an epidemic. Schools were closed until the end of the week, street markets were shut down, and workers were sent out to collect garbage. Air, train and bus routes from other Central Asian nations were closed to non-Kazakhs unless they had certificates proving they were free from infectious disease.

A 2008 scientific report confirms that there really was a cholera threat. The report is among the papers from a conference on "Emerging and Endemic Pathogens" that was sponsored by NATO

Science for Peace and Security in Tbilisi, Georgia, on 22-24 June 2008. On page 18, experts from the Kazakh Scientific Center for Quarantine and Zoomatic Diseases in Almaty and from the Aktobe Plague Control Station say that 65 patients came from Karachi to Almaty over the course of three days. To prevent an outbreak, temporary isolation facilities were set up at Almaty airport with room for 500 persons.

It was just as well that I limited my contact with others and drank my filtered water.

Be Prepared – Early on I discovered that we had to provide lunch for our staff. This employer obligation was a carryover from Soviet times. But it made practical sense for us too. If I released the employees for lunch, they instinctively would go home for lunch. None of them had ever made use of a café, it seemed, other than to attend a celebration of some sort. Moreover, cash was too precious to waste on eating out. Finally, home cooking was generally ranked above eating out. To me, though, the convincing argument was that our office would lose at least an hour or more per day if staff members went home for lunch than if I provided it. To me, still working on UK standards, the cafes were very inexpensive.

One of our translators always carried a folded up shopping bag in her purse and, while we were walking to a nearby restaurant, if she spotted a street vendor selling home grown cabbages or anything else of interest, she would stop, haggle over the price and then bring home her prize purchase. Of course many busy people in the West do some quick shopping on their lunch breaks but they are motivated primarily by saving time, to avoid shopping when they go home from the office. In my translator's case, she was doing what all experienced shoppers knew at that time of scarcity. "If you see it, buy it because it won't be there later."

Homeless People – My apartment building in Almaty is set back from a main street and is fronted by a large fountain, a monument and substantial surrounding gardens. Off to one side is an area almost entirely enclosed by a hedge of about one metre high. In 1993 and 1994, this became the sleeping area for several people while a few others regularly found shelter from the elements under the concrete staircase in front of the building. In the winter, we often found a man sleeping on the floor by a radiator in the hallway by the elevators. Needless to say, security was not very good in our building.

One Sunday a pleasant looking woman rang my doorbell and begged for food. I was so shocked that I could hardly react. My staff had cautioned me not to open the door for anyone, for good reason I suppose. But in this case I really couldn't turn the lady away although, quite frankly, I didn't stock much food in my apartment at that time.

Street Vendors – People were reduced to selling personal possessions on the street. 20 or 30 women lined the street near the Green Market, braving the winter weather and standing in snow while holding up garments and bric-a-brac for sale. A man who specialized in telescopes, binoculars, military items and various instruments, sold his wares on a small and tall folding table on the street near what was then the Marco Polo Hotel (Rahat Palace Hotel).

As I said, this was a tough time to be in Almaty.

Caption: Monument to the Poet Jambul
in front of the author's apartment building.

5

THE MARKET ECONOMY

My understanding is that, without any license, anyone can sell goods in the Green Market or in other areas as long as they can carry what they are selling. This seems to explain why one sees individuals wandering around in the Green Market selling all sorts of things – wooden cutting boards, axes, mop handles, and so on.

It is quite common to see hundreds of women on Zhibek-Zholy Avenue, just opposite to the long cluster of kiosks that are used for exchanging money or selling music tapes, CDs or videotapes. Generally, the women hold two products, one in each hand. These might be a pair of shoes in one hand and a pair of jeans in the other, or a packet of cigarettes in one hand and a woman's blouse in the other hand.

One wintry day in January 1994, when I ran this gauntlet of human merchandise displayers who were standing in the mush of semi-melted snow, my eyes settled on an elderly woman and I nearly shed a tear of deep pathos for her. There she was in this long line of comrades-competitors with their wares held up for examination by the indifferent members of the passing public. This woman, however, stood out from all the others. She was displaying three different items, not the normal two. In one hand she held a pair of shoes, in the other she had a pair of jeans, and there on her chest, held up by a wire coat hanger that was suspended from the top buttonhole of her winter coat, was a blouse. My heart lumped up in my throat, and I hoped that this enterprising, or desperate, woman really did have a 50% improvement in her chances of making a sale that day.

6

DIRECT MARKETING

One Sunday morning when I lived in an apartment in microdistrict Samal II, I heard digging noises outside in the rear of our complex of buildings which formed a kind of courtyard. Not long afterwards, I heard the noise of an injured or distressed animal. I thought it might possibly be a cat which had been run over by a car or otherwise hurt. The sound did not persist and there was no more commotion so I did not bother to peer out to see what was going on. A bit later, however, I did glance out the window and got a rude shock. Two dead sheep were hanging by their rear feet from the metal framework of the public clothesline with blood dripping from their slit necks into the holes that had been dug earlier.

The first sheep to be slaughtered was already being gutted. Within less than one hour both of them had been carved into pieces, sold for the Sunday lunch of residents of the apartment buildings, and the blood gathering holes had been filled in with rocks to thwart disturbance by the pack of dogs that run loose.

I was familiar with dairy people selling their products directly to the public from the back of a tanker or other vehicle, and I had seen people gathering while waiting for a car or van to arrive with freshly butchered meat. I had never before seen a case of shepherds like these bypassing the butchers in order to bring their products directly to the public, with absolutely no middlemen.

This was in the fall of 1993 when the economy of the country was in free fall.

7

HOW TO READ AN INVITATION

If you visit cities in South America and receive an invitation to an event of some kind, you might be surprised to see that the starting time is something like 19:00 "English time". This is not a reference to Greenwich Mean Time; if it was, then this invitation probably is for lunch, not dinner. In fact, the reference to English Time is a polite signal that this function really will start at 7:00 p.m. local time and guests are supposed to be there at that time.

In South America, the English are noted for arriving at the time stated on the invitation, often to the considerable surprise of the relaxed host and hostess who live in a far more carefree society than prevails in the United Kingdom. So "English Time" has become the way of informing all guests, but primarily local guests, that, for this particular function, they should plan their travel so that, when the clock strikes 7:00, they, like the English, will be pressing the buzzer on the entrance door.

Without the prompting of "English Time", it sometimes happens in Latin American lands that guests arrive more or less when they please, virtually without reference to the hour mentioned in the invitation. The host and hostess know that this will occur; the guests know it; and somehow both sides manage to make an evening of it. I guess it is only the English, or English speakers, who are distressed by such a casual attitude about the starting time. They arrive at the official starting time, stay awhile until they decide that the evening is a flop, and then depart, thereby missing the main activity which begins when the locals arrive which is long after the English speakers have gone home.

As the head of the sole international law firm office in Almaty, I received a large number of invitations to corporate and governmental receptions in the early 1990s. Some examples. Center Credit Bank celebrated its fifth anniversary as an independent bank in 1993 at a dedicated function house on the edge of town on what is now Dostyk Avenue. I vividly remember a gathering of miners at the Friendship Palace, next to the Dostyk Hotel, following a machinery trade show. There were also some social invitations, including one for dinner with U.S. Ambassador Bill Courtney at his very nice apartment on Kurmangazy Street. A number of important local people lived on that street in a block of low-rise buildings. In 1993 there still was a guard hut on the curb and huge timbers blocked through traffic. This was a VIP street in the Soviet era, and it still had its former trappings of importance. And so, I had my personal introduction into deciphering invitations.

Written invitations in Almaty do not have such obvious clues as "English Time" to help you to adjust your behavior to the local circumstances. The result is that foreign guests often are nonplussed by what they encounter at a function; they expect one thing, those hosting the function produce something else, and an underlying ill-ease results. Fortunately, local invitations sometimes do provide a few clues and, with some experience and understanding of local ways, one can minimize (but probably not avoid entirely) the risk of making a social misstep.

Whether or not you are skilled in the Russian language, you might have observed that the English text of an invitation often has a termination time as well as a starting time. If you flip the invitation over or read the facing panel, you might observe that the Russian text contains only a starting hour. Is this a secret prank played by the translators of the invitations or is this a printer's error that keeps getting repeated? Definitely not; this is simply an attempt by a sensitive host or hostess to cater to the quite different sensitivities of two quite different groups of people. To local residents, it is impolite and offensive to set a deadline for one's hospitality. How can you graciously welcome someone, give them food and drink, and enjoy their company, and then show them to the door at a pre-designated time that was established weeks ago when the invitations were printed?

To a large part of the English-speaking world, the sensitivities are entirely otherwise. They want (need) to know the nature, extent and duration of what it is they are getting into so that they can synchronize their plans and expectations with those of the host or hostess. They know that an invitation for something that begins at 7:00 p.m. and ends at 9:30 p.m. does not necessarily end exactly at 9:30 p.m. but, from about 9:15 onwards, they will know that the function is winding down and that it is time to start edging toward the door. In some cases, the designated departure time may be an indication that the rented hotel room or reception hall has been booked only for a limited period of time. The start/finish information is also useful for personal meal planning, for making arrangements to be collected by a driver, and for making other plans for the evening that are not inconsistent with the invitation event.

In fact, most functions which have a termination time for English speakers and an apparently unlimited duration for Russian speakers generally work out quite satisfactorily. Neither side is offended by the part of the invitation they read, and when the moment comes for shutting down the function, the English speakers have their pre-orchestrated and written cue as to when to depart and the Russian speakers, generally being polite about these things, start to take their leave when they see others doing so. Nevertheless, it often will happen that that last ones to be seen to be loading up their plates or taking yet another drink – while the English speakers are already saying their goodbyes – are local residents. Thinking that the function was a more or less open-ended activity which would come to its own natural conclusion in its own good time, the Russian speakers pace their activity accordingly. They may have talked longer or drunk more, unaware that the English speakers, who had checked their watches, had already eaten their food and were ready to leave.

Probably the main difficulty in reading an invitation in Almaty is to decipher exactly what the implications are in terms of food. This is such an important topic that it is amazing how many times it is left surrounded by ambiguity. On some occasions, you might rush home from the office in order to grab a quick bit to eat only to discover that a sumptuous repast is spread before you at the function. On some other occasions, you might deliberately avoid eating beforehand in the expectation that a similar sumptuous repast will be there only to be disappointed at the rather thin pickings or, worse, the nonappearance of the food.

For quite a few foreigners in Almaty, the subject of food or no food at the function is very, very important. Many bachelors are tired of their own cooking and are bored with eating in the same handful of neighbourhood restaurants. Many couples find it awkward to shop locally or are fed up with insufficient variety in their own home cooking. Temporary visitors in hotels welcome the chance to avoid the need to plan yet another meal out by instead going to a reception. Thus, the chances are very high that, unless the invitation gives a clear signal to the contrary, many invitees will be expecting food at the function and, like it or not, will judge the event and the sponsors by the adequacy and quality of the fare that is provided.

At least one source of the problem of invitations and expectations concerning food is that the Western concept of the natural time for doing certain things clashes severely with the still prevalent Soviet concept of the natural time for doing the same things. Who on earth would schedule an opera, a ballet or a rock concert at 6:00 p.m. on a week night? Is this hour selected by the local Union of Entertainers so that the performing artistes can go home and get a good night's sleep? Is this hour chosen because the street lights are turned off to conserve electricity? Doesn't such an early starting time violate some natural law of humanity? More importantly – always remembering the importance of the stomach – is one supposed to eat before, during or after? Or do local residents not eat at all on these occasions?

These culture clash problems can be encountered with local invitations. Has the function been called for 6:30 p.m. out of a Soviet frame of thinking with no food being served despite your high expectations? Or is the 6:30 p.m. commencement time on the invitation an obvious and definite confirmation that food will be served, as any normal English speaker would expect? In general, there are no entirely certain answers to these questions. It helps to know something about the people who are hosting the function. A gathering at one of Almaty's many reception halls probably will be accompanied by enough food to constitute a meal though you probably will eat it while standing up and it may not be your idea of a balanced diet. Similarly, a reception at one of Almaty's fine hotels probably will involve a buffet with a good choice of foods. A reception at the business premises of a company may or may not entail a good chance to eat. A Western corporate host probably anticipates your concerns but a local host may not.

Another problem with invitations is that one often does not know if this is such an exclusive or personal invitation that it would be a social blunder to bring along a spouse, a friend, or a date. On some occasions, this is expected (but the invitation does not so state).

Just as many people welcome the opportunity to go to a reception in order to skip the personal bother and cost of arranging their own dinner, so quite a few people welcome the opportunity to take their spouse or a friend to a reception because it represents a break from the routine of life. However, on many other occasions, an invitation really is personal and means that only one person is entitled to attend, leaving you in a rather awkward position if you specifically asked someone to accompany you.

In the West, in the comfort of one's own country, these ambiguities often can be resolved by a simple telephone call. Here in Almaty, the social and language barriers tend to eliminate that option or to leave you as uncertain after you have made the call as before.

Check the invitation very carefully to make sure you understand the starting time. There is about an equal balance between invitations that use the 12-hour clock (e.g., 7 p.m.) and those that use the 24-hour clock (e.g., 19:00).

In some cases, the 12-hour clock is used in English and the 24-hour clock is used in Russian. For those accustomed to one clock or the other, it is easy to be confused when dealing with the other clock. I know. I was still in the shower when the first guests arrived at my apartment at 6:00 p.m. for an open house evening that was intended to start at 8:00 p.m. (which had been misread as 18:00 whereas the party started at 20:00).

Since Almaty is a big village and many foreigners know each other, quite a few cases occur of what would be called gate crashing if it happened elsewhere or among strangers. Here, however, the situations are fairly rare that a reception is so exclusive or the purpose of it so narrowly defined that someone who happens upon it would be excluded. Once, while going to look for someone in the 4th floor bar at the Dostyk Hotel, I wandered into an enormous wedding reception in the 4th floor lobby which sometimes also serves as an art gallery. Flustered, I started my retreat, quite embarrassed that I had intruded. However, I was grabbed by the brother of the bride, given some food and drink and, before I was permitted to leave more than an hour later, I had even danced with the bride. Finally, there is the problem of knowing when to bring the invitation with you to a function. If the invitation was printed, contains your name, and was personally delivered to you, the probabilities are high that you will need to show the invitation in order to enter. The best advice in this regard is always remember to bring the invitation with you. For government functions, embassy activities, and other gatherings where security might be a concern, you definitely will need to bring the invitation with you. Occasionally the invitation actually states that you will need it in order to gain entrance.

8

BANK ACCOUNTS

I opened a personal bank account in Almaty not long after arriving here in January 1993. It was quite easy to open the account, and the only problems I have had with it can be traced to mistakes made by Western banks when wire transferring my funds to me. It has been surprising to me, therefore, to hear about some of the problems faced by others in financing their stays in Kazakhstan.

One of the most amazing money incidents of which I am personally aware occurred sometime late in 1994. I encountered an oil industry acquaintance at the Frankfurt airport at the bar near the gate for the airplane we were going to catch. We bought each other a beer and chatted away the minutes. Eventually my acquaintance excused himself to go to the toilet, and he asked me to watch over his briefcase for him. When he returned a few minutes later, he informed me that he was carrying $30,000 in cash in that briefcase. He needed the money to pay for his apartment, to pay for the office his company leased in one of the hotels, and to pay salary to local staff.

He had had to make extraordinary arrangements in order to collect the money at one of the exchange bureaus at Heathrow airport. They had been given his photograph, his signature, his passport details and a thumbprint, all of which had to be checked before the money was released to him. He then stood in front of the window counting out the money for a rather long period of time in order to make sure it was correct.

I extolled to him the virtues of opening a bank account in Almaty but I think that he never did follow my advice. Perhaps he was concerned about the security of using a local bank. My impression, however, is that he got a bit of a kick carrying around a lot of money.

During the airplane trip to Almaty, my acquaintance solicited my views as to whether or not he should declare the exact amount involved which might attract extraordinary interest in him, possibly creating a personal safety risk after he left the airport. We discussed the merits of disclosing versus non-disclosure for quite a long time. I regret that I never did learn how he dealt with this issue. What I do know is that he did get through customs and into Almaty with all the money intact. He was staying at the Sanatorium Alatau, a very up-market place formerly reserved for use by the country's elite. They had been displaced by oil company executives who were competing for big exploration contracts from the government.

I had two personal bank accounts, one in U.S. dollars, which I was entitled to have as a foreigner, and one in Tenge which I had little use for in the days before local debit cards. The dollar account, however, was highly useful, and not just to receive my funds from abroad for living expenses.

There came a time when I went to my branch of the bank and I was accosted by the Vice President of International Operations who asked me in, for her, a rather stern voice if I was engaged in money laundering. This caught me entirely off guard. For one thing, I didn't know that in those early days, probably the year 2000, that the local banks had implemented money laundering procedures. More importantly, I couldn't, for the life of me, imagine where or how she possibly could have gotten information or the idea that I was engaged in some illegal activity.

It turned out that she knew about the more than U.S. $1 million that had been transferred into my account. In those days, money was rushing out of Kazakhstan, not into it. Probably a lot of people in the bank knew that I had received a huge amount of money.

No, the reason I had that money in my account was that my client was about to purchase a factory in Shymkent (we knew it then as Chimkent). Well, you may wonder, what is a lawyer doing with the money of a client in his personal bank account? Good question. After all, lawyers aren't supposed to mingle the money of clients with their own money. Law firms usually set up client escrow accounts to segregate client money from their own.

The root problem we faced was that a foreign company without any presence in Kazakhstan – no representative office, no branch, no subsidiary – could not open a bank account in Kazakhstan. To compound the problem, local banks did not then have the authority or the knowledge to establish escrow accounts. As a result, if the foreign company wanted to make an investment, such as to buy a factory, and if they didn't want to send the investment money directly to the other side and the other side didn't want to transfer title until after it received payment, they were in a stalemate. So, without a client escrow account and in order not to mingle client money with our office money, I emptied my personal account and for a few days I enjoyed the local status of being a real millionaire!

I already had experience of using my personal bank account in this way. In 1998 my account received about U.S. $300,000. (No one asked me about money laundering on that occasion.) This was for the purchase of a bank. Well, not really a bank. Instead, it was for the purchase of a banking license and a small business premises that could hardly be called bank. It was far more expensive and time consuming to actually form a new bank and to obtain a license for it. Indeed, foreign banks needed to have a representative office for one year before applying for a banking license.

When the day came to complete the purchase and sale transaction, I hired an armoured car from the bank along with two armed guards to being the cash to my office. I also asked for a counting machine. This was a cash transaction and there were eight or nine separate shareholders who were entitled to different amounts of the cash. It turned out that the counting machine was not needed. All the cash was stilled wrapped in its original U.S. Treasury wrappers. We maybe had to break open one or two bundles in order to divvy up a small amount of $100 bills.

When the sellers were satisfied and we had all the required signatures, they bundled their piles of cash into plastic shopping bags and left the meeting.

9

OUR PLASTIC FRIEND

In reading this 1997 article, it bears recalling that, before the introduction of electronic credit card readers and PIN codes, credit cards were processed by swiping them over a paper the size of an old-fashioned airplane ticket on which the details were imprinted. The cardholder then signed the paper, and the cashier at the shop or restaurant then compared the signature on the paper with the signature on the reverse side of the credit card. My, how technology moves on!

Belatedly and slowly, the credit card is making some inroads into the commercial life of Almaty. The emergence of the credit card has not been easy and its future, as seen from the vantage point of 1997, is far from certain. Indeed, one can easily imagine that by the time the economy of this city is ready for heavy use of the credit card, the technology of banking and commerce will already have zoomed ahead to some higher level so that the credit card era, as we have known it in the West, may never actually be experienced here. As shown by cellular telephones, it sometimes happens that emerging countries can skip intermediate stages of development by making a leapfrog of technology.

When I first arrived in Almaty in January 1993 I stayed at what was then known as Residence No. Three of the Supreme Soviet, which is located on Furmanov Street, just down from Abay Street and in close proximity to the Dostyk Hotel. Before travelling to Almaty, I had been assured by our Kazakhstani host that my colleague and I could pay for our lodging and for the meals taken at Residence No. Three by means of a credit card. Not knowing exactly what I would encounter, I brought quite a bit of cash with me to cover basic needs and contingencies, but not enough to also pay the hotel expenses of two people staying for a period of two weeks. On the afternoon before our red eye return flight to Europe near the end of February, I asked for the hotel bill just in case there were going to be any snags. I had not seen any obvious signs that the hotel staff had ever before seen a credit card, much less used one in a payment transaction.

Sure enough, there was a problem. The hotel did <u>not</u> accept any credit cards. It was not that I tendered the wrong card; they simply did not take credit cards. Moreover, they had no idea why I thought they would accept credit cards.

This definitely was not welcome information. I was somewhere near the end of the world, the twice-a-week plane was about to leave, and my luck had just run out. No Western banks had a presence in Almaty at that time; I had only the slenderest of acquaintanceships with some business people in Almaty whose own financial affairs here might have been somewhat precarious; and I was naturally hesitant to throw myself on the mercy of the young American

Embassy, resourceful as it was. I made a desperate phone call to our host and somewhat later I was assured that there was no problem. I merely needed to hand over my credit card to the hotel staff and to sign a large triplicate form, about half the size of an A4 sheet of paper, which had been hastily brought over from the nearby Dostyk Hotel. Later that night, my card was returned to me. Having thus completed the transaction, I packed for the flight and left.

About six weeks later, my credit card statement arrived in London and I spotted an entry for "Fairwinds Trading Corporation" of Tucson, Arizona, a city that I have never visited in my entire life. Fairwinds Trading Corporation was in a joint venture with the Dostyk Hotel, and they had somehow managed to mimic a credit card facility at that hotel that actually operated out of Tucson, Arizona. I am uncertain how they made it work in 1993 but it seems likely that the details of each credit card transaction at the hotel were phoned back to Tucson where they then put the deal through the system as if the purchase had occurred in Tucson. The wonder of the modern credit card had indeed arrived in Kazakhstan.

During 1993, 1994, and 1995, I often ate at what was then the popular and prestigious Dostyk Hotel where it usually was impossible to obtain a room. As a result, I had a large number of credit card transactions that were billed in the name of Fairwinds Trading Corporation of Tucson, Arizona. Anyone who examines my credit card statements for this 3-year period would be led to the inevitable conclusion that I had very heavy business dealings with someone in Tucson, Arizona, but, remarkably, never did anything except eat food in that city.

Four and a half years later, the credit card has still only made a superficial impact on business and commerce in the City of Almaty. A few local residents may possess credit cards that are now available from local banks, but it seems likely that they find them to be convenient primarily for foreign travel and not for use at home. The reason is that relatively few establishments here accept credit cards. The major hotels take credit cards, a few of the more expensive restaurants take credit cards, and only a handful of retail establishments accept them. The credit card business faces the chicken-and-egg problem that arises so often in trying to kick-start a market economy-type business in a non-market economy country. It cannot be transplanted on its own; it thrives only where other independently owned businesses provide the infrastructure of banking and credit rating services that it requires.

The business history of this part of the world is not encouraging for the future of the credit card business. Imagine that you are a representative of a credit card company and it is your task to persuade a local merchant to sign up as a member of your organization. Look at all the advantages. For a modest fee of something like 5% of sales, your credit card organization will take all the credit risks away from the merchant and will guarantee payment to the merchant of around 95% of the value of sales not later than 30 days or so after the purchase. Not only that; sales volume will increase when credit is extended and, besides, cash sales encourage robbery.

This is convincing stuff, right? Well, not exactly. The merchant and all of his or her customers have for decades lived in a cash-and-carry society. 100% cash right now seems, by any reckoning, to be a lot better than 95% or so of the same amount 30 days or more later. There is no credit risk if no credit is extended. Moreover, bear in mind that there is a significant black economy in Almaty and that the credit card inherently involves a paper trail and deposits in a bank account that many merchants would find exceedingly intrusive on their style of doing business.

Even at establishments in Almaty where credit cards are accepted, they do not operate in exactly the same way as in the West. I have not yet discovered a single dining place in Almaty where you can pay a tip using the credit card. Every time I have tried to add a certain percentage to the credit card transaction slip on the line marked "tip" it is refused so that only the basic price of the meal runs through my account. Even the five-star hotels seem unable to conquer this seemingly simple economic task. Presumably the chief accountant at the restaurant or hotel cannot figure out how they could explain to the Tax Inspector or to the Tax Police why it is that they managed to obtain 110% of the published menu price and then distributed the 10% to the staff. The VAT consequences of this transaction probably are utterly horrifying, and the chief accountants of this city probably refuse to accept the heavy burden of newly computing the entire staff's withholding taxes, pension fund contributions, employment fund contributions, health insurance contributions, and so on based on the variable amount of monthly tip income. It is easier to refuse the tip and the benefits it brings than to cope with its enormous accounting, bookkeeping and tax consequences.

I was delighted recently to learn that "Light" Restaurant, where Dostyk Avenue is crossed by Boganbi Batyr Street, was going to start to accept a credit card. They serve good food in cafeteria style, and my apartment is an easy walk away. ("Light" was later gutted by fire, restored and became a retail goods shop.)

I got there one week too soon, however, and was refused on my first tentative try (being something of a disbeliever, I had enough cash with me). On a return visit a couple of weeks later, I casually offered my credit card and it was accepted. There ensued, however, a considerable delay, and I noticed that all of the waitresses were huddled around the cashier's desk. I don't know if they were practicing in unison on my transaction, using me as their guinea pig, or if they were waiting for the call to go through to Moscow to see if the card was stolen.

In due course, the waitress returned to our table and presented the slip for my signature with all the nonchalance she could muster. I signed it. She had flubbed her part a bit, however, because she had already returned my card to me. Feeling that I had a duty to help introduce to Central Asia the business know-how for this advanced technology, I insisted that the waitress compare my signature on the slip with the signature on the credit card. She duly made the comparison and seemed to find it to be satisfactory. I have no idea, however, if she actually comprehended that checking my signature was not just a matter of curiosity but a vital part of a fraud-prevention drill. I assume that signature checking is like most other areas of life -- one really learns only from bad experience, and not at all from good experience. As soon as the restaurant takes a hit on a major purchase with a stolen card, the humor of checking signatures will evaporate.

10
MUCH ADO VERSUS NOTHING

With summer heavy upon us these last few weeks, I am reminded of a picnic I enjoyed so very much in the summer of 1993. Four friends – two of us from the West and two local residents – went on what really was an idyllic picnic on a Sunday round about this time of the year. The sky was clear the whole day, it was warm without being anything like the fiery blast that dominates much of July and August, and there was an occasional breeze that was welcome but not really needed for cooling.

We caught a taxi up near Hotel Kazakhstan, left the city and took a rural road that I probably could not find again if I tried. The route was generally downhill from Almaty and it took us past some wooden flood barriers such as one sees and passes through on the approach to Medeo. The taxi driver essentially took us to the end of a side road and parked unobtrusively behind a bush. We had expected to be dropped off with the understanding that the driver would return for us at a pre-arranged time later in the day, but I guess we had agreed to pay enough so that he was content to sleep away the afternoon and remain with us until we were ready to return to Almaty. He did not ask for food but we had plenty to share with him.

We had parked within 50 meters of one of the many fast-moving streams that carry the clear mountain water to some far away destination. Close to the car was a lonely tree from the roots of which there bubbled up a very cold spring of water that collected in a small pool before draining down to the stream. The pool was large enough to hold our supply of tomatoes, cucumbers, slightly overripe peaches, and a day's supply of beer. We spread out the blankets, put up a couple of umbrellas for protection from the sun rather than against any rain, and claimed our places.

Looking around the broad horizon we could not see any evidence at all of human habitation, and it is my recollection that we did not see even one vapor trail from a jet airplane during the entire day that we spent in the open.

Then, after we had prepared the things we had brought with us, we proceeded to enjoy what was to me and the other foreigner one of the most amazing days that I can recall spending since about the time I was 10 years old. We proceeded to do a whole lot of nothing. We lazed. We dozed. We sat. We strolled. We ate our simple fare. We talked about nothing in particular, the way friends talk among themselves to pass the time. We read books. We dangled our legs in the cold stream. We passed into a kind of listlessness and timelessness that is impossible to imagine unless you have experienced it. Possibly we played a bit of Frisbee but that would have been the most strenuous of our activities if we did it, and the breeze would have taken some of the joy out of it anyway. A few hiking strangers, following the stream, encroached upon "our" territory but continued on their way, briefly puncturing our little universe in which not much else was happening with their own activity.

Quite clearly, the pace of the day was set by the local residents, not by us foreigners. We undoubtedly assumed that there would an agenda of activity, possibly a pre-existing and unannounced agenda but still an agenda. If there was no pre-existing agenda, we initially felt confident that one would soon emerge. It never did. At first, I was somewhat apprehensive. Nothing was going on. The day seemed rather pointless. We were just doing nothing, and a whole day was yawning in front of us that promised a great deal more of that same nothing. What were we supposed to do? Just sit and look at each other?

I know that I am something of a compulsive. I tend to work hard and I tend to enjoy hard. I make up my "to do" lists and my "worry" lists. I live by the clock from morning to night, racing at times to squeeze one more activity into an already crowded schedule. There is seldom an idle moment, scarcely an unplanned minute. It does not help that I am a lawyer whose professional life is measured in tenths of hours of billable time which constantly reinforces my sense of squandering time if the time is not well spent and accounted for.

So, for me it is quite natural when idle to plan how not to be idle and to try to "accomplish something worthwhile" instead of "wasting my time".

But on that day in the summer of 1993, it was driven home to me that there are other ways to spend time which are highly attractive in their own way even if they run counter to the rat race life that we have come to treat as normal in the West.

A couple of years earlier, I had been given a hint that this lolling away of a day or an afternoon in peaceful inactivity may have been a part of the style of life behind the Iron Curtain. In 1989, while working on some construction projects in Warsaw, I met a Polish-born Canadian citizen who was returning to Poland for the first time, now with her Master's Degree in Business Administration and spearheading an investment team that sought to purchase a biscuit manufacturer.

She was in a reflective mood, wondering in particular how Poland might have changed in the dozen years she had been away. She spoke of her youthful years in a small village in Poland, going on weekend walks to see the wild flowers, to chase butterflies, and simply to enjoy the passage of time in the company of comrades and family. She had been aware that her family was poor, economically, but she was also aware then, while talking to me, if not before, that they were living a full and rich family life. Subsequently, having lived in the West with all of its pressures and the seeming need to keep climbing up the ladder of success, she easily wondered if her life then, in 1989, with all its material rewards, was really better and more satisfying than the simple life that she had lived in that village in Poland.

My Polish acquaintance may have been viewing her past through the filter of nostalgia in which the bad is eliminated and the good is accentuated. But that memorable picnic day in the summer of 1993 permitted me a glimpse of an admirable lifestyle that really does exist and that sharply contrasts to my own.

Perhaps the times have moved on so that it is not possible any more to laze away a day such as I did in 1993. Cellular phones are everywhere, and I can imagine lying on a blanket under the sun with no signs in view of humanity when all of a sudden the cellular phone intrudes, a jarring reminder of one's membership in that other, more hectic lifestyle.

11

A DAY OF SLEDDING

Almaty had quite a bit of snow continuously on the ground in the winter of 1993-94. One bright Sunday after a fresh snowfall I went out for a walk to stretch my legs and to find some opportunities to take winter photographs. As I was walking down Furmanov Avenue and approaching Republic Square (formerly New Square) at Satpaev Street, two 12-year old girls, who quickly recognized me as a foreigner, engaged me in conversation so as to practice their English. I have often played the role of "native English speaker" with whom local residents practice their English. In return, I pick up some Russian and learn a bit about local life.

The girls were dragging a sled behind them and it was clear that they too were out to enjoy a nice winter day. I was surprised, however, to learn that they were deliberately heading for the Presidential Palace for their day of sledding. In those days, the Presidential Palace was the large building facing Republic Square up there behind the marble viewing stand. When we got to the Presidential Palace, I could see why they had chosen this place. There are, of course, many places to use a sled in mountain-side Almaty, but the Presidential Palace easily constituted a prime sledding location. The front stairs are quite high and there are intervals without steps which are smooth, making ideal sled runs. Many other children had already arrived at what seemed to be a widely known sled run.

I am aware that the American White House is located on a flat piece of land at 1600 Pennsylvania Avenue, does not have a major outdoor staircase, and rarely experiences heavy snow. However, as I watched the many children enjoying themselves on the steps of the Presidential Palace in Almaty, I tried to imagine the children of Washington, D.C., deliberately going to the White House and being allowed to romp in the snow and to enjoy a day of sledding. Somehow, I could not picture this happening.

12

EATING OUT IN TIMES PAST

I hope I am not encroaching on Russell Ragsdale's culinary territory – his column in *The Almaty Herald* is entitled "Cooking Almaty" - by writing about eating out in Almaty but I shall concentrate on eating out in times past whereas Russ concentrates on times present.

For the early business visitors and first expatriates, the very best place to eat in Almaty was the large restaurant at the Dostyk Hotel on Kurmangazy Street where, for a time, Russ Ragsdale from Arizona and a very early expatriate in Almaty was the chief chef. You entered the hotel, went up the grand staircase and entered the very large, high-ceilinged restaurant that served many of the most popular dishes of the Soviet period, including the local favorites. For some years, it remained an unreconstructed Soviet restaurant. Later, with the influx of ever more foreigners, the menu was increasingly westernized.

There were two large swinging doors to the kitchen and, when opened, one could glimpse the large caldrons of steaming food tended by the cooks in their white outfits topped off with white hats.

Somewhat oddly, a very large white refrigerator stood in the dining room but it probably held cold drinks.

To think about the restaurant in those days is to wish for its revival in present days.

This was the hotel in which the Presidential Administration was involved in management, and this was the hotel of choice by the major foreign investors. The seating was comfortable, the ceiling high, and one usually could see and visit with a wide cross section of the expatriate population in Almaty. And as the expatriate community grew and included spouses and a few children, this was the place to come for Sunday lunch until the Marco Polo Hotel (now the Rahat Palace Hotel) opened on 27 April 1995. (It didn't really open at the Grand Opening. The date of the opening had been set and President Nazarbayev was the featured guest, but as soon as the opening ceremony ended, the hotel's name was covered and the workmen returned. It opened a bit later.)

The restaurant manager at the Marco Polo Hotel had gauged the eating public's mood well. As you entered the restaurant, there was a magnificent display of appetizing food on a long counter just to the left. Fresh fruit and vegetables and a variety of breads. To enter the restaurant was to be enticed, tempted, and encouraged to eat. The Sunday luncheon crowd quickly changed allegiance from the Dostyk Hotel, and soon diners started arriving earlier and earlier still in order to find a table at the crowded new restaurant. Thus was the hospitality dominance of the new hotel ushered in under the Marco Polo mark followed by the Hyatt Hotel. This remained, though challenged, upon the 1996 opening of the incongruously named The Ankara Hotel in Almaty (now the Inter-Continental Hotel) (it was so named in diplomatic reciprocity for a hotel in Ankara named The Almaty Hotel).

The outdoor summer beer garden at the Rahat Palace Hotel also became a gathering place for the expatriate crowd, hotel guests and the general public.

Not long after arriving in Almaty early in 1993, I discovered the Italian Restaurant, a veritable oasis with its authentically Italian style food and particularly with its attractive and well-presented salads. The Italian Restaurant possibly had a name but everyone simply referred to it as the Italian Restaurant, and that was the only name that it needed. It was located deep in the interior of the International Business Center (across from the Kazakhstan Hotel and near to Kazakhstan Eximbank). There was no sign on the building that it contained a restaurant and many expatriates came here for their two or three week stints and went away in ignorance that they had missed the delights of this place.

I remember the two miners whose grub in the hills obviously had been substandard. They ordered up full meals and then, after taking a brief stretch, settled down to order another complete meal each!

The story I heard about the Italian Restaurant is that it served as the canteen for the workers, presumably Italian, when they built the International Business Center, and when the building was finished, the restaurant remained in place to serve the tenants in the building. Word of mouth advertising was all that it needed.

Renate, who operated the Italian Restaurant, eventually moved on to the Circus and then to his own restaurant on a side street not very far from the Circus where he continued to provide his version of some of the mainstays of Italian cuisine.

My birthday in May of 1993 was celebrated at the "Shalom" restaurant but no one called it Shalom. Basically in 1993 if you wanted a respite from local cuisine and if you did not know about the Italian Restaurant you went to the "Jewish Restaurant", the name by which it was popularly known. The Shalom Restaurant was located toward the rear of the Communication Building, the tall building that has external lattice piping about a block away from the Opera. Like the Italian Restaurant, it was somewhat inconspicuous and you needed to know where you were going in order to find it. They had live music and the musicians and their instruments occupied a large percentage of the small floor space. The most prominent feature of the restaurant was a giant star of David which hung like a massive chandelier from the low ceiling.

Yet another inaccessible place for dining was to be found deep in the Interior Ministry building at the corner of Dzerzhiskiy and Shevchenko Streets. It was at this intersection at which one often saw large hand-made protest banners hanging high over the street. The restaurant was actually a flashy disco that happened to serve good food: this was the Italian Disco, a veritable oasis of high tech Western life that was superimposed upon this building. I can't say why it was in the Ministry building other than to note that cash-short ministries were doing all sorts of things to pay for their activities at that time.

When it first "opened" in November 1993, the Italian Disco was actually closed to the public and it operated initially on an invitation-only basis. This was because no license had been issued for the reason that the disco did not have its own toilet facilities. I managed to get in on the basis of being a friend of a friend of the manager, and when that moment came when it would be useful to inspect the porcelain, I was taken on a 10 minutes escorted tour of part of the building, which includes walking through a large theater deep in the recesses of the building. Eventually we arrived at a men's toilet facility which can best be described as in an advanced state of demolition, though perhaps it had been in that state for a considerable period of time.

Even after toilets were installed and the license was issued, it was not easy to go to this disco and to enjoy a late night meal there. Entry was available only to people known to the management. If you did not know the manager, it was necessary to go for an interview accompanied by a written application/resume. Also, entry even by "members" was only by appointment, and the appointment needed to be made by a person whose voice was recognized by the manager.

Finding the door of the Italian Disco was not easy. I remember wandering around several buildings in deep snow while looking for the unmarked door. Finally, I came upon the large gates marked with their prominent red stars. To the left was the locked, heavy gauge cyclone fence gate through which one needed to gain access. There was no sign at all. Upon pressing a button on the wall, a guard would appear with a walkie-talkie. He would speak your name over the walkie-talkie and, if it matched the reservation list for that night, he would allow you in and the exact number of guests that you had said you would bring with you.

The Italian Disco attracted a wide cross section of the affluent of Almaty. On one occasion I met the youthful reputed head of the local Mafia known as "Cat". I don't think he was personally involved, but I did noticed a few weeks later that entry to the place was possible only after going through an electronic screening device, similar to those used at airports. The story was that a fracas had occurred at the disco one night, and pistols were drawn, perhaps used. This was during that period of time when gangs of men dressed in shiny blue track suits roamed the city at night, five or six to the Mercedes car. Presumably they were selling "protection" and engaging in other nefarious activities. Eventually, a major crackdown occurred and many gang members disappeared from the streets. A government official informed me about this when he took me on a tour of Medeo. Cars going out of town were being searched for men evading the dragnet. Ours avoided this indignity after an eye-catching identity card was shown.

The best Italian food, and maybe the best dining experience in Almaty over all while it operated, was at the Adriatico Restaurant. Owned by Giorgio Fiacconi, one knowing reviewer – Dave Essel commenting on Pomodoro - said that this the Adriatico "served real food and wine to a mixed crowd of dangerous local Mafiosi, the first cowboy businessmen, and Wild West oilmen who came pouring into the country in the early days of independence. Back then, one didn't know if there would be water in the taps or electricity in the wire three hours ahead. So a real meal at the Adriatico was a miracle."

I have two strong recollections of the European Restaurant on Abay Avenue a short distance past the Circus and accessible by walking up the outdoor metal steps that vaguely reminded me of being on an apartment building fire escape in New York City. The first memory was of eating dinner there with a companion on a wintry evening. It turned out that the heat to the premises had been cut off and, though the food was hot, the room was so cold we had to keep our heavy coats on. The second memory, which may be related to the first, is of the badly bruised face of the proprietor. He apparently had had a discussion with some enforcers concerning an overdue amount, and presumably he had been insufficiently cooperative.

Later, of course and as we all know, there was a proliferation of restaurants in Almaty when times got better. Some not mentioned above include: Line Brew Restaurant, Old England, Restaurant Borgo Antico on Gorny Gigant on the way up to where several of the ambassadors have their residences, Pomo d'Oro and Pomodoro, Dickens Restaurant, Guinness Pub, Venezia, Arsenal, Dastarkhan, Russ Ragsdale's El Paso Tex-Mex restaurant, and many, many others. The restaurant business being what it is, some of these are still with us, others are not.

13

TELEPHONE MANNERS

In the places from which I come, it is the established convention in the business community for the receptionist to answer the telephone in an effective, efficient and pleasant way. While I am not aware that there are any grooming schools for receptionists, telephonists and others who field the calls from the public and from business customers, it nevertheless is the norm that the telephone must be answered in such a way as to clearly identify the company whose phone it is, to do so in a welcoming way that lets the other party know that his or her call is appreciated, and to accomplish these functions efficiently so that the business of the caller can be achieved quickly. Mostly this is just a matter of good sense and good manners but it is also a matter of projecting a positive public image for the company. Performed properly, all of this can be achieved with very few words, such as: "ABC Company - good morning" or "ABC Company - May I help you?" or even simply "ABC Company." Callers immediately obtain positive confirmation that they have been connected with the company they want and the callers, having been put at their ease, are invited to proceed with whatever purpose they had in calling.

One of the big surprises in coming to Almaty in 1993 was to discover that this convention for answering a business telephone did not apply here. As inconceivable as it was to me, the practice was – and sometimes still is – for the recipient of the call simply to pick up the phone and say "da."

"Da?" That's all? Yup. "Da." In fact, the "da" in question usually is such a toneless and emotionless "da" that it reveals nothing at all about the person who answered the phone except their gender. Sometimes one would not even get the minimalist "da" from the person who answered the phone. You, the caller, could only hear that the phone had been picked up and maybe you could sense that the line was not dead, but nothing at all was volunteered by the person who answered the phone. On some occasions when this happened to me, I actually hung up and redialled, thinking that something was wrong with the line or that I had gotten a wrong number. No one in their right mind, I thought, would answer a telephone by not answering the telephone. Certainly not in a business setting. Sometimes I have gotten so upset at this bad reception that I have adopted the same attitude as the recipient of the call and I have said nothing, waiting to see if the other person will finally make a noise, say "hello", or ask if there is a caller at the other end of the line. So far, I have never won this battle of nerves. The person who "answered" the phone simply hangs up, possibly with a sense of relief that this was yet another successful case of not having to deal with some problem.

Conventions being what they are, it is entirely off-putting or unnerving when a convention is not observed. You dial the phone, you expect to know immediately if the call has gone through to the correct place, and your mental set is that you should be able to proceed with your business. With a "da" reply, and even more with the "da-less" reply, you are thrown off your balance. Has the call gone through correctly? To whom are you speaking? Why in the world do you have to grill the person who answered the phone to find out what they should have volunteered in the first place when they answered the phone? Why is your time being wasted on something as simple as making a phone connection to someone else? When you finally are put through to the person you want to speak to, there probably is an edge to your tone of voice that you might not like to be there. The bad reception given to you might even affect the outcome of your call. Suppose that the purpose of your call was to hire another company to do something for your business. If you don't like the way your phone call was handled by that company, what makes you think you will like their services or goods? It might be better to place your order with a different company.

After encountering this unresponsiveness, this coldness, this possible hostility, this lack of sense of projection of company image, or whatever it was, I tried to imagine why the practice should be so different here from that which prevails in the West. Many people here have long been accustomed to using a telephone in their homes, and my impression is that they make a great deal of use of their phones. Mothers call their daughters every day. Young people call their friends. Everyone calls everyone on New Year's Day. So, why should there be such standoffishness when receiving a call? It is as if people who receive a phone call are expecting bad news or they dread being given an unpleasant surprise. During the Second World War and during subsequent conflagrations in which the United States participated, no one in America who had a relative serving in the military wanted to receive a telegram. A knock on the door and the mere mention of "Telegram" was enough to turn one's knees to jelly. People in Almaty seem to have a similar kind of foreboding when picking up the telephone. By saying nothing or by merely saying "da", do they hope that they can somehow pretend later that they never received the call? Are they preserving for as long as possible a deniability capability?

When I first arrived in Almaty (Alma-Ata at that time) and stayed in hotels, there was a rigorous routine when I checked into a hotel that someone from my office would accompany me to my room. At first I thought this was a nice touch on the part of our local staff. They were making sure that the room was acceptable, and that I was comfortable and safe. Little by little, however, it dawned on me that the real reason for accompanying me was to get a chance to glance at the telephone in my room. I wondered why they were so fascinated by my telephones. Did they suspect that the phones were bugged and that I ought to know about this? Were the phones so decrepit that they wanted to make sure that mine worked? No such thing. This little routine of seeing me to my room and checking the phone was to learn my telephone number.

In those days, and perhaps nowadays in some of the un-reconstructed hotels in Almaty, there was no central switchboard and there was no single listed telephone number for the hotel that the public could call in order to speak to someone at the hotel. Even the front desk of the hotel had its own outside line and when the people at the front desk wanted to speak to someone within the hotel, they didn't dial up an internal number. They simply dialled the correct outside number that your friends and business associates would also be calling. Each and every room had its own direct outside line, and the best and sometimes the only way for anyone to learn that number was literally to go to the room and read the number off the phone instrument. So, if anyone in my office wanted to contact me or to try to keep track of me, someone needed to come to my room, check the phone and write down my number for future reference. Eventually I fell into this same practice. Upon checking into the hotel and going to my room, my hand automatically reached for a pen and a piece of paper while I made a beeline for the telephone.

I thought it must be risky for a hotel to permit its guests to have their own direct outside lines. What if all the guests made expensive international calls and then checked out of the hotel without paying? In the West, hotels control the telephone traffic and add on their own charges besides. I then discovered something else about the telephone system in Almaty that explained why a hotel did not need to worry about the use their guests made of the telephones. There are three different types of telephone lines in Almaty: city lines, inter-city lines, and international lines. Hotels were supplied with city lines and these can be used to make out-of-town calls and international calls only with the aid of a telephone operator who later reports the charges to the hotel for onward billing to the hotel guest.

Speaking of telephone lines, I also learned that, due to public pressure for more telephones than the telephone exchanges could supply, the telephone people here found some way to operate two telephones with different numbers on the same line. In such cases of shared lines, you could call someone and discover that the line was busy even though they later would swear that they were not on the phone or were not even at home at the time of your call. If you had such a line, you could also discover when trying to make a call that your own line was busy.

It has been some time since I have tried to find someone's telephone number by calling the telephone company. I hope that this is another area in which the convention to which I am accustomed in the West has taken root in Almaty and has displaced the local practice that formerly applied. I remember the occasion some years ago when I tried to reach someone whose company had moved to a new office in Almaty. The operator was incensed that I did not know the exact address of the company I was trying to contact, she refused to give their number to someone who was so ill informed as to not have this information, and she hung up in a huff.

14

TAKE THE LOAD OFF YOUR FEET

I am asked on many occasions by people in the West and by visitors to Almaty about living conditions in Kazakhstan and whether things are getting better. In replying, it is necessary to distinguish between living conditions for local residents and living conditions for foreigners. It is also necessary to distinguish between living conditions in Almaty and living conditions elsewhere in the country. As in many other countries, it would be a mistake to generalize about the entire country based upon observations made in the capital. Finally, one must remind those who ask these questions that anecdotal evidence may not be very reliable: Kazakhstan is an enormous country and it seems likely that very few foreigners and probably not so many of its inhabitants have a good grasp of the overall situation.

As regards the situation of expatriates in Almaty -- a topic about which we all have a view -- it is clear that many aspects of life have improved considerably over the past five years. There are more restaurants, more discos, more night life possibilities, more expatriates with whom to carry on a social and private life, and so on. Informal clubs have assembled for various purposes, such as for skiing, dining out, and line dancing.

There have also been some less obvious changes that possibly are beginning to affect the conditions of life for local inhabitants as well as the circumstances of foreigners.

Late in 1992 and in 1993, it was virtually impossible to find a place in public in Almaty where one could simply sit down and relax. Apart from the park benches, there was practically no place to hang out or to congregate for social purposes. The Soviet Union itself may have disbanded but its social and economic structures still dominated the scene. Virtually everything was state owned and virtually everything was state planned. One had the impression, as a visitor, that there was no such thing as a private life that was carried on in a public setting. You checked into a hotel; you assembled as a delegation for a meeting at some Ministry; you went to an organized dinner at a hotel; and then you returned to your room at the hotel. Quite literally, there did not appear to be anywhere in Almaty to sit down and take the load off your feet.

In the winter of 1992-93, I searched for a place to relax without the need to purchase a meal and without going to my hotel room (which, with its eclectic assortment of furniture and chairs with short legs, was not so comfortable). I discovered only the ground floor bar of the Dostyk Hotel and a few park benches. Those benches might be used in the summer by local courting couples and by parents and grandparents minding youngsters but they were pretty useless during the cold of winter. As for the bar at the Dostyk Hotel, it was less commodious than at present but was very inviting. One could sit for hours nursing a drink, or not even drinking, and one could while away the evening in the company of friends or strangers who also were in search of company.

Elsewhere in Almaty, it seemed that a strict line had been drawn between private life and public life. The Hotel Kazakhstan has an enormous lobby but, until recently, it contained only one sofa. That sofa was used at night as the guard's bed and one felt self-conscious or overly conspicuous to sit on it during the day. The Otrar Hotel had a few seats in the reception area but they were too sterile and so under the scrutiny of the front desk that few people used them to lounge away the afternoon or evening. The Alma-Ata Hotel was similarly barren of furniture in its lobby which was made all the more chilling to its visitors by its stone floor.

Inevitably, one came away with the conclusion that, under the former Soviet system, there was no middle area between the private life of an ordinary person, which was lived in one's apartment or hotel room, and public life, which seemed to be carried out in a very structured way, such as in the form of delegation meetings.

The main competitor to the Dostyk's ground floor bar was the Italian Restaurant (does it have a real name?), where many people spent -- and still spend -- a pleasant evening over a genuine cup of coffee or a serving of real ice cream. It is located within the large building directly across the street from the Hotel Kazakhstan, up there above the fountains. The building, called the International Business Center, was constructed by Italians and the future restaurant was the canteen for the construction workers. When the building opened, the chef stayed on to operate a restaurant open to the public.

The one hitch with that was that there was no external sign or any advertisement saying that the restaurant was located there. It was highly popular nevertheless due to word of mouth. I remember encountering a miner there who had just come in from the hinterland and was in course of eating his second full meal at one sitting. He was amazed that the salad looked like a salad he recognized, with lettuce, and the pasta was a real treat. So far as I was aware, the restaurant has no official name, not even on its door when you arrive at it, but every expatriate knew it in the 1990s simply as the "Italian Restaurant".

I suppose it was this lack of function-free gathering places that has helped to make discos and casinos so popular for foreigners. Dr. Bang's Disco (now KIMEP Club) was virtually mandatory even for non-dancers, as one could observe each Friday when the 9:30 p.m. migration started from the ground floor bar at the Dostyk.

"Dr. Bang's Disco" was the informal name of a discotheque that was held primarily for students on Saturday nights at KIMEP, at the corner of Dostyk Avenue and Abay Avenue. It was so called after Dr. Chan Young Bang, an American Korean, who had been invited by President Nursultan Nazarbayev to serve as vice chairman of an Expert Committee that advised the government on economic policy. Dr. Bang subsequently became the founding president of the Kazakhstan Institute of Management, Economics and Strategic Research – hence KIMEP which is now its formal name.

I think it was in November of 1994 that the Italian Disco opened at the former premises of the Interior Ministry/KGB and suddenly it became the gathering place for people looking for something to do. This was despite the fact that entry was possible only with advance reservations, and reservations were available only for people who knew the manager.

In the ensuing years, much has changed and at an accelerating pace. Happy Hour at the International Business Club has become a regular Friday night fixture for many expatriates and local residents.

"Capos" was an instant success, in my judgment, not so much because it offered pizza with real mozzarella cheese, nor because it offered entertainment with the overhead videos, nor the flags on the wall and other decor, but because one could eat or not eat, as one choose, and one could spend the entire evening there as part of a self-selected society and in comfortable relaxation. There is more to life than participating in a delegation while meeting at some ministry, and there is more to life than sitting in a rather barren Soviet-style hotel room waiting for the next formal event or waiting impatiently for the next airplane out of here.

Mad Murphy's came along later, in 1998, and drew away many fans of Capos, having a wider menu, family-friendly atmosphere, and outdoor seating in good weather.

Moreover, the outdoor cafe has burgeoned as a business and as a style of life in Almaty. I think it was only in 1994 that the Dostyk Hotel opened its outside restaurant, but it was tucked away in the rear, enfolded by the building and non-obvious to the passing public. A virtual revolution occurred in summer eating habits and social circumstances during 1995 and 1996. There are more sidewalk cafes than can be counted, and it is pretty obvious that most of these depend for their trade and for their success not on the foreigners, who naturally enough enjoy them, but upon local residents who clearly share in the desire to carry on part of their private life in a public setting.

To me, it is interesting to note that, whereas foreigners have been behind many of the developments mentioned above, local residents have been quick to make use of them and to embrace them as part of their style of life.

15

HELLOS, GOODBYES, AND CONGRATULATIONS

Handshaking is an important ritual of everyday life in Kazakhstan, mainly observed by men. You see handshaking out on the street all the time. When friends meet, they do not simply say "hi" -- they shake hands.

There seem to be many rules and nuances to the shaking of hands. If one man approaches a group of men and recognizes one in particular, the rules call for a handshake. The social issue that then must be resolved quickly is whether to shake a few other hands or to shake all hands. Since Almaty is village-like in many ways, it is likely that the man who approached the group will recognize some of the others. I may be wrong, but it does not seem to be a necessity to know the names of everyone with whom one shakes a hand, and I do not observe that the handshake is preceded by one person introducing Mr. A to Mr. B before the handshake.

Then there is the double clasp. The right hands of two men are in contact when one of the men proceeds to add to the warmth, respect shown or significance of the occasion by enfolding the right hand of the other man with the left hand as well. Often times one sees that the handshake starts with the double clasp from the very outset. One of the men does not simply put forward his right hand. Instead, both arms are outstretched for the double clasp shake. I am still trying to work out if the receiver (the "shakee") must reciprocate by putting out both hands or if it is acceptable to continue to offer only one hand. If only one hand is extended to a man who is attempting a double clasp, is there a social snub involved in there somewhere?

Moving up the scale of warmth, showing of respect or significance of the occasion is the combined handshake-embrace. Right hands are locked together and then the usually under-utilized left arms get their share of the exercise by carrying out a semi-bear hug.

There is a very powerful superstition in Kazakhstan that one must not shake hands through a doorway. It may take a visitor a long time to detect this. Local shakers are very adept at ensuring that a handshake does not occur through a doorway. If you are near a door at a time when a handshake is called for, the local man will either accelerate his way through the doorway or slow down at a distance from you, causing you to move forward through the doorway. The local man may even back away from you in a gesture that could be misunderstood by both parties -- he is trying to be helpful so that you can complete your step through the door but you may sense that this as a sign of standoffishness. This one-sided activity can go on for months without you having any thought that you have been maneuvered into position, but that is exactly what has been occurring. I know one American executive who had been in Almaty for over two years before he became aware of this superstition, and that was only when I told him.

The shaking of hands by men with women can present some awkward situations. Handshaking seems to be not much practiced by some local women but this often depends upon how much contact they have had with foreigners. It may also depend upon upbringing and religious influence stemming from the Islamic practice by which women avoid physical contact with men outside the family. However, the steppe traditions of the Kazakhs, which include handshaking by women, can be stronger than the Islamic influence. Surprisingly, therefore, you may find more often than not that it is the Kazakh-ethnic women who will freely shake your hand and that it is the Russian-ethnic women who will be reticent. In fact, the

Kazakh-ethnic woman may be taken aback that you, a foreigner, are so familiar with their customs!

The upshot of this is that a foreign man may find himself on one occasion undergoing a perfectly routine, trouble-free handshake with one woman whereas the woman standing next to her seems not to know the first thing about how to respond to a man's outstretched hand. The foreign man, unaware that his outstretched hand is causing anxiety to the intended shakee, is slow to consider his options or to retrieve his hand. Meanwhile, the woman, having decided that this problem situation needs to be resolved by her doing something that she would rather not be doing offers a limp and unresponsive hand. Perhaps by then he has already started to withdraw his hand, increasing the embarrassment of the moment. Later he might wonder if everyone else in the room was staring at this unfolding mini-drama of life.

I am still working at the mastery of the mysteries of the handshake in Kazakhstan. My tentative advice to recent arrivals and visitors after much experience and practice in this art is:

(1) avoid doorway meetings or suppress your instinct to raise your hand until the doorway is cleared,

(2) be ever ready to shake hands with men, often and repeatedly,

(3) practice your technique with the double clasp in private with a friend so you will be ready when you are out in society, and

(4) be slow to offer your hand to a woman, allowing her a moment in which to make the first inviting move if she is the sort of person who does this thing, and then be quick to respond, as if it never entered your mind not to offer your hand, if she is that sort of woman.

16
STRANGER STRANGERS

A considerable number of strange people inhabit this planet, so perhaps it is not too surprising that one encounters a number of strange foreigners in Kazakhstan. Of course it may also be the case that a frontier country attracts more than its share of these people. Anyway, I certainly have met my quota of odd, eccentric, bizarre and offbeat foreigners in Kazakhstan. Here are just a few of them.

In 1993 or perhaps early in 1994, while on a Lufthansa flight to Almaty I met a paleontologist. You know, one of those people who study the bones of dinosaurs. At that time, Lufthansa's flight from Frankfurt landed at Tashkent as well as Almaty. In those days, it seems that the few women left the plane at Tashkent, only men deplaned at Almaty, and everyone freely talked to everyone else on the airplane. "Oh, have you been there? What is it like?"

So it was no surprise that I met and got into a conversation with the paleontologist. I was dumbstruck to learn that he had been in Kazakhstan 20 years earlier -- some time in the early 1970's! -- which, so far as the West is concerned, might just as well have been about the time of the traveler Marco Polo.

Having never met a professional paleontologist before, I was very interested to hear what this man had to say. I always thought that dinosaurs lived in hot and humid climates, but I guess that Kazakhstan, in the very distant past, was that way. If we have sea shells in Kazakhstan, then it should be no surprise to learn that dinosaurs once roamed the countryside as well.

Now, if I was struck dumb to hear that this professor had been to Kazakhstan 20 years earlier, I was floored to hear him say that he studied dinosaurs <u>because</u> he was an anti-Darwinian. He was a creationist who believed that God created the earth and all in it, including the dinosaurs, approximately 6,000 years ago. So, here was a man who had dedicated his life to the study of animals that lived millions of years ago for the purpose of proving in some way that they really sprang into existence and then disappeared from the face of the earth within the last 6,000 years. I did wonder what it might have been like to be a student of this man.

At about the same time that I met the anti-Darwinian paleontologist, I also came across some bikers who had arrived in Almaty from Mongolia and who were on their way to some point in the West, on bike. I initially thought they were talking about motorcycles when they mentioned bikes, but they really did mean pedal-powered bicycles. It is difficult to say if these young men were foolhardy or not. They were having an adventure on bikes, which they had done elsewhere and which they now wanted to do in countries newly opened up to their kind of tourism. I met the bikers at the Italian Restaurant, in the International Business Center, where they were wolfing down phenomenal amounts of the nearest equivalent to Western food, something they had not seen for several weeks while eating out of saddlebags.

It was also in 1994 that I first came across the extreme skiers. I am a skier, and I know the difference between on-piste and off-piste skiing, but I had not previously heard about extreme skiers and extreme skiing. These extreme skiers consisted of a party of four, and included the previous year's American woman's champion extreme skier.

Extreme skiers are not merely off-piste skiers who take to the ungroomed trails that generally are found near the manicured ski runs of developed ski areas. No, the extreme skiers went to areas that offered "challenging" skiing, which probably had no association at all with an established ski area. Their runs were accessible only by helicopter, and when they got to the bottom there was no possibility that they could just drive away in a waiting car.

The extreme skiers hired a helicopter and a couple of Russian ski guides. The Russian ski guides tried manfully to keep up with the extreme skiers during the first day. On the second day, however, the guides simply handed a walkie-talkie to the extreme skiers and told them to radio up to the helicopter for help if they encountered problems. On that day and subsequent days, the Russian guides stayed strapped in the helicopter, and they no longer slowed up these strange skiers from the West.

Then there is the case of the solo skier. He went off to remote areas, avoiding Chimbulak and other established ski areas with their crowds and expenses. I assumed that he had his own car but, in fact, he got to the remote areas by bus, hitch-hiking and on foot. When he found a good place to ski, he put on his skis and went as far as he could. He might camp overnight at the bottom of the run, and then trudge back to civilization the next day. A lot of skiers like their sport because it gives them a sense of risk or danger; I guess this solo skiing guy liked skiing more than most of us.

Most Westerners come to Almaty and find it difficult to get out of the city and into the hinterlands of Kazakhstan. Not so with some geologists I met in 1994. Their job was to go to utterly remote areas of Kazakhstan where they embedded rods that emitted laser signals aimed at satellites in the sky.

Many strict criteria had to be met as to where to position the rods in solid rock but, in simple terms, they did not want to place the rods where someone would back into them with a jeep, and they did not want animals to bump into these things or to scratch their heads on them. The whole idea was to use the geo-stationary satellites that hover in space to detect the almost imperceptible signs of continental drift of the tectonic plates which make up the surface of the earth.

The geologists spoke of meeting shepherds and coming across small communities in exceedingly inaccessible areas where the Russian language was unknown and no one could remember ever seeing a foreigner before. These rugged geologists would not seem so strange to you and me. They were normal scientists going about their work. But to the local inhabitants, they might just as well have come from outer space.

About a year ago I met some ecologists. Ecologists? That's what I thought even though the word has a better ring to it in Russian than in English. I know that there are environmentalists, conservationists, and forestry people, but "ecologists"?

The ecologists had encountered some problems and were about to be deported from Kazakhstan to the United States. It seems that, in addition to carrying out an "ecology program" in one of the oblasts, they were evangelistic Christians who used their spare time to distribute a rather large supply of Bibles to local residents. They had attracted local publicity that escalated into national publicity. Their visas, which were up for renewal or had already expired, were not renewed, and they were given a couple of days to pack up and leave the country. They came to me as a lawyer to try to fight their deportation order.

Having heard the facts of the case, I said that I couldn't help them as a matter of law, but I knew a man with influence in high places who could help if he was willing to do so. He had an office adjacent to ours. At my request, he saw them immediately. Our walls were thin, and soon all the members of my staff had their ears glued to the wall as the voice level went up and then up some more. And all of this was in the Kazakh language. He had asked them, as I had, if their real reason for coming to Kazakhstan was to convert locals to Christianity and they, in open honesty, affirmed that that was the case. At the end of the session he told them that he could not help them, which I understood to mean that he did not want to help them. For their part, they remained in good humor and, when they came to me to report the outcome of their meeting – which I already knew – they boldly said: "We will be back!"

To me, one of the most surprising aspects of their case was that these people were fluent in the Kazakh language. When I say fluent, I mean really fluent, like capable of engaging in active debate or argument.

Finally, I guess that I too qualify as a strange stranger just like some of these people I have met. In February of 1993, while shopping in Almaty for a fur hat, I noticed that a woman had come into the shop for the sole purpose of getting a better look at me. She stood uncomfortably close to me for an inordinate amount of time. She just stood there staring and gawking at me. Since I was not acting at all oddly, I guess that my foreignness was so astounding to her that she could not help but take a closer look.

17
FRINGE ADVERTISING

By "fringe" advertising I am not referring to questionable personal advertisements ("dynamic international business executive seeks travelling companion preferably mid-20s") nor am I referring to the more mundane advertisements in supermarket journals or tabloid newspapers, like those in *Caravan*. No, I am referring to the numerous advertisements that one sees on the street, at virtually every bus stop in Almaty, and on apartment buildings. Sometimes I refer to them as "finger" advertisements or "frill" advertisements but local residents, who seem to have no special name for them, know them simply as the cheapest possible way to engage in direct advertising, cutting out all middlemen and yet getting their message directly in front of the ultimate consumer.

These frill advertisements are those ads that take up about one-third or one-half of an A4 sheet of paper where the top part is dedicated to the sales pitch and where the bottom portion might contain 15 or more "frills" or "fingers" hanging down with usually nothing more than a telephone number to call. Prepared in handwriting or on a computer, the intending advertiser cuts easily detached strips along the bottom edge that contain the telephone number and then simply glues the page to a pole, wall, door or any other place where the likely consumers are expected to be found. The idea is that interested readers should remove one of the paper strips to serve as a reminder to make a call when they get to a phone. That the fingers obviously disappear from many of these ads attests to their success.

I have worked in several countries of the former Soviet empire and I do not recall previously seeing frill advertisements. Maybe they are a general feature of the former Soviet Union and satellite countries but I don't know that. Probably I have noticed these advertisements here in Almaty only because I have been a resident here whereas in Belgrade, Warsaw, and some other cities in this part of the world I was merely a business visitor, mainly staying at hotels.

Here in Almaty I can personally confirm the utility of direct advertising by means of a frilly sheet of paper and a bit of glue. In 1994, when I wanted to improve my apartment situation, I discovered that there were not yet any Scot Holland Estates or other real estate brokers available to help me. There were some apartment ads in the local newspapers but it was time consuming and fruitless to make calls to all parts of the city or to go to visit sections of town where I would not consider taking an apartment. The answer for me was to use the frill advertisement.

First, I decided on the area in which I wanted to live in Almaty. Basically this was walking distance away from my office on a well-lit street that was not too far away from suitable shopping places for groceries. My driver drove me around this area and I spotted a recently completed apartment building where the rooms were larger than usual. All of the apartments had been sold and some people had already moved in. In a flash I prepared my frill advertisements and pasted them on the three entrances of this building. Within 24 hours one of the frill advertisements had been totally destroyed – was I encroaching on someone's proprietary turf? But the other advertisements quickly produced results. One apartment was for sale whereas I wanted to rent. Another apartment was far larger than I required. Yet another apartment was available but it was on the sunny side of the building and did not have cross ventilation.

Some other apartments were available but the prices were unusually high. I think I had inadvertently defeated myself in making these advertisements. Although the ads were prepared on my behalf by authentic local residents using their own language, we made the mistake of using high quality normal white A4 paper whereas most local residents at that time were still using the unbleached brown paper produced by the Soviet-era mills up in Russia. So my advertisements probably had "foreigner" written all over them, thereby forcing up the asking price of owners who were willing to sell or rent their apartments at a profit.

18

KAZAKHSTAN'S NATIONAL PASTIME

A "national pastime" is an activity in which the whole nation participates with enthusiasm, even compulsively and perhaps irrationally -- like, say, American baseball. A true national pastime knows no class distinctions, no ethnic barriers, no age limitations, no sexual discrimination. People from all walks of life are involved in a national pastime from the very poor to the very wealthy. A national pastime might even be one of the defining characteristics of nationhood, the sort of activity that sets a group of people apart from others, though perhaps this gives undue political importance to what might otherwise be a rather mundane and inconsequential activity. Of course, there may be some few people who do not join into this activity and some may oppose it. But even these opponents will not be ignorant of the fact that this national pastime activity has considerable importance to those people who do engage in it.

Do you have a candidate for the activity that is the national pastime of the Republic of Kazakhstan? I do. My candidate for the national pastime is the eating of sunflower seeds, and right now in winter time that national pastime is at the peak of its indulgence. The evidence of it is everywhere, such as the husks that I sometimes find on my kitchen floor (and I don't even eat sunflower seeds), or such as the husks that accumulate on my balcony which catches part of the cascade from upstairs.

My guess is that if you spoke to 100 people on the street at random you would discover that about 80% are carrying a small supply of sunflower seeds, and many of these people will be compulsively eating them, with one hand constantly involved in the automatic and rhythmic pocket-to-mouth motion. Quite a few of the seedless 20% probably are on the lookout for a curb side vendor. When they find one, they will purchase a single glass measure of seeds that will be wrapped up in a page from last week's *Caravan* newspaper that has been specially rolled into a cone shape for this purpose.

Sunflower seeds, like popcorn and salted peanuts, have that important characteristic that all food vendors would like their product to have: a nice taste coupled with a virtually inherent incapacity of the product to satisfy the hunger of the user. Of the three, sunflower seeds are the worst. Unlike popcorn and shelled peanuts, which come ready to eat, sunflower seeds in their natural form -- which is the way they are eaten in Kazakhstan -- require the consumer to de-husk them first. The result is that there is a lot of oral seed-cracking activity that produces a rather pathetically small result. Fortunately, man is endowed with a tremendous capacity to carry on several activities simultaneously, all of which, with practice, can occur without conscious thought. Thus, it is possible to go strolling down Dostyk Avenue (formerly Lenin Avenue) while engaging in conversation with friends and at the same time continually consume sunflower seeds.

Do you ever wonder how this city is supplied with sunflower seeds? I can imagine that there must be great long trains, with tandem diesel engines up front and with many freight cars behind, each burdened with tons of sunflower seeds that arrive in Almaty on a daily basis from the Sunflower Belt of Kazakhstan. How else is the necessary supply delivered to the nation's capital and its many consumers of sunflower seeds? I can even imagine that, in future and more prosperous times, there will be competitions to deliver the freshly harvested seeds to the capital amid extensive television coverage. Perhaps these events will be similar to the mad rush that occurs each year to deliver Beaujolais nouveau wine by exotic means from Paris to London so that some prominent restauranteur can announce that he or she is the first one to be able to offer the new batch.

I hope I will be forgiven for saying something now that is very sexist and fails to deal even handedly with the two sexes. As a Western man who has spent a long time in Kazakhstan, I still find it jarring to the senses to see beautiful and fashionably dressed young women strolling down some tree-lined avenue in Almaty, continually reaching into a pocket, popping sunflower seeds into their mouths, and then spewing out the husks over those immaculately painted lips. Having been taught long ago that it is not polite to spit in public, we tend to recoil when we see this happening on the street among local residents. Of course, this isn't really spitting in public -- though that happens often enough -- and in fact there is a qualitative difference in these two activities. The spewing of sunflower seed husks is a mainly dry process, as you will realize when you recall how often you have seen a piece of husk momentarily clinging in unsightly fashion to someone's lower lip.

It would be interesting to know more about the details of the distribution system for sunflower seeds. Who are all those people on the street who sell portions of sunflower seeds and package them up in old newspapers? Do they purchase a few kilograms at the market each morning and then disperse around the city of Almaty? Are these city dwellers who have never seen a real sunflower plant? Or do they drive each day from some remote collective farm in order to raise some untaxed cash? Do they enjoy territorial exclusives out on the street in a kind of primitive system of franchising? Are they exempt from the Weights and Measures Inspectors? Do they pay Value Added Tax? Do they know anything about the national (or even the international) distribution system of which they play such a vital part?

I sometimes wonder if there is a dietary deficiency in Kazakhstan which is overcome by the generous use of sunflower seeds. I grew up in South Dakota which, like Kazakhstan, is landlocked in a great continental land mass, and suffers temperature extremes in the summer and the winter. Iodized salt was invented for us many years ago because our diet on the Great Plains does not include the seafood necessary to protect us from thyroid problems. Has Nature provided the people of Kazakhstan with an alternative solution to this or a similar problem of dietary deficiency?

I also wonder if the passion for eating sunflower seeds in Kazakhstan is connected with the climate. We can have long slippery winters in Almaty, with many treacherous sidewalks and slippery streets. If you place enough sunflower seed husks on those paths, they serve much the same purpose as grit. Are the sunflower seed eaters performing a public service for us when they spew out those husks?

———————

Caravan newspaper was a popular hardcopy tabloid newspaper in the 1990s and beyond. You always knew when a new edition had come off the press because it was immediately hawked at street intersections by men and women standing perilously close to passing vehicles, sometimes in between lanes. Nowadays it is published only in electronic form on the internet so it no longer is possible us use the paper to wrap things to sell.

19

THE UNIVERSAL HISTORY OF PAPER

I was prompted to write this article in 1997 by the announcement that the government had commissioned the writing of the history of the move of the country's capital from Almaty to Akmola (which later became Astana). So far as I am aware, that history has never been published though a lot has been written about the move and about Astana.

The Government of the Republic of Kazakhstan has commissioned the writing of the history of the move of the nation's capital from Almaty to Akmola. The move to Akmola is an important event in the public life of the nation, and it shows foresight for a country which still has many budgetary constraints that its leaders set aside the funds to ensure that the early history of the country is recorded. While I doubt that any official history will ever make riveting reading, this one could be an exception, and at least it will preserve some records of the move to Akmola that will help future historians to write their views on this topic.

My taste in history runs in an entirely different direction. I was never very good at memorizing the names of kings or the dates of major battles, and I have difficulty seeing the sweeping "big picture" views of times past. What does excite me is the history of the common man. I prefer to read about the cannon fodder soldiers who had to slug it out in the trenches or on the front lines rather than to read about the generals who were safely protected well to the rear. I want to know the details of the working conditions and home life of the people who actually built the pyramids, not the courtly lives of the pharaohs for whom they were built. I marvel at the 1,500 year-old leather sandal found in a bog in Yorkshire but get bored by the finery of English royalty on display in London's museums.

If I were to commission a history of contemporary times in Kazakhstan, I would make sure it recorded the minutiae of the present transition period. Twenty years from now, and perhaps much sooner, the way the people of the Republic of Kazakhstan lived in the year 1990 is likely to seem unimaginable, remembered only vaguely by the oldest members of the community to whom details will be rapidly slipping away and what they do remember will seem incredible to the coming generation.

Hopefully, someone out there has been keeping a detailed diary which records, perhaps only indirectly, those little but telling details of how life was lived by the common people of the Republic of Kazakhstan prior to and during the present period of transition to whatever destiny this Republic is headed. Maybe some bus driver has kept a record of the crowded conditions on his bus, the difficulty of chugging up Furmanova Street with a gasping engine, a full load and a broken main spring, and his delight on the day he was given a new bus to drive, one that was imported from Turkey. Perhaps some young mother has recorded her distress at the rising price of sending her child to kindergarten and dealing with the threat of its closure due to lack of parents who can afford to pay the fee for their child. Hopefully, official statistics are available to chart such things as the year-by-year dramatic growth in the number of cars on the street, the rise in consumption of electricity as sales of household appliances grew, and the number of licenses for restaurants, bars and discotheques.

I am an outsider to many of these changes, and I often hear about them by second or third hand. However, I have observed some changes in our office that have affected the way we do things and even the way we talk about them. To take one example, look at what has happened and is still happening to the use of paper in this country.

When I arrived in Almaty more than four years ago, everyone in business, in government and in the home used a kind of textureless A4 paper which failed so utterly in becoming white that it was a faded brown. At that time, it was simply called "paper" because there was nothing with which to compare it. It did not take long before we began to call it "bad paper", and the genuinely white paper from the West became known as "good paper". Both types of paper were used in the office, but one always had to specify which type of paper should be used for which purpose:

- At the lowest level, there was used bad paper. Many people from the West consider that a used piece of paper has already fulfilled its purpose so that it ought to be filed, mailed or discarded. To us, such paper was not suitable for being sent to a client but it was quite acceptable for use in preparing a fax or printing a draft of a document for internal review. Often we used this paper to receive messages in our fax machine but we always had to make sure that the used side was face down. Otherwise, we received garbled messages with the new text printed on top of the old writing.

- At the next level, there was simply the unused bad paper. It was unsatisfactory for use as the second sheet of a letter if the letterhead was printed on white paper from the West but it could be used to send a draft of a document to a client for review and comments. Internal office memoranda could be printed on it but even for this it is not entirely suitable because the paper has so much color in it that it tends to make bad photocopies.

- Finally, there was the white paper from the West. In 1993 and 1994 I lugged in reams of photocopier paper from England from a supplier called "Universal", and for a long time the members of our staff thought that Universal paper was the top line of white paper. Only later did they learn that plain 80 gm/m^2 photocopier paper is at the bottom end of the paper quality spectrum and that better paper is available with texture, watermarks and other quality features. Among us the word "Universal" became an abbreviated way of saying that we wanted high-quality white paper that would knock the eyes off of other local people when they saw it. When we sent letters or documents using this paper, we sometimes received spontaneous complimentary remarks from the recipients -- clearly the medium had importance along with the message.

Nowadays, at least in our office and in many other offices of Western companies and joint venture enterprises in Almaty, the imported, high-quality white paper has become so commonplace and has so entirely displaced the bad paper that the good paper is once again referred to simply as "paper".

So, during these past few years, the language we used was subtly influenced by the high quality of paper introduced from the West. Moreover, local residents who encountered the good paper have been influenced as well to show greater concern about the presentational aspects of written communication. Like it or not, there is a qualitative difference between a perfect sentence printed by a computer on a nice sheet of white paper and the same sentence typed by a mechanical typewriter on bad paper.

In 1993, even the bad paper was in scarce supply. That was the year we suffered from a severe paper shortage, and our office work nearly ground to a halt. Despite the plentiful supply of wood in the Republic of Kazakhstan, it seems that all of the paper for the Soviet Union came from a few giant suppliers in Russia. Those who have witnessed the shortages of electricity and gas in Kazakhstan during the past few winters will be well aware of the disruptions in supply that have occurred in the post-Soviet distribution system.

In the summer of 1993 the time came when we were down to our last few sheets of bad A4 paper, and one of the members of our office staff went with our driver to search the city for supplies. Many hours later she returned to the office empty handed -- there seemed not to be a single ream of bad paper left in Almaty. The next day she resumed the search and eventually came back with some paper. Our excitement at having the fresh supply was only slightly dimmed by the fact that this paper was A3, twice the size of A4 paper. In the coming weeks, everyone in the office had a chance to apply scissors to paper so that we could resume use of our photocopiers, our computer printers and our fax machine.

There also came a time when we neared the closing date for a large, i.e., paper-consuming, investment transaction with only our usual supply of bad paper. The closing was going to be televised and news photographers would be on hand to record this momentous occasion. We did not look forward to using our bad paper to produce the foundation agreement and the charter for the joint venture financial institution and the various other agreements and supporting documents. Fortunately, the Western investors came to the closing two or three days early and brought with them several boxes of photocopier paper as personal baggage.

One of the knacks of running an office in 1993 and 1994 has already become a vague memory to most of us from the West but it may linger on at some of the ministries of government which still cannot routinely afford to purchase white paper. Some of the bad paper was doubly bad because it had been poorly guillotined. The paper probably slips when it is chopped to A4 size at the paper mill. Lacking straight edges, such paper may refuse to be gripped by a fax machine or it may be askew as it goes through a computer printer. One of the tricks you learn in trying to overcome these problems is to make sure when loading the paper that the squarest end is the one that feeds into the fax machine or printer. One also learns to make slight adjustments when photocopying a page that was printed aslant so that the photocopies come out with borders that are more or less uniform in size. Another knack of using bad paper is that, before stapling it, you must thump the top edge on a table, not the bottom edge, because bad paper often comes in variable lengths.

Somewhat later in 1994 one of the members of our staff received a phone call from a relative who had come upon an enormous supply of bad paper. I forget now how many hundreds of kilograms of paper we purchased but I do remember that for many months every nook and cranny in our office was crammed with this badly cut, sometimes holey brown paper which arrived without any packaging other than a rough cord tied around each parcel. In the aftermath of obtaining this supply, we actually started to become careless in our use of paper. We began to throw away paper that had been used on only one side, and some of us started to use entirely clean sheets of bad paper for writing notes of telephone calls. It was only in 1996 that we finally used the last of that huge load of bad paper.

The Soviet Union's legacy of bad paper still lingers on in Almaty. Most of the agencies of government seem to rely still on the traditional sources of supply of paper. Also due to budgetary limitations, most agencies of government continue to be exceedingly conservative in using their paper. We recently sought to obtain a copy of newly adopted regulations of one of the Ministries. We were given what seems to be the only signed original copy of the regulations, and we were allowed to take it to our office in order to make a copy for ourselves but this was on the strict condition that we had to return the original <u>and</u> a good photocopy for use by the Ministry.

20

EAST MEETS WEST OVER THE DINNER TABLE

Although the earth shrinks each year, at what seems to be an accelerating pace, and although one continually senses that the human race is undergoing some type of homogenization process, it remains the case that various groups of people eat differently. This is one of those distinctions that adds to the flavor of life and helps to remind us that there still are real differences among us. We go travelling and encounter new eating experiences. Some we like; some we don't; but they can make for memorable experiences, including here in Kazakhstan.

I have observed that local residents eat with their chins over the dish from which they are taking their food. Often, the chin is not only over the dish, but the chin is also very close to the dish. If you want direct proof, go take a look at the stand-up eating counter at the Green Market.

When I grew up, there was a frequent refrain in our family, and in most of the other families I knew, urging the children not to hunch over their food and to keep their elbows off the table. We were not exactly drilled like the cadets at the U.S. military establishment at West Point, where they must sit ramrod straight while eating, unable to look down at their food. But we were taught to sit back and to keep our elbows well off the table. Napkins covered the lap for the good reason that they might catch something during the course of the meal.

Here in Almaty, it is the norm to hunch over the food, and no one would think it is bad manners to do so. I have wondered often why this should be so. The conclusion I have come to is that this practice arises from the combined effects of a lack of paper napkins or their high cost, and the difficulty of cleaning clothing that becomes soiled by food. Why else is it that 3-ply paper napkins are de-plied into three whole but thin napkins? And, in many restaurants staff members who otherwise might be idle between meals cut the separate plies into halves or even quarters. With such small napkins or no napkins, the very practical local solution to ensure a clean lap is to lean your head over the dish from which you are eating.

How happy some of us were when Hyatt Hotels took over management of the former Marco Polo Hotel (now Rahat Palace Hotel). They operated a dry cleaning business and actively catered to the general public for business.

Another reason for leaning over the table may be historical and irrelevant to much of the modern food that is eaten in Kazakhstan. Not so long ago the indigenous population of this country ate without a lot of cutlery. If one is scooping a wet meal out of a common bowl in the center of the table without a napkin in sight, the natural reaction of most people is to lean forward, over the table and over any dish in front of you.

If you have the good fortune to be invited to eat with a Kazakh family, you will almost certainly eat well and will experience a highly memorable occasion. The traditions of the steppe live on even in the high-rise apartments of Almaty. Strangers must be welcomed, and welcoming means providing food, meaning much food. It also often means providing meat - lots of meat. I have been the beneficiary of much hospitality by Kazakh families. That is to say, I have eaten much. Sometimes so much food is presented that you begin to worry if the family is mortgaging its eating future in order to provide the present meal.

There is among Kazakhs a collective memory of starvation. This may be an age-old collective memory or it may go back no further than to the starvation induced by Stalin's disastrous farm collectivization policies in Russia and Ukraine. Those policies resulted in vast numbers of horses, cattle and sheep being taken from Kazakhs who, being dependent upon meat for survival, died in large numbers. It is no secret among modern-day Kazakhs that, had it not been for those terrible events, the Kazakhs would form a clear majority of the population of the Republic of Kazakhstan today. This collective memory of starvation may help to explain the generosity when serving food -- there's no starvation in this household!

Often, there seems to be no centerpiece to the main course of the meal, assuming that you can discern that there is a main course. There will be plenty of food and lots of varieties of food, but you do not go away and tell people later that you had a steak meal or lamb chops.

One nice practice is the way local men join in serving food to others. My impression is that the dishing out of food at a table is a genderless function. Your neighbor at the table or perhaps someone sitting across from you or even quite a distance away may ladle out some food on your plate and the plates of others. This server might be a woman but equally it might be a man. In the West, a man may carve the meat and serve it, or he might hand out the charcoal grilled food in the back yard, but he is unlikely to put various salads on your plate at a sit-down meal, or to peel an orange for you.

Bread in Almaty retains a kind of biblical importance for local residents, having a centrality to life and to the dining table that most of us from the West no longer experience. Perhaps it is the vacuousness of our bread that separates us from the residents of Almaty. We tend to regard bread as probably fattening and not very nutritious. We generally value our sandwiches for their contents, not for the bready wrapper. Locally, bread is regarded as having a kind of sacredness about it such that one must not waste it or squander it. You and I may discard a piece of bread as a relatively cheap and uninteresting item of food that can be easily replaced. Locally, it is offensive to waste bread, giving rise to a feeling of guilt.

Bread is so crucial to daily eating that, if you invite a local resident to your apartment to share a meal, they very likely will ask for the bread if none is on the table. This is not a show of disrespect on their part nor a sign of rudeness; rather, they probably think that you have overlooked doing something that you almost certainly intended to do, and their request for the bread is really an attempt to be helpful. Would you feel embarrassed on sitting down for a meal in someone's home and asking for the salt? Probably not. Well, to local residents, bread at a meal is more important to them than salt is to you.

By the way, watch the way you put down your bread when you are eating with local residents. If the bread has a natural top and a bottom, such as a sliver from one of those round loaves the size of a large pancake, you need to put it down on its bottom. If you don't, you may make your table companions uncomfortable.

Recently I visited a new supermarket in Almaty. I noticed a long line of people waiting to be served. Curious, I went closer and saw that they were purchasing bread. No one makes much money selling bread, and I was surprised that the bread seller could afford to rent the space. Then I realized that the owners of the supermarket were using modern techniques of merchandising. If you want to draw people into a supermarket, sell something that everyone wants virtually on a daily basis and do so in the middle or rear of the building forcing them to walk past the other counters.

As previously mentioned, meat is very important to the local diet, especially to the ethnic Kazakhs. I remember how jolted I was when serving a well-balanced, Western-style meal to a guest in my apartment one night when the serious question arose as to why it was I was serving cooked vegetables with the meat.

Although the horse is much revered among Kazakhs due to its traditional importance to life on the steppes, it is also much eaten. You do not always know when you are eating horse meat. Many local meat dishes simply contain "meat", probably horse meat. If you have qualms about eating horsemeat, it may help to remember that it is said locally that horse meat is virtually cholesterol-free.

It is likely that a very large portion of the people in the West who have heard of the Republic of Kazakhstan have also heard a story about a guest of honor being served the head of a sheep and of having to eat the eyes of the sheep. This is one of those memorable, if (to us) distasteful, occasions that, for years to come, will be brought up at cocktail parties in the West to amuse and impress others. Many other tales may be told about Kazakhstan but the horror of being served the head of a sheep is within the grasp of almost everyone, most of whom will give a sympathetic shudder even to contemplate the possibility.

Our quick general impression is that local residents do not eat many vegetables, partly due to the emphasis in their diet upon meat. This is probably a misperception based on a bias in favor of what we think of as meal vegetables. Typically, a meal in many parts of the West consists of a piece of meat, which tends to be the foundation on which the rest of the food is selected, and two or three cooked vegetables. It is these vegetables which we consider to be vegetables for dining purposes – such as spinach, peas, Brussels sprouts, beans of various kinds, and even cabbage.

It is true that local meals often are short on segregated cooked vegetables. However, vegetables are used in the delicious soups that are found throughout the former Soviet Union, in numerous stew-like dishes, and there are various meats that are spiked with chunks of carrots or other vegetables. Moreover, there are the virtually ubiquitous tomato and cucumber salads which cause some people from the West to swear that, when they return home, they will never again eat another cucumber or tomato salad. Finally, there are numerous types of salads with chopped vegetables ranging from beets and cabbage to things for which we may not have names in the English language.

Another reason that we do not see so many types of vegetables served in Kazakhstan is that meals in this country continue to be far more affected by the seasonality of the crops than is the case in developed countries in the West. In England, for example, we have virtually all fruits and vegetables throughout the year except for peaches, strawberries and a few others, which makes them all the sweeter for their seasonality. So, in Kazakhstan, you may not see a wide range of vegetables on the table throughout the year but you do see vegetables and the selection does vary seasonally.

As with many countries in the East, tea is very important to the daily routines of life and to the meal. I grew up in the coffee-drinking Midwest of the United States, and it took me a long time to learn to like tea. But, if I think of tea as the local equivalent of coffee, then I begin to understand the role it plays. If you pay even the shortest of social calls upon a local household, you almost certainly will be served some tea. You may or may not be asked if you would like to have a cup of tea – it might simply be set in front of you before you have had a chance to think about what your answer would be if asked. It is more important to the hostess that she offers the tea than that you drink it, but you should drink it.

The first time I ate a full meal as a guest in a local household, I was rather shocked at how utterly rude the other guests seemed to be. The lady of the house, sitting at the head of the table, really did not have a chance to eat because she spent all of her time filling cups with tea. The empty cups were passed up the table without any "please", "thank you", "please pass the cup" or even "could I have some more tea?" I only gradually learned later that this is quite normal, and no discourtesy was intended. Someone must keep the tea supply line open and running, and this is one of the functions of a gracious hostess.

It is revealing of the importance of tea to recall that the World Bank made several loans to the Republic of Kazakhstan soon after independence to ensure the availability of vital commodities. One of those loans was earmarked for the purchase of tea.

Another surprise to me is how the woman of the household often seems not to eat the dinner she has prepared, at least when there are guests. She will be in and out of the kitchen carrying in more food, she will be pressing the guests to take another piece of this or some more of that, and then she will be occupied with keeping the tea cups filled. What a contrast this is with the West. There, a woman may slave away for hours in the kitchen to prepare a sumptuous meal, and then try to sit down with her guests with what appears to be the effortless production of an interesting, well-presented meal. Here, there is no pretense, and the labor-intensive aspect of cooking is respected rather than denied.

21

ENGLISH PENETRATION

Nowadays, quite a few local residents of Almaty speak credible English and large numbers of others are willing to try to communicate even if their training seems to have been based on advertising English, pop music English and TV soap opera English. Many restaurants have bilingual menus, and some waiters and waitresses can take orders in English and perhaps engage in a bit of banter with customers. Hotels that cater to foreign travelers normally have some staff members who can deal with the public in English. Quite a few advertisements can be seen that are in the English language. Some probably are there simply because the importer did not want to spend any money to create authentic local advertisements and merely used the flyers and billboard materials that were received from abroad. But the fact that the importer would consider using the English language advertisements reflects the high acceptability of the English language for this purpose. Clearly there is not a sense of hostility, at least not yet, about this intrusion of yet another foreign language into this culture.

Taxi drivers -- official and unofficial -- often know some words of English, and occasionally one is surprised to encounter a driver who is an accomplished English speaker. Recently, while coming down from a mountainside dacha, I caught a ride with a middle aged man and his wife. Since he initially went past me and my friends and then backed up, I gathered that he did not often accept riders. He had been born and raised in Karaganda, which is not exactly in the vanguard of the influx of foreigners. Nevertheless, he had considerable skills in the English language, which he eagerly spoke with me. My impression is that, despite the large numbers of foreigners in Almaty, he had not previously encountered one of us. Numerous as we are, we are not that numerous. Upon arriving at our destination, the driver refused to accept any money. His reward, if he needed one, had been the chance to speak some English.

Young children who spot an obvious foreigner often try to initiate some practice in the language or will eagerly respond if you give them a "Hello" and a smile. There is a little toddler in my apartment building who is still at the commencement of learning the Kazakh language of his family yet he routinely greets me with a stream of English words, like "Hello-how-are-you?-what's-your-name?-My-name-is-Tuka." Probably he does not know exactly what he is saying, but the fact that he is saying it at all speaks volumes about the penetration of the English language into the homes and lives of people in this city.

It wasn't always so. Early in 1993 one's initial impression of Almaty was that no one spoke English other than specially trained interpreters. There was a good reason for this. The Soviet heritage meant that speaking English to a foreigner was highly suspect, and might even be followed by official questioning and a black mark on your record. With that kind of attitude, it was safe to be an accomplished English speaker only if you were a translator or interpreter whose job it was to help officials communicate with English-speaking foreigners.

If you spoke German but not Russian, then your chances were quite good in 1993 that you could get around on your own. German was probably the leading second foreign language in Kazakhstan up to the onset of perestroika, and of course it continues to be a popular language today even if English has rocketed past it. The fact that some millions of ethnic Germans settled in the Republic of Kazakhstan and wanted to keep their language and culture alive certainly helped. But they were not the only ones interested in the German language. Many ethnic Kazakhs voluntarily took up the German language as their second or third language. Up until the Berlin Wall fell, Eastern Germany, depressing as it was to Westerners, represented the highest level of achievement in science and commercial production for the whole of the Soviet Union, and it was the nearest thing the Soviet sphere had to a "Western" country. Also, during the Second World War vast numbers of prisoners of war learned the German language in German prison camps.

Very large numbers of local residents who are now 30 years old or younger studied English while at school. Their problem, until foreigners came here in large numbers, was that they never had a chance to use the English language and certainly not with a native English speaker. It often happens, therefore, that if you meet a young adult in Almaty and you are unable to communicate in Russian, the chances are pretty good that you can communicate in English. It may be halting English, with lots of pauses, with missing articles, with "he" and "she" being entirely interchangeable, and all the other typical problems that Russian speakers have with the English language, but it is real communication.

I have had the rich experience of making a gift of functional English to several people in Almaty. They had had formal academic training a few years earlier but had never made any use of the language during the intervening years. The thought had never entered their minds that they might ever go on a trip abroad where they would use the language. Then I met them. I virtually pulled the English language out of them. There was a time when three or four young people practically turned the Italian Restaurant in the International Business Center into a club, baiting me to stay on with them for hours while kick starting their English or getting the rust out of it. I imagine that my experience has been repeated by many other foreigners who have come here.

Not all English speakers in past years came from the Language Institute with the objective of being translators or English teachers. Children of Soviet diplomats attended International Schools in Cairo, New York, Tokyo or wherever the diplomatic career took their parents. Quite a few local residents learned the English language from Christian missionaries, particularly Baptist missionaries. By the time I arrived here in 1993 they had already been here for a couple of years, ostensibly to teach the English language but running Bible study classes as a sideline, also in English. I know some people who took both kinds of classes, not with the idea of converting to Christianity but simply to gain more exposure to the English language.

I met a quite unusual man while looking for office space about two years ago. I had spotted his advertisement for a building in an excellent location and we set off to take a look. On approaching the building, I saw a driver washing his car. He had a certain age, was an ethnic Russian, and gave every appearance of being the driver. I asked to see the owner. Sensing that I was a native English speaker, he immediately switched into English with one of the best accents I have heard here during five years. It turned out that he was the owner of the building, and he showed us around. The building turned out to be unsuitable for my purposes but we had a pleasant exchange of views that finally led me to ask how it was that he spoke such good English. His response bowled me over. He said that some years earlier he had been a shepherd in the mountains and he spent months up there in lonely isolation. He had one book with him which he read from front cover to back cover and then from back cover to front cover, in English. I never did figure out if this was his way of saying that he had been a high level officer in the KGB but I suppose it was possible that he had been a shepherd and that he did have only one English book with him. Probably there was more to the story of his language skills than he told me.

Earlier, I had once been trying to locate the office of a new client which was in an apartment building up near the Hotel Kazakhstan. They had given me a description over the telephone that seemed quite accurate, but when I arrived in the courtyard of the building, I discovered that there were many more entrances to the building than I had been led to believe. A gardener in the courtyard who had rough hands and soiled boots saw that I was in a quandary. He strolled over to me and asked, in English, if he could help me, which he then did. I was impressed with his language skills but equally with his friendly willingness to help a stranger.

It is difficult to imagine what will be the role of the English language in this country in future years. The Kazakh language is vibrant and on the rebound; time is on its side. The Russian language is resilient, even among many ethnic Kazakhs, and there are too many ethnic Russians in Kazakhstan to permit the Russian language to be displaced, at least not quickly. Moreover, Moscow continues to be a kind of cultural magnet or beacon, and not simply to ethnic Russians. This is a dynamic mixture which will require a generation or more to work itself out. In the meantime, the English language continues to sweep across the globe making itself the unofficial universal language of mankind while locally, here in Almaty, English language skills open employment opportunities and improved salaries for those who have mastered the language.

22

ENGLISH AS SHE IS SPOKEN

Increasingly I have become aware that I need to watch my language. I think I first became conscious of the fact that I had drifted dangerously far into "Mid-Atlantic English" in November 1978. We were going to host some of our neighbors in England to an American-style Thanksgiving Day dinner. While on a business trip to the United States a couple of weeks earlier, I heard myself telling my American relatives that I had purchased several "tins of yams" to take back to England to add an authentic American touch to the meal. The words just came rushing out of my mouth and I was immediately taken aback by what I had said. I realized that I was no longer fluently bilingual in English in that I had used English English with Americans and not American English to describe the "cans of sweet potatoes" that I had purchased.

Not long afterwards another incident like this occurred in my office in London. One small room had been pressed into use as an administrative office even though its entry door was uncomfortably low for a tall person like me. While showing some equally tall American visitors around the premises, I cautioned them to "mind your head" when entering that door, to which they commented that this was a rather quaint way to say "watch your head". Again I had slipped, this time so far that I did not even realize that I had used non-standard American English when speaking to Americans until my error was drawn to my attention.

I grew up speaking General American English, which is sometimes called Broadcaster American English. In the part of the

United States from which I come, we think of ourselves as speaking an accent-free form of English of the American type, the same language that numerous radio broadcasters and TV newscasters speak on the national media in the United States. If you check out the origins of the likes of former TV news anchormen like Chet Huntley or David Brinkley, and scads of other radio and TV personalities from the earliest days of nation-wide broadcasting in the United States right down to the present time, the vast majority of them, perhaps surprisingly, are from the thinly populated middle part of America from which I come -- the area that the British Broadcasting Corporation not so long ago referred to as the "flyover" part of America, you know, the part that most people see only from the window of an airplane as they travel from one heavily populated coast to the other.

The General American English that is my birthright is kind of like having type O-positive blood, the universal donor blood. Everyone seems to be able to hear us without having to strain when we speak whereas we often must cock our heads or ask someone to repeat what they have said if they speak Southern to us, have an Indiana twang, use too much Valley Speak, or murder the English language in New Jersey.

I have lived in England for nearly 30 years and people there often comment on how remarkable it is that I have not lost my very American accent. I sometimes reply that I was chiselled out of South Dakota granite. On the other hand, people in America who do not know me tend to think that I might come from Canada. I guess my pronunciation of vowels has been affected by living abroad far more than I can hear. For my part, I cannot discern any accent in my voice but, by contrast, I certainly have become aware that a lot of English expressions have worked their way into my ordinary speech, and I am getting slower and slower in my ability to filter them out when speaking to Americans. Okay, being "at sixes and sevens" is still to me a very English expression (meaning that someone can't make up their mind). And I still cannot manage to say "whilst" with a straight face but lots of other English ways of saying things have entered my vocabulary and I no longer recognize their English origin nor the fact that the time worn meanings in England may not be understood by Americans.

Sometimes in England I find myself repeating what I have said in the various ways that I know how to say the same thing, using both English English and American English, sometimes without certainty as to which is which, hoping that the listener will pick out the one that has meaning for him or her. It is not very efficient to tell someone in a kind of Anglo-American babble to "take the elevator/ lift to the second/first floor" or to "get the tools out of the trunk/boot and then to make some repairs under the hood/bonnet" of the car but I assume that the listeners hear only the parts that have meaning for them. This can be tedious for me as well as boring to them, and probably is no more effective than speaking English quite loudly to non-English speakers in the hope that they will better understand by this means a language they do not speak.

I have discovered in Almaty that I face even greater difficulties than in England to try to retain my mother tongue as it was handed down to me. In particular, my English often becomes degraded when speaking to local residents (and to some foreigners who are not entirely comfortable in the English language!). My speech does not exactly turn into Pidgin English nor even into a simplified Esperanto but it definitely is not the full-spectrum English that I know and would use with native English speakers.

Frequently I become aware while speaking that I have ceased using the articles "a", "an" and "the" which are so essential for speaking English with precision and clarity, but which do not have counterparts in the Russian language. Other words that are not essential for the point I am making also tend to get eliminated. Out go the adjectives and adverbs. If you sense that the listener is struggling to comprehend each individual word that you are uttering, the natural instinct is to economize on the number of words being used. This is a case of "the less said, the better" because the fewer the words spoken, the more likely it is that each word will be understood, or so it seems.

Other times I realize that I have slipped into using what might be called "translator English". This is where the English word is selected because of its close proximity to the Russian equivalent rather than because it is the best way to express oneself naturally in the English language. I am certain that, as time has gone by, I have also become rather tolerant of translator ways of saying things in English which in previous years I would have corrected. I know what the words or phrases mean because I have heard the same things said in the same (non-standard English) ways before but someone less tolerant of the non-standard use of the English language or less familiar with the severe demands placed upon translators might not be so accepting. Even here, however, I have never found myself using the much overworked "till" of the translators which would better be rendered as either "until" (an ordered deadline) or "by" (a permitted period) and almost never as "till" (which I tell the translators to reserve primarily to refer to the drawer that holds the cash in a cash register). Also, I still go on "a business trip", not "the business trip", but maybe in a few years I too will go on "the business trip".

Another common problem with my English when speaking to local residents who have a somewhat tenuous command of the English language is that I repeat myself, sometimes tiresomely, using the exact same words that I have already said. In England, I repeat myself by using different words in a combination of English English and American English. Here, I echo the exact same words, like a broken record. It is as if I am assuming that the listeners will not comprehend what I said the first time around so I had better give them yet another chance to hear the exact same thing repeated for their benefit without waiting for them to ask for the repeat. This self-echoing on my part is something that a few local residents have (to their credit and to my considerable embarrassment) drawn to my attention and questioned. (I think I have never gone so far as to say "How are you? How are you?" but I probably have come close to it.) In fairness to myself, for the last five years I have constantly been teaching English, and repetition is an essential part of the process.

I also tend to eliminate idiomatic expressions when speaking to local residents, thereby stripping much of the color out of the English language but perhaps increasing the likelihood of achieving effective communication. This has more advantages than disadvantages. I recall a recent occasion at a press conference in Bishkek where an idiomatic expression that was intended to stress the main point of the presentation in fact became a major diversion which almost undermined the purpose of the meeting.

The conference was held by a high level official of one of the major international lending institutions in order to announce an important new investment to the assembled members of the press corps and government officials. His flawless English presentation was smoothly translated by an excellent interpreter but she lost her stride and his presentation came temporarily unstuck when he made reference to how there ought to be a "level playing field" (fair or neutral rules that do not favor one side or the other) for foreign and local investors. The press conference came to an abrupt halt as the interpreter searched her mind to try to comprehend what he had said in English and then to find a suitable Russian-language equivalent. Various members of the press corps and several of the other assembled dignitaries offered up their versions of what might possibly be meant by "level playing field" and how best to say the equivalent in the Russian language. I am not sure that a satisfactory result was ever achieved but a good time was had by all in the linguistic free-for-all that ensued for several minutes!

The banker, to give him due credit, quickly spotted the problem he had stumbled into and he tried to restore the decorum of the occasion. However, he then faced a problem that was no less excruciating for him than the one he had earlier created for the interpreter, namely, to find a way, under the glare of the TV cameras and the urgency of the moment, to say in plain English that which had been so much more easily and more graphically expressed by using an idiomatic expression.

23

THE PERILS OF THE OPEN ROAD

The street in front of my apartment building in Almaty recently acquired an open manhole. This new peril previously was well covered by the requisite manhole cover but that cover either was stolen by someone in order to cover yet another exposed hole elsewhere or it became broken and has not yet been replaced. To me there are two or three things that are remarkable about this newly opened manhole.

First, it has been some time since I can remember seeing a conspicuously open manhole in the middle of a street in Almaty which poses danger to passing cars and to inattentive pedestrians. Oh, I know that there is still that depression in the sidewalk near the kiosks on the corner of Dostyk (Lenin) Avenue and Shevchenko Street which is about the size of a manhole but which is only about one foot deep. And I also know that, if you deliberately go scouting around in Almaty, you undoubtedly can find some other open manholes and similar perils in the streets and on the sidewalks. There are, for example, some open holes or teetering covers on the side road as you walk down toward the main gate of the Green Market. But it seems to me that many of the former dangers to drivers and pedestrians in this city have been fixed, and it also seems that there is a more deliberate effort now, as compared to just a couple of years ago, to keep the streets and sidewalks safe.

Second, there have been obvious attempts by someone, perhaps the people who live in my neighborhood, to try to alert drivers and others to the existence of that gaping manhole. At first, a cardboard box was placed over the hole but it either blew away or was struck by some hapless driver. Then a tree branch was stuck into the hole to alert oncoming traffic that the hole is there. It is not for nothing that most cars in Almaty are operated by drivers who make a living from the road and for whom alertness to danger is part of their job. My point is that, only a very few years ago, it seemed to me that no one went out of their way to alert others to such dangers. Can it be that there is in Almaty an emerging sense of civic responsibility?

Third, rather quickly after the open hole appeared in my street, some efforts were made to repair it. I think it took only about one week for a new round cover to be placed over the manhole. This is a quicker response than I can remember in the past to fix other open manholes. When our office was located near the intersection of Abay Avenue and Seifullin Street, there was a rectangular hole in Seifullin Street that went wholly or partly uncovered for many, many months. Despite the caution shown by many drivers in Almaty, several cars ended up with a wheel stuck in that hole and maybe with a broken axle. I do not want to denigrate the repair effort on my street so I will only quietly observe that the replacement cover also experienced problems within one or two days with the result that the manhole out there in the street is open once again.

I used to have an apartment up in micro-district Samal II, and I often walked up and down Furmanov Street just opposite to where the new Presidential Palace is located. At that time, in 1993 and 1994, the area just above the National Museum was desolate and overgrown whereas today it is a nice looking public garden. At the edge of the public pathway and in the midst of the overgrown area there were quite a few open manholes near which children played and, if you took a look down, you could see steam pipes running beneath at a breath-taking drop of about four meters (say, 15 feet). I was horrified. At night the street lights were turned off very early to conserve energy and these open holes were there as a constant source of danger. But I never saw a child -- or an adult for that matter -- come to harm and it occurred to me that local residents had learned to live in the midst of a high degree of peril that we from the West found objectionable.

I wondered in 1993 and later why it was that there should be so many open manholes in Almaty. Manhole covers are durable and generally have no alternative uses. Once covered, a manhole normally stays that way. Were covers in short supply during Soviet times? Did the Central Planners underestimate the need for the covers but not for the manholes themselves? Did the city in the Soviet Union that specialized in the production of manhole covers fall behind on production? Did the Manhole Combinat outproduce the Manhole Cover Combinat? Thoughts like these went through my head and were unanswered, but it was obvious back then that there were quite a few peculiarities and dislocations in the industrial sector and in the distribution system in Soviet times and after the collapse of the Soviet Union.

The winter of 1993-94 was a rough one with long periods of snow, cold, and fog. Everyone wore fur hats. The leather coats and jackets from Turkey were nearly ubiquitous. But gloves and mittens seemed not to exist, and raw, cold hands were a natural condition of life. It was as if the Soviet Union, having evolved in relative isolation, had overlooked developing something to cover the hands. Probably I am mistaken about this, and local residents have told me that, while there was indeed a leather shortage several years ago, people did use gloves. Nevertheless, five years ago, if you wanted to make a favorable impression with your local friends in Almaty, a new pair of gloves was regarded as a special treat. My impression persists that gloves continue to be little used by many local residents in Almaty. Do old habits persist even after gloves become available? Have the international traders failed to spot this niche market?

The question of what is and what is not a danger, like open manholes, is a subject that can be much debated, and the answer clearly depends upon the country or society in which this subject is raised for discussion. When I lived in Paris in 1965, I was interested to see that Paris still had its ancient green buses with the rear platform on which people could stand and onto which many people took a running leap if the bus pulled away before they had had a chance to get on or from which people alit even if the bus was still moving. One's initial impression was that these buses were open invitations to personal disaster but, despite the countless rides I took in all weather conditions and despite observing many people jumping on and off while the bus was in motion, I cannot recall seeing anyone have an accident. In London, we used to have trains with doors that opened outward and that could be operated by the passengers at any time. Many passengers, particularly during morning rush hour, would jump off the moving trains upon arriving at a train station in order to beat the rush to the ticket collectors at the gates. Again, this seemed to me to be a recipe for disaster and I am sure that some passengers fell when taking premature departure from the trains and I am also sure that some passengers waiting on the platform got struck when doors of approaching trains flew open. Remarkably, however, the overwhelming majority of travelers who used these high-risk forms of travel in Paris and London went unscathed day after day.

I may not have seen any accidents when people jumped on buses in Paris and I may have witnessed only the occasional slight mishap of people alighting too early from trains in London, but the fact is that you can no longer jump on the back of a green bus in Paris and, so far as I am aware, all trains with passenger-operated outward opening doors have been withdrawn from service in London. Presumably the very small number of people who could not cope with these "normal" risks of daily life stung the operators with such large lawsuits and settlements that those operators made the decision when looking for new equipment to specify higher safety standards.

My feeling in Paris and then later in London was that the American public has been conditioned to expect far too much protection against public danger and has been lulled into relaxing the sense of responsibility that each individual should feel for his or her own safety. Plaintiffs' lawyers in the United States make the claim that they hold the key to the improvement of safety in the United States. They also justify the use of the contingency fee method of billing as one of the dynamos for social change. If, for example, you break your leg on bad public paving and are too poor to sue the city, don't worry; a lawyer with a contingency retainer agreement will quickly redress the balance, sue the city, get you an award and get the lawyer a nice fee in the bargain. The city, having paid out a large award, is stirred into taking preventive action so as to avoid similar suits in the future. A large court judgment tends to grab the attention even of city officials.

It is possible to hold the view that plaintiffs' lawyers are among the scum of the earth -- you don't even have to be a non-lawyer to hold that view -- but there is much to be said in favor of the principle that no one is accountable unless there exists an effective mechanism for holding them accountable.

While in college in the United States, I spent a couple of summers working as the cashier at a drive-in restaurant in Alpena at the upper end of the lower peninsula of Michigan. I soon learned that I could tell at a glance the cost of a tray of food being sent out to a car. I am not some kind of mathematical wizard, and it probably is the case that I now would use a calculator if I had to figure the cost of a tray full of burgers and milk shakes. But I know that all of us have within us a kind of skill at numbers which is available for use if we want to use it but which lies dormant if we constantly rely upon a calculator to do the figuring. Maybe the skill of living safely in the presence of peril, such as open manholes, is somewhat the same as the skill of doing numbers in your head -- you have the skill if you use it and otherwise you lose it.

———————

I brought all the members of my small team in Almaty to London for a visit in August 1994 to let them know more about the world outside the confines of Almaty and to reward them for their good work. Lawyers, translators, chief accountant, and even the driver came in two consecutive groups. They marvelled at many things but one of the sights most commented on to me was the smoothness of the streets and highways. It also caught their attention that I personally drove my car on our excursions. It hadn't quite dawned on them while in Almaty that cars could be driven by someone other than a professional driver.

Some years after this article was written, the Akimat of Almaty purchased a US$1 million street paving machine. It gobbled up the street in front of it, added in extra new material to improve the mix, and then spread new pavement out from the rear. After years of suffering from potholes, deteriorating road surfaces and bad patching, the city finally had a resource that was marvellous to behold in action.

24
CONSUMERISM IN KAZAKHSTAN

Nowadays, most consumer goods are available in abundance in Almaty. It has taken seven years since the breakup of the Soviet Union to bring the goods of the world to the market place with the result that there are car showrooms, shops galore, some almost opulent, and all kinds of things can be found in the kiosks. Even a shopping center is under construction at Samal.

In fact, however, many of the improvements in the past few years have been only in the packaging or presentation and not in the availability of the products. Previously cars were available from the outside world but they were bought in crummy rundown places. Now we have fancy showrooms. A few years ago imported clothes were available but only in the Green Market or the Chinese Market. Now they are in fancy shops.

Indeed, I was told a few years ago that, despite appearances, everything is available in Almaty. You might have to put up with last year's model or it may not come from your preferred manufacturer but it is available. I can give some personal examples of successful shopping before the arrival of all the modern shops.

In the summer of 1993, I discovered that our office caught far too much sunshine and it was a very uncomfortable place to work. I decided to buy an air conditioner. Someone from our office was dispatched and later came back with a new window air conditioner from Azerbaijan, where the Soviet Union had concentrated the manufacture of air conditioners. I was very pleased and the price was quite reasonable. The only problem was that this brand new air conditioner did not work when plugged in despite the fact that it was straight from the factory. I could not believe it but the members of my staff calmly accepted the fact that something new from a factory might not work. We located a repairman who diligently worked for three solid days on this example of Soviet consumer products. At the end of this there were several bits and pieces on the floor and I imagined that here was yet another case of someone taking a clock apart and not being able to get it all back together. The difference is that this time the air conditioner worked, and it continued to work for the next five years without any further attention, until we moved to a new office where it was no longer needed. The cost of the repairs, labor and parts included – a mere $16 – but then $16 in 1993 bought a lot more than it does today.

In the winter of 1994-95, I decided to buy my own skis in Almaty. At that time the rental skis at Chimbulak were quite bad and the boots were worse. (I remember one occasion when, on getting off the chairlift, I had to push my way down the mountain, so burred were the edges and so rusty were the skis. On another occasion I skied all day with a left boot with no buckles.) By now, I had my own boots and I wanted to improve the quality and safety of my weekends at Chimbulak by getting better skis.

A ski friend told me to go to the Green Market where I could find a ski shop. Ski shop? 1994 and a dedicated ski shop? I went to the Green Market's main entrance, as directed, and looked all about. I checked out both sides of the street and could not find anything resembling a ski shop. Just as I was about to give up a hopeless task I stood back, surveyed the entrance of the Green Market and my eyes were drawn upward and there, over to the left and on the second floor, was a shop called, in English, "Ski Shop". I dashed up the stairs and saw, to my amazement, that they stocked perhaps 100 pairs of skis, with several choices in my preferred length. They also had a wide selection of bindings. It did not take long for me to make my purchases, at very competitive prices, but when it came to the crucial service of joining the bindings to the skis I encountered a problem. Yes, the shop had skis and, yes, the shop had bindings, but for putting them together it was necessary to go to the hotel at Chimbulak, to go down the stairs and to proceed to the second door on the left. There was a shop where the bindings could be affixed to the skis.

The author at Chimbulak
with his locally purchased skis.

Somewhat wary that I was about to blow a few hundred dollars but anxious to improve my skiing pleasure, I took the leap of faith, purchased the bindings and the skis and headed off to Chimbulak the very next day. I went to the hotel, descended to the basement and found the second door on the left in the dim hallway. Here was an unkempt machine shop with no evidence of having been cleaned at any time since the collapse of the Soviet Union. There were no pneumatic drills or overhead lines for compressed air, such as one sees in the ski shops in Vail, Colorado. Instead, there was a table-mounted electric drill with a hand-operated lever that shouted out to me that my skis and bindings were about to be greatly abused.

Although my antennae were out, working overtime and worrying about my future safety on the slopes, I handed over my skis and bindings to one of the two workmen and stepped back to watch the possible mutilation. I then witnessed one of the marvels of pre-microchip Kazakhstan. Out came a clamping device that, when affixed to a ski, pre-set exactly where a hole should be drilled for a screw that would attach the binding. Although I had been worried about the depth of each drilling, I then saw that there was a depth regulator on the drill shaft. Contrary to my fears, the drill could not go all the way through my skis. It was pre-set to go only so far as was needed in order to admit the screw and give it the required purchase for proper seating. The pressure settings were adjusted and off I went for a day of skiing.

One year later a ski instructor from the West spotted my skis and bindings and asked me where I got them. He was very impressed when I said that I had purchased them locally. So far as he was concerned, they were state-of-the art ski equipment and he could not believe the modest price I had paid.

I also wanted to buy a pair of long johns to wear while skiing. I didn't have proper ski clothing and it seemed useful to have an extra layer under my jeans and jacket. For this I returned to the Green Market and wandered from stall to stall searching for the insulated underwear. While I still feel confident that I would have found the warm underwear if I had spent more time looking for it, I compromised by purchasing a Polish-made tracksuit which served the immediate purpose and also provided me with some jogging gear at the same time.

The buying of the track suit reminds me of one of the rules of Soviet shoppers: "buy it if you see it." Perhaps this rule no longer applies but only a couple of years ago all the adult women of Almaty carried with them at all times a plastic bag or other carrier. Things were available but you could never depend upon the same thing being found in the same place for two days running. Accordingly, if there was something you needed and you saw it, the rule was to buy it there and then or face the peril that you would never see it again. Probably the current younger generation is growing up without this sense of urgent purchasing but habits die hard with the older generation and I imagine that many elegantly dressed women of modern Kazakhstan still carry with them a hidden plastic bag which can be produced in a flash if a purchasing opportunity presents itself unexpectedly.

The first classy showroom for cars opened on Kurmangazy Street across the road from the Dostyk Hotel and half a block to the left. It developed a thriving business. Unfortunately for the owner and other car dealers who made investments for a future in the car sales business, the government slapped a special tax on imported cars. I seem to recall that it effectively added 25% to the tag on a car. Without notice, the demand for new cars had been killed. This drove the dealers out of business. The shop on Kurmangazy closed, still looking freshly painted.

An official, who had opposed the tax, told me that the cash-strapped government expected to tap a rich new source of revenue but had received virtually nothing from this tax. In those days, the government acted in a kind of a bubble, out of contact with the world outside. No one seems to have consulted an economist on the likely implications of the law; no hearings had been held; the affected industry was not consulted. Seems that no one had heard of price elasticity of demand. Later, I was told that the effective date of the law was deliberately delayed until after a train load of Mercedes-Benz cars had crossed the border going into Kazakhstan.

25

CRANES, TAXIS AND EXPENSIVE CARS

Several months ago (before the financial crisis in Russia in August 1998) I had the occasion to confer with an economist from one of the large international financial institutions and to discuss with him the progress being made by the Republic of Kazakhstan as an "emerging economy" country.

I was informed that the growing financial resources committed to Kazakhstan were such that his employer had decided that the time had arrived to send someone like this economist to undertake an assessment of risk. Kazakhstan now ranked in the top 20 or 30 countries in terms of their financial commitments. Presumably all member countries are entitled to a certain amount of financial help for the private sector as well as the public sector without undue concern about risk. But when the numbers get big, as they clearly did in Russia and now also in Kazakhstan but on a much smaller scale, even international financial institutions need to show concern about how their money is being used and to take a view about the prospects of getting repaid one day.

It seemed that the economist and I were about to settle in for a pretty heavy discussion of macroeconomics, the balance of payments position, indices and indicators, the big picture, and a lot of economist jargon. However, I was quickly put at my ease in this regard. The economist told me that he had asked for time to speak to me as an expatriate with considerable experience in Kazakhstan and that he merely wanted anecdotal evidence to confirm (or disprove) his other findings. So, he had already looked at the big picture, he knew the balance of payments position of the country, the history of the value of the Tenge, and so on. Now what he wanted, from me and a few other "old hands", was local color or characterization to support or rebut his more scientific findings. He had been to one of the other CIS countries a few years earlier but he candidly acknowledged that he was not familiar with this part of the world. All the more reason, therefore, he told me, to seek anecdotal evidence from those with more experience of the country to help to round out what he had learned by more statistical methods.

I was then told that risk assessors, such as him, often used three soft or informal indicators to evaluate the progress of emerging economies. As you might guess, soft indicators are like the "Big Mac Index" where the local currency cost of a Big Mac hamburger from a McDonald's restaurant is compared, country-by-country, in terms of the U.S. dollar equivalent. This informal Big Mac Index is far from scientific but it is more than a joke (except that it still does not work here in Almaty); it often does give one an instant feel for the cost of living in a particular country.

In this case, the economist told me that he and colleagues of his in the emerging markets risk assessment business used three factors to see how a country was doing: the number of construction cranes to be seen on the skyline of large cities, the number of taxis, and the prominence of luxury cars to be seen on the street. Quite frankly, the economist told me, Kazakhstan seemed to flunk all three of these tests of a successful emerging market based on what he had seen in Almaty.

Looking out of his top floor hotel room -- he seemed to take the hotel for granted and not an indication of the emergence of a successful economy -- the economist had not seen any cranes on the skyline. (It probably was just as well that he had not spotted the innumerable derelict cranes rusting next to the semi-completed buildings that dot this city.) Although his hotel had some taxis of its own, he had not seen any taxis out on the street. And, to complete the apparently depressing picture of this country, he had seen only a very few posh cars in the city.

I can be as critical as the next person about the shortcomings of this country but, in this context, I suddenly found myself rising to the defense of Kazakhstan.

As to the first point, there had indeed been some prominent cranes on Almaty's skyline but they were removed upon completion of the new buildings such as the Marco Polo Hotel (later the Hyatt Regency Hotel and then the Rahat Palace Hotel) and the Ankara Hotel (later the Regent Almaty Hotel and then the InterContinental Almaty Hotel), and upon the near completion of the Alem Bank Towers (eventually the Samal Towers). (The three sheep I witnessed being slaughtered in the basement on the occasion of the ceremonial pouring of the concrete foundation seem not to have been sufficient to bring good luck to this building. They were at least one sheep short of that, and this green high rise building up in micro district Samal II regrettably holds the distinction of being the first semi-completed modern office building in Almaty.)

More importantly, the main development going on in this city during the past few years has been on a smaller and less conspicuous scale but it is significant nevertheless in terms of the emerging market economy. Quite a few modern shops have been developed on the ground floor of what otherwise might be a decrepit building. It is true that there have been few big demolition projects followed by the 18-month to two-year development of some Twentieth Century architectural marvels. A lot of the real estate development is still in the category of mama-and-papa achievements. A boutique is carved out of the ground floor of an apartment building with a doorway knocked out of a wall and a fresh façade imposed on the exterior of the old building. Or a free-standing building is tarted up with a fresh coat of paint, a new entry way, some "quick-build" interior partitions, and a wrought iron fence around the perimeter. There may not be a lot of new apartment buildings but large numbers of individual apartments have undergone much needed extensive renovation. Finally, one only has to look at Kok-tube to see some pretty lavish houses.

This is progress and cumulatively it is quite significant. Okay, there is no obvious property development boom or investment bubble such as often occurs with depressing frequency in the boom-and-bust economy of so many countries, like those that are still suffering in Asia, but progress is occurring.

I emphasize that this conversation took place before the collapse of the Asian economies and the financial bust in Russia. I imagine that the economist might be somewhat chastened about his informal indicators if he revisited Almaty today. Many of the countries that he might have had in mind as classic cases of the booming economies of emerging countries are now in tatters, leaving international investors licking their wounds.

As for the second point, dealing with the number of taxis on the street, I informed the economist that, quite to the contrary of what he thought he had been observing, we have a very large number of taxis in Almaty. There are, of course, some conspicuous yellow cabs but these are only a small minority of the taxis that work the streets. Long before the yellow cabs arrived there were, and still are in Almaty, a large number of radio taxis that work efficiently in the service of the community. In the Soviet style, however, they were not conspicuous and bore no advertising and, until the yellow cabs arrived, no one thought that advertising of taxis was appropriate or necessary. They were simply plain cars with a radio. I surprised the economist by pointing out that in addition to responding to phone calls, the central dispatcher would inform the caller of the license plate number of the responding taxi so that, upon entering the cab, the hiring party could obtain the comforting confirmation that this was indeed the cab sent in response to the request. How many cities in the world with an abundance of apparently more advanced taxi cabs provide such a civilized taxi service?

I started to point out to the economist the widespread use of ordinary cars for local transport – the gypsy taxi business – but this turned out to be part of the economist's message to me. To him, gypsy taxis reflected a failure of business development, not an achievement. Of course they work and of course they are useful. However, their very existence, which undermines the organized taxi business and probably results in a lot of unreported (i.e., black) income, is a mark of the failure of the development of the economy of Almaty and, presumably, the greater economy of this country.

We then turned to the subject of luxury cars. I pointed out that this is a mountain town. If four-wheel drive cars were included in the category of luxury cars, along with the Mercedes, BMWs, Jaguars, and Bentleys that might be seen in Singapore and other apparently successfully emerging countries, this city probably would leap to the top of the scale in the luxury cars per capita indicator of success of an emerging country. One has only to view the parking lot at Chimbuluk on a good day for skiing to see that an enormous amount of money has been spent on personal transportation vehicles.

I also had the occasion to point out to the economist that this is not yet a country in which conspicuous consumption has found its place. (Okay, so I played down the parade of New Kazakhs in beautiful cars tooling through the Chevron and Mobil filling stations, and some of the other situations where the consumption by local residents borders on or achieves the level of being conspicuous.) Possibly there is an overhanging influence from Soviet times. Possibly there is a fear that flashy wealth will attract unwanted interest by criminal elements. Possibly in Almaty there is some other levelling factor, such as applies in Minneapolis, where some of the wealthiest people in the United States are quite indistinguishable in many outward aspects from merely well-to-do people. They all buy their suits from Dayton's department store and almost everyone drives his own car.

———

If the economist in the above article had visited Kazakhstan in 2007 rather than in 1997, he would have made quite different conclusions about Kazakhstan. He would have found an energetic emerging market with an annual GDP growth rate of 10%, lots of high-rise cranes and so many expensive cars that there was little need for taxis. Yet by October 2008, after the global financial crisis struck, the property bubble had burst, banks were hurting badly, the growth rate had sagged to 5%, and business confidence was way down. So much for shallow economic litmus tests.

The financial crisis in Russia mentioned above struck on 17 August 1998. The Russian Central Bank was forced to devalue the ruble and the country defaulted on its debts.

The Big Mac Index was introduced by The Economist magazine in September 1986 as a semi-humorous illustration of "parity purchasing power" and has been published annually since then.

26
PAPER WEIGHT

Kazakhstan has performed wonders in the past 15 or 20 years in reducing the burden of bureaucracy, cutting out needless red tape and simplifying government oversight of business. The country's ranking improves each year in the "ease of doing business index" published by the International Finance Corporation.

The following article was written in 1997. At that time, the Tenge was still a new currency – it came into circulation on 15 November 1993 – and an established abbreviation had not been settled upon. A common abbreviation was "Tg." as used in this article but later this was largely displaced by "KTZ".

This country's leaders are trying to attract new foreign investors to Kazakhstan. Much needs doing and it all costs money. Vast resources in this country remain to be tapped. The infrastructure needs to be rebuilt and developed. Soviet-era industries need to be privatized or closed. The bills of the State need to be paid.

A key element in the attraction of foreign investors is the adoption of legislation of importance to such investors. Starting with a burst of enactments in 1995, we saw the adoption of a new company law, a law on the registration of legal entities, securities legislation, a banking law, a bankruptcy law, and, recently, the law on state support of investments which permits the granting of tax and other incentives to investors. So, from the big picture point of view, the legal structure for investment in Kazakhstan is dramatically better in 1997 from what it was in, say, 1994. Viewed from headquarters in New York, London or Houston, things look pretty good.

From the small picture point of view, however, not a lot has changed from Soviet times -- you know, at the ground level, at the stage where day-to-day business is carried out by a manager in the field, where the simple building blocks of implementing an investment have their reality. Have improvements really been made in the practical aspects of investing, such as in the hiring and firing of employees, the paying of invoices, the leasing of space, the organizing of lunches for staff, and so on? At this level, the unmistakable impression is that the millions of bureaucratic Lilliputians of Soviet times continue to thwart and hamstring this country from being the economic powerhouse that it could be.

To be the boss of even a small office in Kazakhstan is to devote a large part of your life to masses of paperwork that have no counterpart in the West. The simple task of paying Tg. 7,500 for a magazine subscription, for example, is already a complex and time consuming transaction. A duly signed and stamped invoice must be obtained before making payment. Either the publisher will send its driver to your office with the invoice or, more likely, you must send your driver to fetch it. Then your chief accountant must prepare a payment order to your bank which the boss must sign and stamp. Very probably, the chief accountant will personally take the payment order to the bank. The bank then transfers payment to the bank account of the magazine publisher. Although you know that you sent the money, which is now missing from your bank account, you need proof that it was received by the publisher so you ask for a receipt. This requires yet another round of signing, stamping and delivery by their driver or collection by yours.

If your bank account is short of Tenge, you will need to convert some dollars from the currency account into Tenge. Two copies of a currency exchange contract with the bank must be completed (to be signed by the boss and stamped), one copy for the bank and one copy for your business as evidence of the deal.

Don't even think about cutting through this maze of paperwork by paying cash. Previously, each enterprise, regardless of size, was subject to a monthly limit of about Tg. 1,000 (about $13) for cash purchases. The purpose of this rule was to drive the black economy out of business (it has not succeeded), but the practical effect was to thwart consumption and to saddle legitimate business with an enormous administrative burden. That rule seems to have disappeared only to be replaced by other rules that make getting money out of your own bank account about as easy as pulling good teeth. This is because the National Bank has made agreements with the Tax Inspectorate under which banks actively assist in the enforcement of the tax legislation.

If services are required by your enterprise, there must be a contract for the services. You don't just call up a lawyer or an accountant and then wait for their invoice after they have done some work. Instead, a kind of framework agreement is signed in which the service provider promises to provide the services that are ordered and the orderer promises to pay if any services are ordered and performed. These agreements are drawn up in duplicate, signed by each boss and stamped. Later, invoices are sent pursuant to the contract. This is followed by the bank transfer procedure: the chief accountant fills out the payment order, the boss signs and stamps it, and the chief accountant once again goes to the bank to deliver the order. (It is a fortunate company whose office is located next door to its bank.) One might think that this is the end of the procedure but, no, the service provider probably will ask for an "Act" at the end of the year which officially acknowledges that the services that were ordered and paid for were in fact rendered by it and received by the orderer.

Payday is mainly a nightmare for the chief accountant but most of the papers that she -- I have not yet met a male chief accountant -- produces must again be signed by the boss and stamped. Although computer programs can assist with payroll calculations, it often happens that tax and the other mandatory payments to the State budget must be separately calculated for each employee each payday. This is due to exchange rate fluctuations, changes in the tax rate as the cumulative amount of pay works its way up the progressive tax rate scale, and varying amounts of extras in the form of meals or other benefits which affect the gross amount of compensation. All of the payroll taxes and contributions to the various funds must be paid promptly in conjunction with payment of salary, each one entailing computations, papers, signatures, stamps, and trips to the office of each fund to obtain receipts.

If an employee goes on a business trip, an Act ordering the trip must be prepared and then signed and stamped by the boss, whereupon the Act is numbered and entered into the company's Book of Acts. Funds for the trip can be withdrawn from the bank after submission of proof of the duration of the trip which enables the bank to calculate the prescribed "norm" of permitted travel expenses as well as the 15% withholding tax which is applied to amounts in excess of the norms. To prove that the trip actually occurred, the employee must carry a document to be signed and stamped by someone at the destination. Instead of encouraging business travel and consumption which generates revenue and taxes from suppliers of goods and services, this cumbersome system discourages travel and invites evasion.

The paperwork nightmare reaches its awful finale during the annual audit by the external auditor followed by the submission of the tax return which then leads to the grilling by the Tax Inspector. This is the season of the year when your lingering suspicions about your own chief accountant are absolutely confirmed; you now know for a certainty that she works for the State or for a competitor and that her real job is to destroy your business. Everywhere there are problems; nowhere, it seems, are there solutions.

Whereas the world standard is that the external auditor must make random or sample checks to its satisfaction to ensure that accounting procedures are correctly observed, in Kazakhstan an auditor must check every document of which, obviously, there are many. Even if your chief accountant is very conscientious, it is likely that, during the annual audit, new forms will emerge which require the boss's signature and stamping, some being pieces of paper the likes of which you have never seen before which seemingly do nothing but re-confirm that which has already been well confirmed.

At agencies of government, almost every conceivable task seems to have been divided into separate units, each one performed by a different individual. Often the last step involves getting the approving signature of the boss. If this individual is ill or on a business trip, the paperwork generally stops until he or she returns to work.

Difficult as the external auditor can be, the problems and the angst get much larger when the Tax Inspector enters the scene. Typically this is a woman, and her chief objective in life seems to be to make life so difficult that you finally take her aside and make an offer to end your agony and loss of time.

Now let's see how things work in practice or, more accurately, do not work. A Westerner working in Almaty had some business in Bishkek in the Kyrgyz Republic and, while there, visited the market. He spotted some ceramic tiles that would look nice on the walls of his bathroom in Almaty, and he bought $100 worth of them. Anticipating that he would have to show documentary proof of his purchase at the border, he insisted upon being given a receipt, something the market traders do not offer but which they can supply. He loaded the tiles onto his small flatbed truck and started on his way to Almaty.

The tiles were not wrapped or concealed in any way. At the border, the Kyrgyz officials refused to let him pass despite the presence of the invoice because he lacked an export license. Exactly why this should be required is uncertain since the ceramic tiles were not inherently valuable, had been imported into the Kyrgyz Republic in the first instance, and were not a controlled substance or mineral. Besides, isn't there some kind of customs union between these countries? Determined to keep the tiles, the man drove the 25 kilometers back into Bishkek. With the help of friends who know their way around, he found the relevant Government office and obtained an export license. He returned to the Kyrgyz border post and presented his documents. The export license was in order but now the border officials explained that the man lacked proof that his seller had legally imported the goods. Perhaps import duty had been avoided by that person. Still determined to keep the tiles but agitated at the snarl of officialdom that was besieging such a simple economic transaction, the man again drove back to Bishkek and found his seller in the market. Amazingly, the trader had documentary proof of the legal importation of the tiles into the Kyrgyz Republic. Happy that his documents were truly in order, the man raced back to the Kyrgyz border and once again presented his documents. They were indeed in order and, greatly relieved, he was waved through the border post.

After passing over the bridge, the man was stopped by Kazakhstan's border officials who checked his small cargo. He presented his packet of documents for the $100 worth of tiles. The man's breaking point came when the officials on Kazakhstan's side of the border asked for documentary proof from his employer in Almaty that the tiles had been purchased for self-use and not for re-sale. Exactly why anyone would think that someone at the border who has just made an impromptu and personal purchase of small value, having nothing to do with his employment, would have such a letter beggars belief. The officials would not accept telephone confirmation from the employer, and they would not let the tiles into Kazakhstan conditional upon subsequent presentation of the confirming document. Driving into Bishkek for a document was one thing; driving for five hours to Almaty and back to obtain something from his employer was another. And so, defeated by the system, the man returned to Bishkek for the third time where he abandoned the tiles with his friends, perhaps to await a future trip to Bishkek with the required letter from his employer.

About a year ago, a friend of mine decided to purchase a used car from someone who was leaving Kazakhstan. My friend had excellent command of the Russian language and had lived here for more than four years. To say that he had married a local woman and ran a business is also to say that he was very familiar with the bureaucracy that impedes nearly every action. He knew, therefore, that a car purchase transaction merely began when the price is agreed and the money is handed over. For nearly a full week, my friend worked diligently at completing the paperwork, going from the long queues of one agency to those of another in what seemed like an unending circle in which each agency could not act because some other document, to be obtained elsewhere, needed to be presented before they could issue their own paper. Nearly exhausted and certainly frustrated after his week of effort, my friend duly announced, with triumph, that the car had become deregistered. That is to say, the car had been disconnected from its previous owner and was now in a kind of legal limbo of not being owned by anyone. My friend could now begin the process of registering the car in his own name. He assumed that this registration process would be as daunting as the deregistration process. It was.

My impression is that the registration of the car was the last straw for my friend whose natural good nature deteriorated rapidly. Having achieved the Herculean task of becoming a car owner, my friend's thoughts increasingly turned to the joy of returning to the West, and not so long after buying the car he departed, yet another victim of "Kazakhstan field fatigue". I never did learn if the person who bought the car from him had a smoother ride while registering a further change of ownership.

It is said that any foreign company that engages in business in the Republic of Kazakhstan needs an American lawyer and someone from India on its management team. The American lawyer will worry endlessly about how to keep the company from committing violations of the legislation, which are inevitable. In other words, a very serious but not entirely successful effort will be made to comply with the legislation. Meanwhile, the Indian executive will simply ignore the legal problems and carry on with the business. He is used to a business environment in which almost everything is illegal. With this powerful combination of talents, the company has as much assurance as possible that the business of the company will be carried out legally and it will also have assurance that the business of the company will in all events be carried out.

It is important, of course, for this country to have good company legislation, tax laws and so on to spur the interest of foreign investors. However, what this country really needs right now is a Law "On the Elimination of Paperwork that Impedes Business and Cripples the Development of the Market Economy", a further Law "On the Establishment of the State Commission of the Republic of Kazakhstan for the Elimination of Paperwork, Procedures and State Jobs that Cannot be Reasonably Justified on the Grounds of Protecting the Interests of the State", and a Law "On Finally Removing the State From the Private Sector of the Economy".

27
TAKE IN A WEDDING!

I have attended several weddings or wedding receptions in Almaty. All were delightful occasions, as one might expect. Some were in the Russian style while others were in the Kazakh style. Vivid scenes come to mind. The presentation of the large loaf of bread and the salt, Russian style. The wedding couple greeting arrivals at the reception but also taking in money, Kazakh style. I was particularly excited about attending weddings at the Palace of Weddings. One of those weddings prompted me to write this article.

Okay, so you're feeling a bit jaded. You have been around Almaty for a while and you have done all of those things that people do when they come to Almaty. You are starting to get bored with it all as you begin to realize that most of what you are doing you have done before, sometimes very often, sometimes on a weekly basis. Here you are again at the International Business Club; yet again dining at that same restaurant -- good yes, but wouldn't it be nice if they changed the menu (or actually served everything that is listed on it).

So, you have:

- been to Medeo to watch the skaters and climb all those stairs (or, more likely, watch someone else climb those stairs);

- eaten the chicken lunch at Chimbulak and watched the skiers coming down the mountain (or queuing for a lift);

- climbed up to the waterfalls off the fork in the road on the way to Medeo;

- "done" the National Museum up by the Presidential Palace;

- been to the opera;

- been on a picnic out in the country where there was not a telephone wire in sight and where there was not a sign of human presence except for the airplane vapor trail in the sky;

- taken the helicopter trip out to the "Grand Canyon";

- eaten the sheep's eyes when the head got served to you on some special occasion.

Interesting, yes, every one of them, but finite, limited, repetitive, and eventually boring when repeated.

My advice for those of you who need a jolt, an uplift, a change of pace, a tonic, a balm, a relief from the confines of being too long away from home in the West is -- take in a wedding. If you want to have a reminder that you are some place that is different, I mean really different, from everything you know from your other travels, then take in a wedding at the Palace of Weddings.

The Palace of Weddings is located on Abay Avenue fairly close to the Circus, just across from the Stadium but on the other side of the canal. It's that round building where the traffic builds up almost to a standstill on Saturday.

The Palace of Weddings is a purpose built, single-purpose building, solely for the conduct of weddings. In fact, it is designed and built not merely for weddings but it is designed and built in order to achieve weddings at the rate of four per hour, all day long.

The building has two floors. On the ground floor there is the staging area, where the various wedding parties congregate in separate function rooms, biding their time until they are called to the grand staircase. There are several of these staging-post rooms or bullpens:

in one a wedding couple is getting ready to go up the staircase and become joined in matrimony; in another room, panic has not yet set in because their wedding is scheduled for somewhat later and there is time for a haze of smoke to come billowing out as the nervous couple indulge a last smoke or two; in a third room, the newlyweds have just returned from upstairs to collect their personal things so that they can scoot about town with blaring horns to the various monuments; in yet another room, the couple is just arriving with the first of their family members, and they are starting to get the hang of how things will go as they watch the other wedding parties.

Upstairs, the friends and the slightly remote relatives of various couples are gathering around the large balcony that overlooks the entire downstairs of the building and which allows a view of the grand staircase.

Wedding guests crowd the balcony at the Palace of Weddings.

Off on the right-hand side of the balcony is the passport room. This is a room that looks something like a passport warehouse, with an impossible number of passports awaiting the stamping and endorsements that will permanently show for the record that the passport holder is now "married". Presumably this is a highly professional operation in which, out of seeming chaos, all newly married couples are efficiently reunited with their modified passports shortly after the ceremony is over.

One of the most amazing features of each 15 minute wedding is the "Happy Lady". This is the lady who stands at the top of the grand stairs who so enthusiastically leads the singing and handclapping to Mendelssohn's "March" -- or "Wedding March" -- as each couple mounts the stairs. Her face radiates happiness; she claps enthusiastically; she sings with gusto. Her smile is infectious. If marriage is anything like this, it must be bliss. The really amazing thing about this woman is that, 15 minutes later, she will be back in action, cheerleading the next couple up the grand staircase.

Alan Delp and Maira Makisheva going up the
grand stairway at the Palace of Weddings.

I have often wondered if the Happy Lady is happy only as a professional matter, or is she this way all the time?

The marriage is performed by the Presiding Officer, a sturdy woman of indeterminate age who seemingly would be comfortable rapping a gavel to call the City Council meeting to order, but I do not recall any actual gavel being used. She speaks into a public announcement system that seems to have been manufactured by those same people who make bus station systems that, while amplifying the noise, cannot be understood even when you strain to listen and even though you are likely to know much of what is being said.

28
THE DANGERS OF DRINK

I think I have finally discovered why the fast food chain restaurants still have not arrived in force in Almaty.

For the most part they are not here despite the fact that the Republic of Kazakhstan has been independent for several years, foreigners have arrived in abundance, and there is evidence of a certain level of affluence among some local residents.

The problem, in my opinion, is to be found with the iced drinks that are prevalent at the fast food outlets and which may be a key to their profitability. Here in Almaty, local residents simply cannot bear to drink cold beverages, particularly in the winter.

They react to a cold drink in much the same way as you and I would if someone suffering from Black Plague invited us to share a drink with them out of their unwashed drinking glass.

If the fast food chain restaurants sent their marketing people into the Republic of Kazakhstan, they undoubtedly found that their usual economics just don't work in this country. In the West, someone discovered a long time ago that ice is cheaper to serve to customers than the drinks they chill.

The result is that the "how-to-franchise" books probably recommend the practice of loading up the paper cups with exceedingly generous amounts of ice so that there will be room for only a splash of the beverage served over it, like some kind of coloring for the ice.

If you have ever asked for an ice-free soft drink at a fast food restaurant, you probably noticed how the manager blanched as your server repeatedly pushed the "fill" button to persuade the machine to squirt out the equivalent of four or five servings of the fizzy drink in one cup.

Now, just imagine a whole city of customers lining up for a try at the first real fast food restaurant to open in Almaty. Customer after customer – and not just some occasional weirdo from the West – asks for the ice-free drinks, and when the cashiers tabulate the results for the first frenetic day of operation, they will realize that the profit just isn't there. The ice making machine was a totally wasted investment, and the customers are in effect drinking away the profit.

This concern about cold drinks goes to extremes. Last summer I saw someone purchase a plastic litre bottle of Coca-Cola which had been stored (baked) on the sunny side of a kiosk, and the purchaser immediately started to take swigs from the bottle. From where I come from, that is practically unpatriotic. You simply do not treat Coca-Cola with that kind of disrespect.

When I went to Bishkek during the winter, several of us sat in the ground floor bar of the Dostuk Hotel while awaiting the arrival of other members of our group.

It was a cold night and one of the hotel's guests from Kazakhstan ordered a beer. It was served in what seemed to be a pre-chilled mug, well frosted on the outside. I couldn't figure out if it came from a freezer or if it had been sitting on the window sill.

The guest immediately asked the bartender to give his drink a zap in the microwave oven behind him and, without batting an eyelash, the bartender did so with a well-practiced punching up of the timer. I guess this was not the first time the microwave oven had been used for this purpose. Only those of us from the West who were sitting in the vicinity of the microwave oven instinctively ducked our heads as the mug of cold beer slowly rotated under the burning rays. No one else in the room thought that this procedure was in the least noteworthy.

Previously, I had no idea that cold drinks are associated with catching a cold or getting a sore throat or coming down with the flu. Throughout the year I drink my cold drinks and I still enjoy what seems to be robust good health.

In the meanwhile, my local friends, neighbors and colleagues who observe my cold drink drinking habits get nearly apoplectic at the apparent carelessness I take with my health. They guard their health far more carefully yet spend several days a year on sick leave while I, for all my ice-cold drinks, return to work day after day.

I guess that local residents take excessive precautions to avoid sickness because many of the remedies we take for granted elsewhere are unavailable to them or are not trusted, and small symptoms can quickly deteriorate into a major illness for which the local hospitals may not be well suited to give treatment.

Those of us from the West may be willing to take a small risk by drinking cold drinks in the comfort of knowing that we can control the consequences. Local residents may feel required to avoid the same risk entirely, if possible, not because the risk is greater to them than to us but because they fear that they cannot cope with the consequences.

So, now we understand the local aversion to cold drinks. Or do we? If cold drinks are so inimical to health, why is it that local residents eat so much ice cream even in the winter?

29
SPOTLIGHT ON LIGHT BULBS

One can believe that the residents of Almaty actually prefer unlit stairwells in their apartment buildings. Why else are they such a universal feature of life in this city? Indeed, having seen some very nicely decorated and well-furnished apartments in Almaty, it occurs to the observer that the darkened stairwells and beat-up entryways could be part of a deliberate ruse to avoid unwanted interest in the building. But, then again, are the residents really so fearless of muggers and whatever other dangers may lurk in those darkened passageways?

Some long time ago, two expatriate representatives of foreign companies discovered in separate ways that it is possible to keep the lights burning in the stairwells of apartment buildings in Almaty.

The representative of Company S imported a very large supply of ordinary light bulbs for use in his apartment building. Without consulting anyone, he proceeded to install light bulbs at all levels in the stairwell of his segment of the apartment building. As he had anticipated, the bulbs started to disappear almost immediately. Undaunted, the representative replaced the missing bulbs, and then he replaced them again, and then he replaced them yet again. By the end of the first week the rate of replacement had fallen considerably, and by the end of a few weeks it became necessary to replace bulbs only if they actually burned out. Obviously a level of saturation had been achieved in the building; the "supply" of light bulbs in the stairwell had finally outpaced the "demand" of someone to have a reserve supply of bulbs.

The representative of Company M took a somewhat different approach to lighting up the stairwell in a nice apartment building on Abay Avenue. Concerned that his neighbors might be upset by the appearance of light in their long-darkened stairwell, the representative conducted apartment-by-apartment interviews to determine if any of his neighbors in the stairwell would complain if he personally sponsored the installation of lights. To his delight, no one objected to the lights so long as they did not have to pay to install the fixtures or for the electricity. He solved those problems by running a line from his electricity meter all the way up and down the stairwell. He also solved the problem of bulb snatching by installing neon lights. They are economical in their use of electricity; they are comparatively long-lasting; and, while someone might snatch neon lights for re-sale elsewhere, virtually no one in Almaty uses neon lights in their apartments.

I never bothered to ask the representatives of Company S and Company M if they acted as they did out of fear for their personal safety, or if they were conducting personal crusades to introduce to Almaty a familiar feature of life as it is lived elsewhere, or if they had other motives.

It has been some time since I last visited these two apartment buildings in Almaty, so I cannot report on their current condition, but I know that those two stairwells were for many months shining illustrations of the fact that the residents of Almaty really do not prefer the darkened stairwells to which we have become so accustomed.

Local residents tell me that various other techniques are used in order to outwit the bulb snatchers. One is to install the light fixture so high as to be out of easy reach. Of course this carries the disadvantage of making it difficult to replace the bulb when needed. Another technique is to use bulbs of such low wattage that no one will be tempted to take them. The next time you enter a dimly lit hallway, just remember that it is dimly lit for your convenience, not for your inconvenience.

One of the most bizarre stories I have ever heard about light bulbs in Almaty involved an unusual form of recycling. The story is so farfetched that I am convinced that it is true even though I have never been able to locate the vendor at the heart of the story. Truth is not always stranger than fiction but I doubt that anyone would fabricate such a strange tale.

In the summer of 1993 I was told that there was a place in the main green market where someone routinely sold <u>burned-out light bulbs</u>. Burned-out light bulbs? That's right. This was not a case of fraud in which a trickster sells useless goods to an unsuspecting public; this was an honest merchant supplying a public need. Of course the bad bulbs didn't command a very high price but they nevertheless had considerable value. Indeed, it could be said that their value is nearly the same as the price of a new bulb.

But who would knowingly purchase a burned-out light bulb?

Are you as stumped as I was? Well, the answer is that a burned-out light bulb has great utility to someone who wishes to purloin a good bulb from their place of work. If good bulbs consistently disappear from an office, suspicion is aroused. However, if a spent light bulb is left in the place of a good one, suspicion is not aroused; the employer simply replaces the bulb and life goes on.

30

RULES OF THE ROAD

The automobile is a very important feature of modern life, and it is particularly essential to business and private life in Almaty. Almaty is a sprawling city with a diffused center (in what seems to be the Soviet style) so that going from point A to point B frequently involves covering large distances. People speak of places being located in central Almaty but one sometimes has the impression that "central Almaty" occupies about 90% of the city.

Very few foreigners drive their own cars in Almaty. Undoubtedly the number of foreign drivers is growing, but so is the expatriate population. Most foreign firms provide transportation for their staff by employing drivers who furnish their own cars. Many practical considerations support this practice:

- It takes far more concentration to drive a car in Almaty than in most cities in the West due to the bad condition of the roads and the large number of new and/or bad drivers on the street.

- Uncertainty about effective insurance coverage affects everyone, whether or not you drive your own car, but most foreigners probably assume that, if you are in an accident, you are better off being in a car owned and driven by your driver rather than driven by you personally.

- One of the benefits of having a hired driver for your car is that you can drink alcoholic beverages at daytime receptions and evening parties without having to worry about driving your car afterwards.

- Another benefit of having a hired driver is that he attends to the car when it is not in active use. Drivers snooze in idle cars, wash and wipe them down, and generally watch over the car. The fear is widespread that an unattended car will soon be vandalized or stolen. Witness the number of missing car manufacturer medallions. (The missing windshield wipers usually symbolize fear of theft, not actual theft; normally they are tucked away inside the car waiting to be re-installed when it rains.)

- Fear of a mechanical breakdown probably stymies many foreigners from taking up the challenge of driving in Almaty, particularly if they are not very capable in the Russian language. Most local drivers have high maintenance vehicles for which they do their own repairs and as to which they are constantly on the alert for small telltale signs that something needs attention. By contrast, many foreigners only have experience of driving low-maintenance cars that require high technology repairs when something goes wrong. The absence of a driver-friendly and helpful automobile association or radio-controlled recovery vehicles adds to the worry of experiencing a breakdown.

- Almaty was not built to accommodate a large number of cars, with the result that parking can be difficult. The problem is eased by having an employed driver. He can temporarily pull over in a spot where you would not leave the car on its own, and he can park in a way that blocks other cars because the driver will be available to move the car when the others want to leave.

- The recent appearance of modern filling stations has only just started to reduce the headache of keeping cars filled with gas.

- If these problems are not enough to dissuade foreigners from driving, then the prevalence of the traffic policemen on the street probably is. They routinely flag down large numbers of cars, seemingly without reason, causing uncertainty and unease among foreigners as to exactly what this document inspection/vehicle inspection process really entails. Foreigners readily conclude that local residents are far better at handling these encounters than are foreigners.

If male owner-drivers are somewhat unusual due to the standard practice of using hired drivers, then private female drivers are even rarer. However, there are enough of them so that now it is generally unremarkable when one sees a woman behind the wheel. Not so long ago that was a head-turning event in Almaty.

A woman driver can still catch the attention of local residents. Only last summer I saw several drivers looking a bit stunned when they spotted a woman driving a flashy convertible with the top down – I think it was a Mercedes – but it seemed that what stunned them most was the fact that there were three <u>male</u> passengers. It just seemed incongruous that men could be passengers of a woman driver.

My impression is that the number of car accidents has declined during the past couple of years. It used to be commonplace to see brand new cars from the West in head-on collisions or in intersection incidents, typically hitting an old local car, and one had the strong suspicion that the new car had an equally new driver behind the wheel who had not properly learned how to drive.

It is said that driving licenses can be purchased. It seems that, if someone fails the test or fears that they will fail the test when they take it, it is possible to arrange to pass the test in order to become licensed. If true, this would help to explain some of the bad driving that one sees and the number of accidents that still occur.

British people in particular should be careful when using the zebra crossings in Almaty. Those are the special pedestrian crosswalks that are painted with white stripes. In the United Kingdom, the pedestrian has a clear right of way in such crossings. Drivers definitely must yield when a pedestrian plants a foot in such a crossing. In Almaty, the painted crossings seem to be a fairly recent innovation, and drivers and pedestrians are still trying to work out how to use them. The crossing at Dostyk Avenue (formerly Lenin Avenue) and Zhambul Street, near the statue of Poet Zhambul, is a good example at a busy time, such as when children are going to or from the nearby school, and you can see this process being worked out. Some drivers stop for the pedestrians; some do not. Some pedestrians safely make it half way across the street and then become stranded because drivers going in the other direction do not stop for them. Sometimes drivers stop very abruptly for the pedestrians, causing or nearly causing the following car to rear-end the car that stopped. In general, do not regard yourself as being any safer by reason of being in a painted crosswalk than if you were jaywalking without any pedestrian rights at all. *[Times change. Nowadays in Almaty drivers routinely yield to anyone who steps into the crossing.]*

Another rule of the road that seems to be a recent innovation is that drivers who turn at an intersection must yield to pedestrians who are trying to cross the street. Thus, a driver whose car is going up Furmanov Street and who wishes to turn right on Abay Avenue must yield to pedestrians who are trying to cross Abay Avenue. Some drivers do not know this rule, choose not to observe it, or cannot cope with the judgmental factors required for the operation of this rule, with the result that pedestrians often are hesitant to claim their right. This throws the drivers into confusion if they know the rule and this encourages drivers to proceed if they do not know the rule or wish to ignore it. In general, be cautious when crossing a street but remember that, if the driver seems to be yielding to you, it is not merely out of courtesy and you can exercise your right-of-way as a right and not as a privilege.

It always surprises me when I see drivers making a U-turn at a busy intersection of two major streets, usually after waiting in the left-turn lane until the light changes. It seems that this is legal and is brought about because it is not legal to take a left turn out of a driveway onto a 4-lane, 2-way street. So, if drivers cannot take a left turn out of the driveway, they turn right and then pull a U-turn at the next intersection.

One noticeable feature of nightlife and life on weekends is the relative absence of teenagers out on the prowl in cars or drag racing each other. Cars are too expensive for many families to own one and they may be too valuable to be entrusted to a young person if the family does have a car. Also, quite a few of those important or well-to-do people who, in many other countries, might be expected to own a car or two of their own, may not do so in Almaty because a chauffeured government car or company car is at their disposal. Consequently, even if the younger members of the family hold drivers licenses, they often do not have access to a car.

The non-availability of cars to many young people may help to explain why promenading is still such a popular activity for young people (as well as for older people). In the United States and other countries in the West, young people spend much of their free time cruising around and looking for action in a car. Here, much of the equivalent activity seems to take place on foot.

There was a period of time in 1993 when all of us, including the drivers, started using the seat belts in the front seats of cars. Foreigners took to this with ease even though many local cars had badly installed static belts rather than inertia-reel belts. Many of them were also filthy with dust and grime from lack of prior use. Most local drivers and their riders felt uncomfortable about using a seat belt, and they quickly adopted the practice of simply draping the belt loosely across the chest, giving the general impression to the observing police that the belts were in use. Seat belts in those days didn't automatically retract. Often you became aware that a policeman had been spotted by the driver when you noticed him making his loose seat belt a bit more conspicuous until the car had gone past the policeman. I think the enforcement of the use of seat belts must have been a one-time campaign waged by the police department because it did not take long before the use of seat belts declined to the point where it is highly exceptional to see local residents using them.

As a law-abiding driver myself, I regard the recent innovation of "lane invention" to be exceedingly annoying. Lane invention occurs at busy intersections such where two important streets cross each other at a traffic light. Typically, these streets have room at the intersection for two lanes in each direction. In other words, four lanes meet four lanes. There is room for the slow-moving left-turn lane and another lane on the right for through traffic and right-turning cars. Lane invention occurs when a very macho, high-testosterone driver jumps the queue and opens up a new lane, usually by the left-turning cars, thereby potentially blocking the oncoming cars. I have witnessed double lane invention where two lanes become four lanes. It's amazing that there are so few obvious road rage incidents in Almaty.

31

TRIPPING THE LIGHT FANTASTIC

I got my first inkling that social dancing was important to the people in this part of the world in August of 1965, when I paid my first visit to the Soviet Union. After receiving my law degree in 1964, I studied in Paris for one year in order to polish my skills in the French language. While awaiting the results of our final exams, many of us students sat around in the student cafes dreaming of ways to pass the time and making plans for how to spend the summer. A friend of mine owned a VW Beetle and the two of us with a third friend decided, for reasons that I cannot now remember, to travel through Eastern Europe and the Soviet Union. Money was in short supply but we calculated that, by pooling our resources, we could manage a few months on the road if we travelled as campers.

People in the West who heard in the late 1960's that I wandered around the Soviet Union by car in 1965 were flabbergasted. The Soviet Union was such an impenetrable country that the United States had to use U-2 aircraft to take photographs from 70,000 feet in the air. And here I was with my friends driving in by car, camping at public camp sites, meeting local people, and generally having one very interesting time.

Local residents in Almaty who learn in the 1990's that I visited the Soviet Union in 1965 are quick to remark that this was during the Golden Years of the Soviet Union. My impression was distinctly otherwise in 1965 but of course I recognize that everything is relative. I saw squat peasants coming to our camp sites to buy cucumbers for their breakfast and I saw very long stretches of roads with no private vehicles on them, and I wondered why it was that the CIA continually rated the Soviet Union as a threat. We met a psychiatrist in Smolensk who was reduced to hitch-hiking to Moscow to attend his wife's graduation with a specialist degree in medicine. Had no one else been here to see what it was like? Judged from the inside, however, it may be that things had never been better.

My two friends and I were at the wrong end of the financial supply line after a year in Europe. Law school had destroyed my personal finances and I had barely scraped through the year in France by working in a bar at night. My two friends were not much better off. Nevertheless, we used much of our dwindling supply of hard currency to prepay for the campsites and for the gasoline for the car, and off we went, following the then flooding Danube River on into Budapest and beyond.

Only after entering the Soviet Union a few weeks later did we begin to comprehend that the ruble was vastly overvalued in relation to the dollar. The official exchange rate gave a kind of parity of the ruble to the dollar but young children would come up to us and offer one or two rubles for a stick of chewing gum. We soon learned the ropes for getting on in this environment, and it was then that we discovered that we had rather more money for discretionary spending than anticipated. We were also minus some of our Western clothing. Moreover, after shopping at GUM, just off of Red Square in Moscow, and seeing its empty shelves, we concluded that there was nothing, not even a trinket, that we would consider buying as a souvenir. So it came about that, instead of eating cheaply in the commissariat at the campsite just outside of Moscow, it was possible for us to eat in the very best of the Intourist restaurants.

One day, while eating lunch in some brightly lit grandiose restaurant that was situated in the ballroom of a major hotel, a band started playing music. This was an all-women's brass band with a heavy-footed drummer, and the matronly musicians played quite martial music. The Beatles and Rock n' Roll music were in full tide in the West but there in Moscow, in the heart of the Communist world in 1965, all of that was officially held in low esteem.

I was caught off guard when women from nearby tables began to come over to ask us to dance with them. The lights were wrong; the time of day was wrong; the mood was wrong; and the music was terrible. The women were seated with their own men at their tables and were not obviously hustlers. The fact that I could engage in conversation only in English, French and halting German was not a barrier to dancing with the local women who spoke only Russian. After each conversationless dance, the couples returned to their respective tables, whereupon some other women would appear at our table to seek their turn for a dance.

So, as long ago as 1965 in a brightly-lit ballroom at lunchtime in Moscow to the fox trot music of a brass band composed of rather dumpy-looking women, I learned that dancing was an important feature of life in the Soviet Union. Nothing in my experience in

Almaty has persuaded me that anything has changed. Of course the lights now are low or flashing or strobing, the music is Rock n' Roll, and the women seem much thinner, but dancing continues to play an integral part of the life of an exceedingly broad cross section of the local population.

Westerners who first came to Almaty flocked in droves to Dr. Bang's Disco. It still operates in KIMEP in the same place as in 1993, only now it is called KIMEP Club. Lacking other places to meet, Dr. Bang's Disco became the ex officio weekend meeting place for just about all expats. Some never left the upstairs balcony, preferring to remain close to the beer supply and to look down on the dancers below. Most, if not all, however, found themselves drawn down to the dance floor at some time or other. Maybe they had not really enjoyed a spin around the dance floor since they left university but here they were, in the middle of nowhere, dancing to state-of-the-art music. With the opening of so many hi-tech discos in the past two years, KIMEP Club has lost its role as the weekend mecca for the foreign community and has reverted to serving its own student community, but many old hands in the foreign community in Almaty remember the place with a certain fondness.

An early competitor of KIMEP Club was the disco at the Otrar Hotel which drew a substantial expatriate crowd on weekends from the International Business Club just a couple of blocks away. One minute the International Business Club would be overflowing with customers; but when dance time came, it would empty in a flash and the disco at the Otrar Hotel would be packed with people.

As noted, Almaty has experienced the development of an abundance of discotheques in the past couple of years. One can easily conclude that the city has attained an excessive supply of discos but the weekend prowlers do seem to keep many of them busy. Each next new disco seems to attract the trade for a period of time and then the dancers start to return to their former haunts. The closure of one disco, which ought to chill the enthusiasm of investors, is often followed by the opening of yet another new one. I have the impression that discos in Almaty are somewhat like new highways in the West. Building more does not solve overcrowding; building more simply calls into existence ever increasing numbers of users.

A disco that long was a magnet for the expatriate crowd was the Havana Club. It was in the basement of that building on the grounds of the Rahat Palace Hotel, which was then called the Hyatt Hotel, to the right just after going through the front entrance gate. It was new, large, and flashy, with a super long bar, a balcony above and an impressive entry staircase. Inside, drinks and goods were purchased using "Havanas", plastic coins in different denominations that were purchased when entering the club. Unfortunately, it all came unstuck when the owners hired a strong-willed bouncer who offended so many people that they migrated their nocturnal business elsewhere.

Many expatriates in Almaty suffer from lack of physical exercise. Getting around to sports venues can be difficult, not everyone can afford the membership fees of the health clubs at the main hotels, and skiing (thankfully) continues to be a somewhat exclusive sport. In some respects, therefore, an energetic night out in the discotheques each weekend is one way to try to fight the flab. One advantage of doing the discotheque scene is that this is an all-season sport.

Many large-scale private parties in apartments start off as not much more than beer busts where the intention of many seems to be to forget the past week and to get anesthetized for the next. But it is very common, at around midnight, for the carpet to be pulled aside and for the music system to be turned up to full blare for the dancers. In the apartments, as in the discos, local residents can be very insistent about getting the more sedate foreigners to join in the dancing. People who have not danced for years or for whom Rock n' Roll is a fading memory from their youth will find themselves dragged out onto the dance floor.

I have the impression that local residents do not consider that there is any age at which it is no longer appropriate for them to join in the dancing, including, for the most part, the lively dancing that sometimes is involved with contemporary Rock n' Roll. Every wedding party I have attended has involved dancing, and it seems that everyone, from the youngest to the oldest, joins in.

Not everyone dances every dance at the discos and it is true that many people prefer to stay on the side line, saving their feet or preferring their drinks. But there are more than a few favorite songs that, when the opening bars come blasting through the amplifiers, inspire a rush to the dance floor. These songs are deeply compelling, as if local residents have an itch in their feet that needs to be satisfied. This itch knows few limits. Women can dance alone or in groups. Men can join in or not. No one cares. Men can dance alone, or with friends or with strangers. A kind of camaraderie of the dance floor takes over and normal rules for formal introductions take a back seat.

Once, while taking a stroll on a Sunday afternoon in Panfilov Park which surrounds the wooden Ascension Cathedral (also known as Zenkov Cathedral), I heard some live music being played and I approached to see what was going on. I found a group of about 30 rather aged pensioners dancing in the hot July sunshine. A small cardboard box had been placed on a nearby park bench into which contributions could be placed. It was immediately clear that these old people were in need and that this was their way of doing something to earn the money they were too proud to beg for. It was difficult to say if the dancers were enjoying themselves. They gave some gusto to their dancing, if gusto is the correct word for the way quite old people dance. I marveled at their grit in trying to do something which would attract contributions by dancing on a public pathway. This was back in 1994 or 1993. I have never again witnessed the old folks dancing for money so I surmise that this is not ordinary. Yet, it tells us something that, when they decided to raise money, it was through dance.

In a previous article in *The Almaty Herald*, I noted the hospitality of local people, particularly toward foreigners. There was that time when I wandered into a wedding party on the fourth floor of the Dostyk Hotel. I sought to back out of the room so as not to intrude but I was grabbed by the brother of the bride who insisted that I must join in the toasts. In no time at all I found myself out on the dance floor and eventually had a dance with the bride.

I have long been amazed at how quickly music from the West finds its way to Almaty. One day I hope to find out more about how this occurs but it seems that a few disk jockeys from radio or from the discos have their contacts in the West and thus manage to keep up with the latest releases. At least one radio disk jockey has a brother-in-law in the West who remains very close to London's music scene, and I have carried in more than a few "Not to be sold" promotional albums which have helped to fuel the music market here.

I went skiing at Vail, Colorado, a few years ago. "Crash Test Dummies" had just issued their first single ("MMM MMM MMM MMM") in October 1993, and it was making its way around Vail's dance spots. It was months before I heard this group in England, which is far from being underprivileged in terms of music, but upon returning to Almaty from Vail, "Crash Test Dummies" was already being aired over the long defunct Radio Max and at the discos.

———

My 1965 trip through Eastern Europe and the USSR almost aborted when Winston Churchill died while our passports were being slowly processed by the consulates of Hungary, Czechoslovakia, Poland and the Soviet Union. Churchill died on January 24, 1965, and his funeral promised to be a spectacle of a lifetime. It was mighty tempting to dash across the English Channel to see what we could see of the funeral and take in other sights. Moreover, I had never been to the United Kingdom. In theory, there was ample time for my friends and me to go to the funeral and also on the later trip to the Soviet Union. The catch was that we would need to retrieve our passports to go to England and then there might not be time for some of the Eastern countries to process our visa applications. The further problem with deciding what to do was that, if we skipped the funeral in order to go on the big trip and if one of the countries then rejected our applications, we might miss both big events. In the end, monetary considerations forced the decision. We couldn't do both. We skipped the funeral. The visas applications were all approved and we went on the trip

32

TAXI! TAXI!

So many people drive their own cars today that it is difficult to remember that in the early 1990s there were three kinds of cars on Almaty's streets: large numbers of government-owned cars driven by chauffeurs, known only as drivers; privately owned cars whose drivers mainly patrolled the street as gypsy taxis; and actual taxis. The streets were so empty of cars that congestion might then have been defined as when more than seven or eight cars were parked on Lenin Avenue (Dostyk Avenue now) in front of Hotel Kazakhstan. Otherwise, the streets were entirely clear of parked cars. Really. That's hard to believe with people now having become so accustomed to the difficulty of finding a place to park. It's as if cars descended on Almaty like a swarm of locusts and forgot to move on.

Private individuals who could afford it, were in a rush, or couldn't conveniently go to their destination by bus used the gypsy taxis. Virtually everyone had experience of hailing down a "taxi" on the street, knew how to bargain about destination and price, and was well aware of the rules for safely arriving at their destination. The following article speaks of conditions in 1997.

143

———————

Western security experts strongly advise foreigners not to use "gypsy" taxis. What they mean is that, in the interests of your safety, you should not take any of those vast numbers of cars that circulate around Almaty during all hours of the day and night, which seemingly are taken without fear by local residents and which are vital to the functioning of this city.

It is not just the security experts who can testify to the need to be careful when taking taxis. Quite a few foreigners, and more than a few local residents, have been "taken for a ride" and given pretty nasty treatment, though I have yet to hear of anyone being murdered by a gypsy taxi driver. I know of one case where two men (who had been drinking and it was very late) were taken into the mountains, separated, beaten, robbed and left stranded, with each one fearing that the other one had come to a far worse end than he himself had experienced.

Some people are so used to taking any car that stops that they may be surprised to learn that there really are licensed taxis in Almaty. Not just taxis with the word "taxi" on the side or with a lit-up sign on the top that vaguely hints of the Checker Cab logo but truly licensed radio-controlled taxis.

Local residents often seem not to distinguish between licensed taxis and gypsy taxis. Indeed, they are so accustomed to taking any car on the street that stops for them that they might wonder why on earth foreigners are so fussy about a distinction between so-called gypsy taxis and regular cabs. Certainly the gypsy taxi drivers seem to know their way around Almaty as well as the licensed taxi drivers. And the gypsy taxis often are available deep in the blackest part of the night when you might find it difficult to locate a licensed taxi prowling for work.

The main advantage of the licensed taxis is that they are available by telephone and by appointment at a particular time. Moreover, for your further safety and so that the taxi driver knows that he has located the correct passenger, it is the practice when booking a taxi to be given the license plate number of the car that will be dispatched. Thus, on going outside to find your taxi, it is possible to determine with certainty, even before opening the cab door, if this is your intended taxi. A further advantage is that you can ask the dispatcher to telephone you to let you know when the taxi has arrived outside the building to which the driver was sent.

Expatriates would be wrong to assume that local residents are cavalier about taking gypsy taxis or that they regard themselves as immune from harm. On the contrary, if you observe closely you will see that safety precautions often are taken by local residents. If a woman needs a ride late at night, she may be seen to wave off a car that has begun to stop for her in the event that she is ill at ease about accepting a ride in that particular car. For example, if the car has a man who is accompanying the driver, the woman may very well give them a signal to carry on driving. The drivers seem not to take umbrage at this.

It could be that the extra man is simply a friend helping the driver to pass away the hours and also helping to ensure the safety of the driver. (The danger out there, incidentally, is not all one way.) Equally, the two men could be a couple of tough looking customers for whom trouble is no stranger.

If the woman spots a car with only the driver, she is more likely to take the car. Even then, however, it is the custom to engage in a bit of bargaining through an open window or open door, before getting into the taxi. The driver may not be interested in taking the person to their particular destination. He may consider that the destination is in a dangerous area or he may be working his way toward his home in a different direction. Also, it is useful for the intending passenger to gain some clarity about the cost of the ride. During the moments of this interchange, the woman probably is making a risk assessment in the back of her mind and, once again, if she has any unease about taking the taxi, she can still break off the conversation and start looking for another taxi. In short, local residents are also concerned about their safety and they do exercise prudence but they do so in a way that is inaccessible to those foreigners who are not capable of assessing risk through the fog of language and cultural barriers.

It often happens that the second person in the front seat of the taxi is a woman, typically the wife or girlfriend of the driver. She may not add as much to his safety as a male companion but at least she can spend time with her man while he is out on the street and, more importantly, she serves as a very important advertisement to the public that this is a safe taxi, and not just for women.

There is a local custom that may come as a surprise to you, especially if it has not occurred to you that taking a taxi can be dangerous. This practice is for the passenger to phone the people they have just left after they reach their destination in order to announce their safe arrival. For example, if you have been visiting someone or if you drop someone off at their apartment before going to your own, it is a nice touch, even very late at night, to phone them simply to say that you are home. If this arrangement was not made before you left the apartment of a local resident, you might occasionally be surprised to receive a phone call from that person checking to see if you got home safely. Your first reaction may be that it was rather pointless for them to call simply to see if you would answer the phone, but it makes a lot of sense to the caller.

It is a little unclear what actions could be taken in the event that someone called to you and you were <u>not</u> safely at home; however, the main point of this phoning exercise may be to let those people who did not travel retire for the evening in the peaceful knowledge that something that might have gone wrong for others has not gone wrong.

Techniques for catching a taxi vary. Normally, all that is required and all that is given is a motionless outstretched hand, usually with the palm facing the oncoming traffic. Sometimes, one sees the first and second fingers outstretched together with the thumb while the ring finger and the little finger are curled up. Another method is to outstretch the first two fingers and to snap them down in an authoritative way, as if commanding the next driver to stop. This gesture imports a sense of urgency or importance. My impression, however, is that the methodology for hailing a ride is not particularly important. The drivers are pretty anxious to get passengers, and the slightest show of interest by a pedestrian in getting a taxi is likely to produce results in short order. Indeed, when I wait on the street for my firm's driver to collect me in the morning to go to work, I need to show studied indifference to the oncoming traffic if I want to avoid being bothered by eager drivers who want me as their fare.

Except when going to a very prominent destination which the driver cannot fail to know, the universal practice is to state the destination in terms of the intersection of two streets. Typically this is done by running the two street names together as if they were a single name, e.g., FurmanovAbay. This might be the actual destination but often it is simply an approximation. When nearing the destination, the passenger can give additional instructions so as to alight in the correct spot, which could be a few blocks away.

One never gives instructions to a taxi in terms of the number of a building unless the name of the closest intersecting street is not known. Giving the intersecting streets is very efficient. Moreover, local residents tend to be quite protective and secretive about their private lives, giving out information only when there is a demonstrated need to know. I imagine that they instinctively want to avoid letting the taxi driver know the exact place to which they are going.

One of the mysteries of life in Almaty is knowing in advance the correct amount of money to offer to a gypsy taxi driver. Some drivers seem totally indifferent to the amount of money offered, accepting any quantity of Tenge offered, sometimes without even giving it a cursory examination. On other occasions, usually late at night, the driver may demand a high price and may want pre-agreement by the passenger that the price has been settled before the trip begins. Not so long ago Tg. 50 would finance a trip to most points within central Almaty during daylight hours. Currently the price seems to be at least Tg. 60, or Tg. 80. Later in the day, at an hour that cannot be predicted exactly but probably coincides with the onset of darkness, the price climbs upward. My impression, however, is that the cost of late night trips has levelled off, even for foreigners.

Local residents seem to have a grapevine knowledge of the going rates based upon the interplay between the distance and the hour of the day. If you ask a local person who can afford to ride by taxi what you should pay to get to a particular destination, that amount almost certainly will be accepted by the driver when you tender it. There are exceptions. If you take a taxi to a 5-star hotel, the driver's expectations may go way up. I have witnessed hotel doormen rescuing foreigners from potentially nasty situations where the price had not been pre-agreed and where the amount tendered was rejected. You can avoid problems like that simply by giving the destination to the nearest intersecting streets but you will have to walk the last 100 meters to the hotel door.

33

UPSIDE DOWN, INSIDE OUT
AND BACK TO FRONT

It is amazing how many things are said or done differently here in Kazakhstan compared to what I had previously come to think of as normal, correct or usual. I accept that there often are two or more ways to do the same thing in the West, and I have also come to learn that "average" covers a whole lot more of the spectrum than I thought not so many years ago. Even so, the incidence of matters that are "out of proper order" in this country seems rather large, at least to me, and they take some getting used to.

In England, where I have lived for many years, we have witnessed the invasion of the litre and the displacement of the Imperial gallon but this was somewhat unexpectedly accompanied by the invasion of the comma and the partial displacement of the decimal point, at least at filling station pumps. I guess there is no domestic U.K. manufacturer of filling station pumps and so the Continental comma was brought in along with those metrified pumps. You know, you look at the meter and it says that you must pay for 53,4 litres. This happened a long time ago but I still have never heard anyone in England pronounce the comma when referring to the price or to the amount of gasoline being purchased, as in, "I need to pay for fifty-three comma 4 litres". Equally, I have never heard anyone mispronounce the price or the quantity by uttering "point" or "dot" as in "20 point 5 litres", despite the fact that the decimal point is no longer used. Perhaps we are all awaiting the development of a social convention as to how to handle the intrusive comma and meanwhile we politely ignore it.

Anyway, having grown accustomed to this "misuse" of the comma in England, I was not too surprised to see it put to a similar use here in Kazakhstan. I was jarred, however, to see large numbers printed virtually without punctuation, with no embarrassment at all, as if this is entirely natural, and who would think that a number like 435 555 438,90 needs any more punctuation? I have seen numbers like this for five years and I still feel ill at ease, wanting to do something to dress up such a naked number, to remove that blasted comma and to restore the rightful decimal point.

Another twist that takes some getting used to is the reversal of the family name and the first name on calling cards and other printed renditions of personal names. Except for a stint in the military and except for attendance lists at school, I have always been Thomas E. Johnson. And even in the military I was JOHNSON, Thomas E., with that useful comma calling attention to the fact that the usual order has been reversed for the convenience of presenting the family name in alphabetical order. Here, people live rather naturally in a world where the family name is presented first and where the first name follows without that comma to show that something unusual has been done with the name. Fortunately, at least some local people helpfully spell their family name in capital letters on their calling cards, assisting those of us who are used to a different convention to decipher which name is the family name and which is the first name.

Part of the skill of being bilingual/bicultural is to be able to present your name orally in one order in English and in the reverse order in Russian, without pausing and without blushing.

One of the challenges of business card printers is to decide whether or not to translate the Russian/Kazakh version of the name into English in the same order or to use the English convention on the English side and to use the Russian convention on the Russian/

Kazakh version. My impression is that there is no general agreement on this point so that some English names retain their order in Russian, to the possible confusion of non-English speakers, and some Russian names retain their order on the English side, to the confusion of non-Russian speakers. This may not be so bad when one of the names is an obvious first name, say, Boris, as in YELTSIN Boris (or Boris Yeltsin, as you may prefer) but a lot of names in Kazakhstan are not obvious first names to many foreigners and they are accompanied by other names that may not seem so obviously to be family names either.

Where I come from, when you purchase a bouquet of flowers, you hold them stalk end down, flower end up. Why we do this probably has no reason but this is the way we do it. Previously I had no occasion to think about why we hold the flowers in the same posture in which they grow in nature, flower at the top and stem at the bottom. We just do it, and when I try to think of some reason for this it occurs to me that, if the flowers had been resting in a vase of water, it is a pretty good idea to hold the drippy end down.

Now, the only reason that I have tried to think of why we hold flowers in the direction in which they grow in nature is that the vast majority of people in Kazakhstan naturally hold the bouquet in the other direction, drippy or dry. Little children follow the style of their parents, and so generation after generation they observe a convention that I could not even have imagined before I landed in this country more than five years ago. (Were the people here isolated from the mainstream development of humanity?) The justification that I have imagined for the flower-on-top rule obviously does not apply here. I have asked some local residents why they hold the flowers "in the wrong" direction. The usual answer, if they can think of one – conventions normally exist below the level of consciousness – is an economical one, namely, that the petals will stay on the plant longer this way. I kind of have my doubts about this but I have never yet bought two bouquets in order to see which one starts shedding petals first. My guess about the reason is that it is easier to see the path ahead if the flowers are upside down, and in this city it is still useful to keep your eyes on where you are walking.

I won't comment at length on the presentation of months, days and years in Kazakhstan. The United States has been in the minority for a long time. Most of the world knows that 12/01/98 is January 12 and would be surprised to think that anyone would be confused enough to read this as December 1. I have lived in a bicultural world for many years and my own adaptation as an American has been to follow the military style of 12JAN98 so that all of my addressees will read the same date.

Another surprise to me on coming to Kazakhstan is the apparent gracelessness with which the Russian language usually is typed. It seems as though no one has any concept about the proper packaging of words. Of course the message is important but the medium is not irrelevant to that message. What really grates me is the absence of two spaces between sentences.

Probably I am close to having a fetish about the need to hit the space bar twice after a period that ends a sentence. I had a rather demanding typing teacher when I braved the derision of my classmates and took a secretarial class at the age of 17. Ever since, I have come to accept that the two spaces are important for the visual presentation of a sentence. When reading down a page, these two little spaces alert the eye to the natural pauses in thought and content of what one is reading. Without them, one needs to study the page more intensely in order to grasp what is being said. I think this must be true in Russian as in English; indeed, probably truer, at least when some of those convoluted Russian sentences are used where we would simply make a direct statement in English.

Whereas in English the packaging of the page is important, it seems that in Russian it is more important to ensure that as much as possible of the page is covered with print. I have yet to figure out if this is intended to prevent fraudulent alteration of the written material or if this simply reflects the perceived high cost of paper.

Yet another topsy-turvy aspect of life in Kazakhstan is that local residents peel their bananas from the wrong end. Watch them, and you will see an unexpected social practice in action. Except for a few well-travelled local residents, they are totally unaware that there is anything wrong with their behavior when eating bananas.

A couple of years ago, when I commented to my relatives in the Washington area on this observation of mine, they scoffed with disbelief. They enjoyed my tales from Kazakhstan but this was so incredible that they assumed that I had started to invent far-fetched tales for their further amusement. Fortunately for me, an acquaintance of mine from Kazakhstan was studying in Washington at that time, and my sister kindly invited him to join us for a Sunday afternoon out in the suburbs. This included a traditional (for us) Sunday lunch. For dessert my sister presented a large bowl of fruit. All eyes were glued on our guest as he reached out his hand for the irresistible banana. And all of us broke out in uncontrolled laughter when, as I had predicted, he started to peel it from the wrong end. The unbelievable was happening right before our eyes. It took some fancy footwork on my part to explain our rude behavior to our guest who was as completely incredulous as my family had been that his entirely normal conduct should excite any comment from us at all.

When asked why they peel the banana as they do, most local residents reply in effect that the stem usefully serves as a kind of lollypop stick while eating the banana.

If you think about it, that probably is a better justification than ours for approaching the banana from the other end. We use the stem to break the banana open, which gives us a momentary advantage, but after that we no longer have that woody piece to hold as we near the end of the fruit.

34

IN PRAISE OF
APARTMENT BALCONIES

I lived in New York for seven years in an apartment with no balcony and it never occurred to me that the absence of a balcony was a kind of deprivation, a sort of second best situation that ought to be improved upon at the first opportunity. Here in Almaty, I don't know what I would do without my balcony, and I have come to think that life in a balcony-less apartment really is second rate, a deprivation, a handicap in life and society.

Although not every apartment in Almaty has a balcony, large numbers do, and they are highly valued by the residents and put to many, many uses. You can see many of these uses if you scan some apartment buildings on your next stroll around town.

Storage: Probably the most common use of the balcony is for storage space. Local residents make intensive use of their apartments. You and I might feel a bit cramped living alone in a 3-room apartment of 70 square meters or so but, locally, a husband, wife and three children might be making do in a mere 55 square meters. To them, the balcony may be the only place where seasonal items can be stored, like a sled in summer or a bike in winter, or where the extra chairs are kept until needed when company arrives. Sometimes even the balcony is inadequate to fulfill the storage requirement, and in those cases various items might be hung over the edge of the balcony. One time I saw a wheelchair dangling on a hook over the edge of the balcony -- saving it for some rainy day in the future?

Larder: Quite a few people use their balconies to store home preserved food for the winter, this being a special form of storage. In the West during the winter we eat frozen food, canned food, and fresh food that has been flown in from the far parts of the world. Home preserving is something most of us remember, if at all, only from our youth. Here in Almaty, many people still engage in putting up home preserves and so, late in August and during much of September, they buy fruit and vegetables in large quantities at the market, when they are inexpensive, and then spend long hours cooking them and putting them up in those large glass bottles that one sees from time to time. By late September, the temperature is usually right for putting the bottles out on the balcony where they will stay chilled until needed during the winter.

Smoker's Haven: Another very common use of the balcony is as a smoker's den. Although local residents smoke cigarettes a great deal, often without regard to the desire of non-smokers to have good air to breathe, it appears that many of them are not allowed to smoke inside their own apartments. My impression is that this has little or nothing to do with concern for health and the desire of non-smokers to avoid secondary inhalation. Rather, smokers seem to be banned from the apartment in order to protect the furniture, wallpaper and paint. Anyway, it is a common sight in Almaty during all of the seasons to see smokers out on their balconies taking in the local sights, leaning on the edge of the balcony and smoking their fags.

Apartment Extension: The universe of apartment dwellers in Almaty divides neatly into two opposed camps when it comes to the enclosing of balconies. Some residents insist that balconies can only be enjoyed and can only serve their true purpose if they remain open. Other residents -- often influenced by the high density of occupation of their apartments -- have no qualms at all about enclosing their balconies. Indeed, judging from many buildings in my neighborhood, it seems to me that the enclosure people far outnumber the free air people.

Several arguments are made in favor of enclosing the balcony. An apartment becomes much warmer in the winter if the balcony is enclosed. The down side of this, however, is that apartments also tend to be hotter in the summer if the balcony is enclosed, due to the baking effect this produces. Drafts are reduced if balconies are enclosed, with the result that less of Almaty's very fine dust finds its way into the apartment. If properly enclosed, the balcony can become entirely integrated into the apartment as an extra room, giving the apartment an element of roominess even if the narrowness of the balcony makes it somewhat impractical as living quarters.

Clothes Drying: Even enclosed balconies continue to serve the purpose of hanging clothes out to dry. In many cases when balconies are quite small, a couple of metal poles are extended over the edge of the balcony and 5 or 6 wires are stretched between them as clothes lines.

Play Area: Many balconies are safe for even quite young children, particularly when the balcony has a concrete wall rather than railings. In such cases, the balcony often serves the mutual purpose of letting the children get away from their parents and letting the parents have some time when they are relatively free of the children.

Selective Nonconformity: I have the impression that many apartment dwellers use their balconies as a way to make a statement of their individuality or nonconformity to the usual norms of society. Many apartments in a large building are much the same on the inside, i.e., monotonous, but when you look at the exterior of the building, the maze of enclosed balconies are all different. It seems that no two balconies were enclosed by the same carpenter. At first I thought this was regrettable. Can't people get organized to use the same carpenter so as to have uniformity in the balcony enclosures? Then it occurred to me that uniformity is already too prevalent in apartments and their furnishings, and that perhaps the last concern of an apartment dweller when he or she orders the enclosure of their balcony is to make it look exactly like other balconies in their building. Most enclosures are made from soft, unpainted wood, but some have a horizontal plane, others have a vertical aspect, some are entirely made of glass whereas others have boarded up parts.

Dog House: Many of those improbably large dogs that one sees emerging from cramped apartment buildings spend much of their lives out on a balcony, which may help to explain why so many dogs join in the barking in the middle of the night.

Botanical Gardens: The balconies on the southern side of my apartment building have a lot of ivy vines which serve the very practical function of shielding us from some of the sunlight in the summer. However, I can see quite a few window boxes with flowers and several potted plants, and it seems that balconies offer the space for these horticultural pursuits which are not so feasible within the confines of a crowded apartment.

Overflow Capacity for Parties: It is not just the expatriates in Almaty who make apartment parties seem like a kind of telephone booth stuffing contest. And for this purpose, the balcony offers relief or expansion space, a place to cool off if the party happens on a hot summer's evening, a refuge for the smokers even in the depths of winter, and a place for lovers to try to gain a moment of privacy. The balcony also offers storage space for the large amounts of beer that tend to be drunk on some of these occasions.

35

LUCKY TICKETS

When you last took a bus ride in Almaty did you examine your ticket closely? Okay, judging from the foreigners that I do <u>not</u> see on the buses in Almaty, maybe it has been some time since you have ridden a local bus or perhaps you have never had this experience at all.

Many local residents who do use the buses examine their bus tickets with care every time they purchase one. They are looking for a "lucky ticket". If they have such a ticket, their spirits might brighten up considerably, a warm feeling may go through them, and suddenly a rush of hope rises up for something good to happen to them.

A bus ticket is lucky if the first three digits of the ticket number add up to the same total as the next three digits. For example, the ticket I most recently purchased was not a lucky ticket because it bore the number 692347. Adding up 6 + 9 + 2 yields 17, and adding up 3 + 4 + 7 yields 14. So, I had just another normal ticket. A ticket with 692593, however, would be a lucky ticket with 17 for the first three numbers (6 + 9 + 2) being the same as 17 for the last three numbers (5 + 9 + 3).

The rules for the lucky ticket seem to vary from person to person, depending upon your informant. However, it is widely thought that a person who gets a lucky ticket receives more than a simple omen of happiness. The lucky ticket is not just a coded "Have a nice day!" message. The holder of the lucky ticket is supposed to be able to make a wish that will come true. There is less consensus about what must be done with the lucky ticket itself. Some people believe that the holder of the lucky ticket must swallow it in order to realize the good luck represented by the ticket. It is unclear to me if this must be done immediately upon discovering that the ticket is lucky or if the holder can at least wait until getting off the bus – which might be a good idea in case the ticket seller demands to see the ticket later in the ride.

I have met some people who claim to be regular recipients of lucky tickets. Some even claim to know in advance when they will receive a lucky ticket. However, one young adult I know swears that she got her last lucky ticket when she was a mere 12 years old, and she has been faithfully looking for another one ever since.

36

CLOSE SCRAPES

The terrain described near the end of this 1999 article has been entirely transformed during recent years. At the time of the incident described, Ramstore had not yet been built and the site was a jumble of rubble, small trees and bushes. The Samal Towers stood as empty hulks collecting rainwater in their shared basement. There was a semi-completed Soviet-era stadium at the far end of the land now occupied by Dostyk Plaza. Much of the area around those structures consisted of holes and piles of rubble with not a single street light in sight.

Two friends of mine and I went on a self-drive car/camping tour of Eastern Europe and the Soviet Union in 1965 – yes, 1965, one of the Golden Years of the Soviet Union. And, yes, by car, a durable

Volkswagen Beetle that survived the USSR's low octane gasoline that overheated the engine so much that we couldn't turn it off merely by using the key. Instead, we had to kill the engine by engaging a gear and hastily letting out the clutch. We often wondered if the engine would totally seize up, leaving us stranded behind the Iron Curtain. We had many interesting experiences on this tour but this is not the place to recount those adventures of long ago. Except for one.

While looking for a place to park our car near the Kremlin in Moscow's Red Square, we obviously did something wrong. We were approaching the dedicated parking lot near St. Basil's Cathedral, when a policeman flagged us down and wrote out a ticket. We had to pay it on the spot. This was for us a new experience. For six weeks, we had driven through Hungary, Czechoslovakia, Poland and deep into the Soviet Union without any problems with the police, who naturally were minding us much of the time.

We were at a loss as to how to cope with this situation. Between us, we spoke several languages but only a few words of Russian. This non-functional Russian was not enough to clue us in as to what we had done wrong. We seemed to be in a driving area – admittedly this was none too clear in Red Square with all of its parade markings – and we were aimed at exactly where other cars were already parked. So, having paid our penalty, we continued on the same path as before. Oops. Another gesture by the policeman. We were arrested again and had to hand over more rubles for the second ticket. Maybe the policeman took pity on us about this time, or maybe he had run out of tickets. Anyway, it now became clear that we were trying to enter the parking area – which seemed to us to be wide open and unregulated – by means of the exit. By gesture and a few words we learned that the entrance was on the other side of the cathedral.

So it was that I learned, and probably over-learned, that it is best to avoid encounters with policemen with whom one cannot adequately communicate and who, in a strange country, may hold awesome powers. All of which leads to my stories about close scrapes with the street level of authority in Almaty.

My present apartment is a couple of hundred meters away from the Zenkov Street police station, at the intersection with Kalinin Street. If you live in this area and are out on the street when the day shift ends at 7:00 p.m., you will quickly gain the impression, which undoubtedly is true, that the average Almaty policeman is an ordinary person who, after pounding the beat all day, is happy to go home to wife and family for some dinner and a chance to watch television, that favorite household pastime which continues to dominate family life in this country. The policemen leave the station in groups, truncheons at ease, talking small talk as they wander over to the bus stops on Dostyk Avenue. Quite normal guys just doing their jobs.

On seeing these real human beings, one can easily forget that some of them are the same fearsome representatives of the awful power of the state, guys who, for example, spend their days pulling over motorists for document reviews and more. This road patrolling is by far a more conspicuous daily reminder of state authority than we from the West are accustomed to, and it intimidates many expatriates from attempting to drive their own cars.

One of my idiosyncrasies is that I don't like to take people to restaurants, bars and discos that I have not previously attended. I need to know what I am getting into before I dare to risk involving friends or clients as well. So it was that, some years ago, I found myself checking out the Dostar disco, quite a ways down the mountain and just off Furmanov Street. I had heard several people mention this place favorably, and I was anxious to add yet another night spot to my short list of decent places to use.

On the understanding that the Dostar was primarily a disco, I went at what I thought was a suitably late hour. However, on entering the place I was given ticket No. 002 for my coat, and I noticed that mine was the only coat on the coat rack. Indeed, after entering the cavernous disco, I quickly concluded that patron No. 001 had already given up the night as lost and gone home. Oh well, you live and learn. Being alone and without the chance to join anyone for companionship, I pulled up a stool at the bar and proceeded to nurse a beer in the hope that the evening's action would start before too much longer.

Various employees conversed with me. One, a delightful young lady, was a violinist who was pursuing a career as a serious musician but here she sang and did karaoke for the late night guests. She made a stunning $100 per night and worked 7 nights a week. Curious about how local residents keep their cash safe, I asked where she kept this veritable avalanche of money. She replied that she really was not saving anything – yet. Her earning power had been harnessed for the benefit of a rather extended family, and it seems that her earnings for the next few weeks were already committed for various needed purchases.

Patron No. 003 finally showed up about the time I finished my second beer and I concluded that my bedtime occurred before this nightspot came alive. Out on the street there was not a taxi to be had and I was all alone. I pondered the alternatives and finally decided to hoof it to Samal II, where I then lived -- a long way up the mountain. The moon was out, the temperature was not so bad and, as a life-long desk jockey, I needed the exercise.

About one block away from the Dostar I spotted three young policemen or army men walking down the same sidewalk that I was walking up. My heartbeat picked up and thoughts raced through my head. Should I cut across the street to avoid encountering them? Or would that simply attract their attention and thus increase my peril? Should I turn around and hightail it back to the Dostar and re-think how I was going to get home?

In the end, I concluded that my best bet was simply to proceed up the street. On approaching the young men, they stopped me. Now my heart was not just beating faster; it was rapidly working its way up into my throat! They were armed and, in the dim moonlight, they looked pretty rugged. I had heard stories about young men from the country who live a rough life and find it hard to cope in the city, and it was easy to assume that I was now facing three of them.

It was then that they asked me politely for the correct time. They had been patrolling the streets for a long time and were hoping that they soon could go off duty. I dug out my watch and informed them of the hour. They thanked me and proceeded on their way. (I cannot recall any subsequent occasion of going out on my own to check out a new night spot.)

On a more recent occasion, a friend of mine and I shared a taxi home after a late night out on the town. We live near each other and we exited the taxi at a spot midpoint between our apartments. That was not a good decision. As I walked in the dark on the last couple of hundred meters to my apartment, a police jeep came along and I was arrested, or so it seemed. Anyway, I soon found myself in the jeep on my way to the Zenkov Street police station. It was not immediately clear what offence, if any, I had committed. Okay, I was out on the street at a late hour, but I was not drunk, I was well dressed, and I did have my passport with me. There were the seemingly routine questions about did I have any drugs (no) or did I have a gun (no).

After being escorted into the police station, we quickly arrived at a kind of standoff, with me being seated out in the open reception area. They didn't charge me with any particular crime but they also seemed not to want to let me go. I thought about offering a contribution to the Policemen's Retirement Fund, but I lack experience of finding financial solutions to non-financial problems. The minutes went by and there I remained. Eventually I used my mobile phone to call a friend of mine, a well-known local personality, who agreed to help. She charged into the police station at what was then 3:00 a.m., asked in a very accusatory tone if I had been harmed in any way (no), and grabbed me by the arm to lead me out. The policemen were models of courtesy, and I shook all of their hands as I departed. I guess my rap sheet in Almaty is still clean.

A far more ominous encounter with the police occurred several months earlier. Although I no longer lived in Samal II, I had agreed to help a friend install some kitchen cupboards up near my former apartment. Drilling the mounting holes in hardened concrete took longer than expected, and so I found myself heading out to Furmanov Street at dusk on an autumn evening. The street was well lit and people were gathered at the bus stop close to the where the Butya shopping center, better known as Ramstore, is now located. I heard someone calling from behind me but ignored it as it was unlikely to be directed at me. The calling continued and I turned to see what was going on. That may have been my big mistake of the evening. Some policemen were gesturing toward me to come to their car. I approached and they asked to see my passport. I had left it is my apartment that afternoon, which was another mistake. Ralph Lauren shirts are nice but lack pockets, and this was my weak excuse for leaving the passport behind.

I was ordered to get into the car, as I did, and found myself crowded in the backseat with the man in charge and another policeman, with a driver and a young policeman up front. At that time there was a slip road off of Furmanov Street that led to several of the buildings just up the mountain from the National Museum. Instead of going on to Furmanov Street proper, and then to a police station, these men drove me past the buildings of Samal-I and onward, almost to Lenin (later Dostyk) Avenue into that very dark and desolate area by the semi-completed stadium. If you want to find a spot in Almaty where you can be totally alone, this is it. The car stopped and the two youngest policemen got out for a cigarette – or were they too young to witness what was about to happen? The hands of the remaining guys were all over me, into my pockets, feeling my legs and arms for a hidden gun or drugs, and I could smell more alcohol on the breath of the head guy than is good for his health.

It was impossible to find out what they wanted. All I could think of was that they were intent on intimidating foreigners. If so, they were making progress. There was no reason at all to kidnap me. They asked or accused me of having a pistol. No such thing. They accused me of being drunk. Also no such thing. Although I provide my share of support for the brewing industry, this had been an entirely dry afternoon, with nothing more to imbibe than a cup of tea with a bit of lemon in it. They accused me of having drugs. Nary a trace of it. They examined my wallet time and again, possibly hoping that incriminating evidence of something would pop out. They claimed that I had jay-walked on the slip road. They were not mollified when I replied that everyone in Samal II crosses the road where I did.

There was some grim humor that night as I sat trapped in a police car in a deserted area of town wondering if I would ever again see the light of day. I had a black beret-like hat with me and a black bag of tools which also contained a small flashlight. I had been in the vicinity of the Presidential Palace. I fully expected that I was about to be charged with some as yet undetected burglary. No such thing happened, however, and my Western tools were well admired.

We arrived at a kind of impasse. I had obligingly allowed them to search me. They found nothing of interest and I seemed not to be intimidated. (Hey, I did my main military training at Ft. Bragg, North Carolina, and my MOS numbers include one for Battle Police – and don't dare ask me what they do in the army of a democratic nation!) Of course the thought occurred to me that they wanted money but they had done nothing to help themselves to any of the cash in my pockets or wallet. Not having any experience of paying off cops, I at one point made the slightest and most ambiguous of gestures about the money. This produced a very stern retort – no money!

With their permission I used my mobile phone to corroborate the fact that I had helped a local resident install kitchen cupboards. This seemed to be a turning point of the evening. Eventually I was asked one of the most surprising questions that I have ever heard in my life, proving that context is everything. "Would you like a taxi?" Boy oh boy, you bet I would! Surprise of surprises, the police car was the taxi. They drove me to the vicinity of my apartment for a pre-agreed fare of 150 Tenges, which was a rather inflated price but this did not seem to be the moment to inform them that the going rate for such a short trip was closer to 70 Tenges.

As I got out of the car, the well-oiled leader asked if he could use my mobile phone. I was wary of some last-minute trick but handed over the phone and he proceeded to call his girlfriend, probably for the first time by cellphone. Presumably he did not know that her telephone number was being electronically recorded for posterity and for possible use at his disciplinary hearing. Having made his call, the policeman returned my phone, bade me farewell and they drove off.

I thought for a long time about how to react to this outrageous evening. Eventually I decided not to report the incident and not to seek revenge. Of course I had been in fear of my life, and the conduct of the policemen was utterly reprehensible. The head man ought to be charged and convicted of serious misconduct, possibly with the loss of his job or worse. On the other hand, I had not been physically harmed, nothing was taken, and I also did not want to get involved in a bureaucratic procedure which might increase my risk by alienating the officer. What would you have done? Weeks later I reported the incident to the U.S. Embassy for statistical purposes but without mentioning the incriminating phone call.

37

THE EXPATRIATE COMMUNITY

When I moved from New York to London in 1971 in order to expand my international practice of law, I found that there already was a small band of American lawyers who had stumbled across each other in London and who had formed a loosely-knit luncheon club. We met occasionally for the purpose of getting to know each other, of sharing information of mutual interest, of seeking to gain some advantage from the other members while, hopefully, giving away nothing which could be of advantage to them, and probably to look each other over for possible affiliation or employment or office sharing.

One of the American lawyers in London had, rather exceptionally, been there since shortly after the end of the Second World War. He had been in the U.S. Army during that war, became badly wounded, returned to his home state in the United States, found that he could not settle down, and had come back to Europe in order to work something out of his system. The rest of us arrived much later but we were still the early birds in the founding of the American legal community in London.

Our luncheon group expanded so much as time went on that we had to find a new venue in which to hold our meetings. We got more organized, elected our leadership, and started circulating written notices of meetings, and once in a while we even had a guest speaker. A bank account was opened for the group and we no longer paid for each lunch by chipping in cash to cover the bill at the end of the meal. Instead, there was a check-in and payment process at the door. The character of the group changed too. Initially, the luncheon group was composed of a hard core of independent minded and self-employed lawyers with a long-term commitment to the international practice of law based in London and, as I recall, all of us were men in those first several years. Later we were inundated by lawyers on relatively short-term assignments to London, most of whom worked for banks or other multinational corporations and some of whom were women. Eventually we old-timers began to lose interest. Going to a quarterly luncheon meeting populated by people you increasingly did not recognize and who probably would have returned to the United States by the time of the next meeting was not so interesting or productive. So, somewhere in the late 1980's our group evaporated. It had lost its definition and much of its purpose. And the particular glue that held it together – those of us who had started it and gave it continuity – came unstuck.

The life history of the American Lawyers Luncheon Group in London is not necessarily the profile of every other expatriate group in every country of the world, and that history is not necessarily predictive of anything. But I imagine that many readers who have been here in Almaty for an extended period and who participate in the life of the expatriate community with some energy will recognize in my little tale about American lawyers in London some elements or patterns that may be emerging in their own circles here in Almaty. Nothing is guaranteed about life. No pattern is fixed. Everything changes. The pattern this year, which seems nearly permanent, changes under the tide of external events or as people come and leave, and a new pattern emerges which seems utterly natural to new arrivals but which seems rather strange to you who have been here for some time, and then yet another pattern of social activity emerges, and so on and so on. You cannot freeze a social process. You can treasure your memories, but you cannot guarantee that things won't change.

My advice, therefore, is not to hold back and wait until everything is clear and settled but, rather, to join in the life of the community now. This is one of the reasons really that I volunteered to *The Almaty Herald* to write some articles that I thought might possibly be of interest to its readers. We are a kind of community even if some of us have never met each other, and one of the things that holds us together is an English-language newspaper, like *The Almaty Herald*, which performs some of the functions of a community bulletin board or even of a town hall. In many ways, my "Almaty Perspective" column is my personal way of trying to participate actively in this rapidly evolving and changing community of expatriates and local residents who happen to speak some English. This is also my way of trying to put something back into the community and not just always to be taking out of it.

I don't remember the first issue of *The Almaty Herald*, probably because I did not receive a copy of it and didn't even know where to get a copy of the newspaper at the time. For that matter, I may not have seen several of the first issues of that newspaper. Entrepreneurs don't start a new enterprise in its full blown mode overnight, and it takes some struggle and the passage of time before a newspaper finds its public and also before the public searches out the newspaper.

I do remember, however, the journalists of *The Almaty Herald* from the very beginning. They were covering some event that I attended two years ago and they wore prominent badges which proclaimed that they were journalists but, probably more importantly, the badges had the side effect of announcing for all to see the fact that something called *The Almaty Herald* existed. I even remember writing down the name of one of the journalists, thinking at the time that it might be useful to remain in contact with an emerging English-language newspaper in Almaty. Little did I imagine at that time that I would later become a frequent contributor to *The Almaty Herald*.

On the occasion of the one hundredth issue of *The Almaty Herald* on 22 January 1998, I offer my congratulations and best wishes for its future success. I have no idea what is in store for any of us as the future unfolds but I would like to wish the newspaper long life and prosperity as it continues to serve valuable functions for the expatriate community as well as for many local residents.

38
THE GOODBYE PARTY

There are clearly discernible phases to the development of the expatriate presence and community in Almaty. In 1993, it seemed that all foreigners stayed in hotels, went to Dr. Bang's Disco (now KIMEP Club) at 9:30 p.m. on Friday night, and met for Sunday brunch at the second floor restaurant at the Dostyk Hotel.

Then there was a period of delegation visits – foreign aid hit teams – such as numerous World Bank squads, the IMF teams, the Arkansas chicken farmers, and the 52 Dutch potato farmers.

There was the hi-tech disco era which started when the Italian Disco opened in November of 1993, in the Ministry of Interior building at the corner of Dzerzhinsky and Shevchenko Streets. It quickly became a veritable oasis of Western high life, making it possible during the evening to step outside of Almaty and the former Soviet Union, and to imagine that you were somewhere else. Soon, Space Disco opened at Daulet Club, which was more accessible to local residents, and then a series of other discos started.

When Happy Hour started at the International Business Club on Friday nights, it seemed that whole new vistas of possibilities were being opened up for expatriates. One no longer had to dance or to lean on the balcony at Dr. Bang's Disco in order to meet other expatriates or local residents. At some point during this period foreign women and children arrived in Almaty, adding an important dimension to what otherwise had been in danger of remaining a community of bachelor, or virtually bachelor, foreign men.

One of the current themes of expatriate life in Almaty, primarily indulged in by the single expatriates, is the goodbye party.

It would be nice to think that a goodbye party consists of a gathering of close and intimate friends and associates who desire to assemble on the eve of someone's departure in order to say their fond farewells, to raise a glass in a sentimental toast, and perhaps to think sober and deep thoughts about friendship and the harsh demands that life places on all of us.

The truth about contemporary goodbye parties in Almaty, however, is that they more closely resemble something out of "Animal House" than a diplomatic dinner. The departure of someone who has been in Almaty for a significant period – more than a couple of months but probably not more than a year or 18 months – is likely to be simply an excuse for a group of expatriates to do what they probably would do if no one was leaving, i.e., to hold a kind of mixer-beer bust party. In this regard, a goodbye party is almost indistinguishable from a New Year's party, a Victory Day party, or a Valentine's Day party. A determined group of people is intent on having a good time, and the reason for the gathering is more or less irrelevant.

It is difficult to say when these parties took hold as a prominent and sustained feature of expatriate life. Certainly they were a regular part of the social whirl during all of 1996 and during 1995 as well. Before that there were not so many foreigners and most of them still stayed in hotels; and many of the foreigners were not here long enough to inspire someone to sponsor a goodbye party for them when they left.

It is impossible to predict when the goodbye parties, like the Disco scene, might fade from being one of the outstanding hallmarks of a social life among expatriates. Of course parties to mark the occasion of departure will be around for as long as foreigners continue to work and live here, but at some point they will become cultivated affairs, to be given among people who really do know each other quite well and who genuinely want to say goodbye in a pleasant and memorable way to someone they have come to know, to like and perhaps to admire. Maybe when USAID and other foreign assistance programs, which rely heavily upon short-term employees, pack up and leave Kazakhstan, the goodbye party will once again start to resemble a polite dinner party for those who are near and dear and want to see off good old Charlie. For the time being, goodbye parties are mostly just parties, with the "goodbye" element being the thinnest of veneers.

Analytically, here are some of the main social facts that, when combined, brought about the phenomena of the goodbye party as it is known today:

A sufficient pool of foreigners, mainly single. Not so long ago, one could also define this pool as being almost exclusively male. While the pool continues to be male dominated, the men have been joined in the past couple of years by quite a few single women from abroad.

When you attend a goodbye party and gaze around the room, it is possible often to have an overwhelming sense of déjà vu – aren't these the same people who assembled last Friday to see off what's-his-name? And for someone else the week before? And for yet another person a week earlier?

In many ways, the goodbye party is a special species of rent-a-crowd. There is in Almaty a mixture of expatriates with lots of free time on their hands and quite a few locals who desire to meet and mix with expatriates. Given a venue in Almaty and a starting time, it is possible for anyone who is willing to serve beer and a modicum of food, to quickly assemble the ingredients for a successful party.

There probably is a hard core group of around 200, perhaps more, committed partygoers, being a mixture of expatriates and local residents, whose membership will make up a high proportion of the attendees at any given goodbye party. On the night in question, many of these people are not available. Some are out of town, some have business or social commitments, some are recovering from the night before and, the invitation process being haphazard as it is, some may not have heard about the party. (If a host or hostess fears that they will have a low turnout at their social function, all they need to do is to find some way to tap into this hard core of partygoers, and then stand back and let nature take its course.)

To keep matters in perspective, I must emphasize that there will also be in attendance at a goodbye party some genuine friends of the departing person who truly will be sorry to see that person leave Almaty.

A sufficient pool of local residents, mainly English-speaking. This group tends to be predominantly female in gender and single in marital status, offering a complementary match to the majority of the other pool of participants, but this one also includes a number of local men. Many of the members of this group are employed by foreign companies, which is how they hear about the goodbye parties and feel comfortable about attending these unusual functions.

A fairly rapid turnover rate among many of the foreigners, thereby providing the excuse for the goodbye party. Many factors lead to a high turnover rate among the foreigners in Almaty. Foreign government employees usually work on fixed assignments and then rotate out of here for their future career development and promotion. USAID contracts are limited by U.S. budget requirements and, even if the contracts are renewed, most contractors engage their staff members for temporary periods. Multinational companies, like foreign governments, need to reconcile career development paths, promotion cycles, and personal interest of employees in any assignment. And, let's face it, some foreigners find life difficult in Almaty. Some families prefer to remain in the West while the breadwinner works in Almaty for a limited period of time. Other families join the breadwinner and then discover that social, linguistic and other barriers are higher than expected. Some husband-wife teams come to Almaty when one of them is assigned here, and then learn the unhappy truth that the job market for the accompanying spouse is exceedingly thin. Finally, when the Republic of Kazakhstan opened up to foreign investment, there was no pre-existing base of long-term expatriates already living here who could ease the entry of those riding the wave of inward investment. The social infrastructure for expatriates has had to be built from scratch, and some of that infrastructure remains pretty rough and tentative.

The existence of a central point of information which is widely accessible. The starting point of the invitation process for many goodbye parties is the cafeteria at the American Embassy. Many of the departing expats are government employees who have completed a tour of duty or are short-term employees of USAID contractors, and they and their friends are regular customers of the cafeteria. Many other foreigners and quite a few local residents also use that cafeteria each week. So, the practice has arisen of posting announcements on the entrance door and the adjacent wall of the cafeteria, and of leaving a pile of invitations where people will see them and take them away while standing in line. Who would believe the sociological structure of the invitation process that takes over the minute the invitation is released? The fax machines start working; the photocopiers roll; and the telephone syndicate swings into operation. Only the jungle drum is missing as a means of passing on the message.

To those in the know, the party invitation can be spotted from a distance of 30 paces. It occupies an A4 sheet of paper with a simple indication of the purpose of the party (if any), a diagram of where to find the party venue, and the key words of date, time, address and phone contact number. These diagrams can be challenging. In this town, you never know if "up" is north or south or somewhere else.

Depending upon the computer skills of the person who prepared the invitation, it may also contain balloons or other graphics to help convey the mood of the party. Oh, yes, the invitation also gives the first or last name or both of the person who soon will take their leave of Almaty.

The result is that large numbers of people gather together for the goodbye party despite the fact that many of the attendees have never heard of or met the departing person. My strong impression is that it would be quite possible to hold a very successful goodbye party for an entirely fictitious person. Few, if any, would cotton on to the fact that the guest of honor does not exist and was incapable of coming to his/her goodbye party. And no one would be disappointed if they did learn the truth.

On a recent occasion as I was walking down Dostyk Avenue late on a Saturday afternoon, I encountered a Western couple with whom I have a nodding acquaintance. They asked me where "the party" was going to be that night, and I told them about the only party of which I had knowledge which I assumed was the party they were asking about. Three or four hours later, I encountered them at that party, and they expressed their pleasure at having located it from my instructions. It then emerged that earlier they had had no idea that any party was being held that night and they certainly had not received any invitation. No one questioned their presence at the party or challenged them in any way.

I imagine that more than a few people have located a party (of the goodbye type or otherwise) simply by prowling the streets of Almaty on a Friday or Saturday night listening for the tell-tale noises emanating from an apartment building. If English is heard over the din of the music or other sounds, the chances are good that this is an open-house type function, or near enough thereto, to which entry will not be refused. In fact, if you are a recognized member of the Goodbye Party Club, it is likely that, upon entry, you will spot many people you know, and many of them will assume that you are a bona fide, invitation-carrying guest.

The availability of a venue. Now that large numbers of foreigners live in apartments or, in a few cases, in houses, there seems to be no lack of places at which to give parties. At least a few apartments are put to recurring use for this purpose. Some dachas have also served this function, particularly when the event has a company sponsor.

I have not yet heard of anyone being ostracized from a party because they always attend parties given by others but never host one in return. That kind of sentiment is for a future period of higher civilization and culture.

The relatively high entrance cost at many of the commercial establishments which might otherwise serve the mixer function of the goodbye party. Single foreigners continue to attend discos, eat out at restaurants, go to the company-sponsored receptions, and seize the other one-off opportunities that come their way to meet and mix. However, the discos tend to be too expensive – with entry fees set at Tg. 1,500 or more per man and at, say, Tg. 1,000 per woman – for this to become more than a once-a-week activity. That leaves up to six other nights per week that many foreign single people would like to fill with a less expensive activity. The handy solution that currently fills some of this need: the goodbye party.

39

GOOD NEWS REPORT

There have been some attempts to publish "good news" newspapers in the United States but my impression is that none of them has succeeded for long. You can argue with the reading public all you want that they should not be so attracted to reports about car accidents, violent crimes, scandals, wars, revolutions and disasters but the public buys those newspapers. As for the good news newspapers, they are ignored and die unless they have independent financing. Oh, it is possible for the dire news newspapers to print the occasional happy piece of news. One sometimes sees a story with a happy ending about the reuniting of families that got separated years ago or about childhood sweethearts who finally marry at the age of 75 after some stupid mistake set them adrift decades before.

On the basis that there is at least some tolerance by readers to good news stories, I thought the time was ripe to tell a few good news stories about life in Almaty. Of the other kind of story, we hear a great deal. For example, every month at the U.S. Embassy's Business Roundtable, a written and/or oral security report provides details of those bad events which have been brought to the attention of the Security Officer at the Embassy. These reports cover all such security incidents, not just those involving American citizens or American companies. These reports chronicle everything from the theft of windshield wipers, to attempted or actual breaking and entering of apartments, to muggings, to extortion tries, to the grisly murder a few months ago of an American journalist.

My impression is that there are quite a few good news stories that people have to tell, and which it might be interesting for expatriates to know about as a balance to the bad news stories. Unfortunately, good news being what it is, we don't much hear these stories.

One month in 1996, the Embassy's security report provided details and a warning about the "wallet trick". This trick has variations but basically the Almaty version goes like this. You are walking along minding your own business when suddenly someone coming in your direction reaches down to the ground and picks up a wallet. He shows surprise and hands it to you as he dashes off after the person who presumably lost it. Soon the finder returns with another man who, on checking his wallet, "discovers" that $50 is missing. He accuses you of the theft and threatens to call the police unless you "return" his money.

On the very next day after hearing that Friday report on the wallet trick, I went to the Green Market to do my weekly shopping. Needing some Tenge, I exchanged $100 at one of the currency exchange kiosks and received Tg. 7,240. As I walked away after pocketing my money, a young man tapped me on the shoulder and handed some money to me. Wallet trick? Where's the wallet? Wary to the extreme after hearing about the wallet trick, my hands shot into my pockets and I tried to ignore the young man but he persisted long enough for me to comprehend that he was handing me my own money. Sure enough, I had Tg. 7,000 in my pocket; I had dropped the Tg. 240 on the ground. I was so flustered by this unexpected turn of events that I believe I never even thanked the pleasant young man and I certainly failed to give him any reward for his honesty which, I would like to emphasize, was not solicited in any way.

Only a couple of weeks later I personally experienced the wallet trick. I was walking down Kunaev Street (Karl Marx Street) next to the Dostyk Hotel and was within 10 meters of Kurmangazy Street when an approaching young man reached down to the curb (just out of my eyesight) and "picked up" a newly found wallet. Again, my hands shot into my pockets as I continued to walk down the mountain while the con artist went through his much practiced story about how I should hold the wallet while he dashed off to find the person who lost it. Knowing what the trick was all about was helpful to me but it also made the young man appear to be so foolish that I nearly laughed at him. So far as I could tell, he had pulled the trick without an accomplice (did I look that gullible?), and there was not a person in sight behind me on Kunaev Street all the way from Kurmangazy to Abay Street, the direction being pointed to by the con artist. Maybe he was practicing (the sleight of hand was very good). Maybe he had heard only part of the trick from the real con artist and was beginning to wonder why he was not having much success.

When I mentioned my little tale about my returned money to some other expatriates, one of them told his own story of returned property. He had been out to the airport to collect someone and upon returning to his apartment he realized that he had lost his cellular telephone. It had been in his coat pocket, and he assumed that it had fallen to the ground when he bent low to get under a barrier. This was on a Saturday and he was very concerned that the finder might run up enormous long-distance charges before the owner could ask the phone company on Monday to terminate service on his instrument. He was also concerned about the cost of replacing his phone. Then the owner of the phone had the bright idea to call his own cellular telephone number. Sure enough, the finder answered the phone. The quick-witted owner asked the finder his location and told him to wait there for 15 minutes. The finder duly waited and gave the phone back to its owner. Not one call had been made on the phone. The honest finder was well rewarded by a very relieved owner.

I too had a fortunate experience with honest local residents at the airport. A few years ago I arrived in Almaty with 10 identical boxes of office supplies as well as a suitcase and briefcase, making a luggage count of 12. It was in the winter and the airport was very crowded. I was met by two people. While I guarded my hoard in the terminal building, they shuttled the items to the car. As a result, it was difficult for me to keep track of everything and it was impossible in the crowded car to see if all items were on board. When we arrived at my apartment, it was clear that one of the identical boxes was missing. We search the car, the hallway and the lift without finding it. I had counted everything correctly when presenting myself at customs control but now I was short one box. I still had my luggage claim tickets so I knew exactly which box was missing. My driver, like many local residents, was prepared to believe the worst of other local residents, and was absolutely convinced that we would never again see the box. He thought it was useless to phone the airport for information but he willingly drove all the way to the airport to try to learn what had happened to the box. Two hours later he returned to my apartment with the box in perfect condition. Some honest person had noticed that it had been left behind at customs control and turned it over to the customs officials. They in turn gave it to Lufthansa personnel who were holding it for identification and collection.

I also had a recovered phone experience but I never did learn if this was good news worthy of reporting. While shopping one weekend at the Green Market, I was a victim of a pickpocket. Many people warned of this danger so I was not overly surprised when it happened. I was wearing a long but light coat, a kind of raincoat with the familiar Burberry lining, and in my left pocket I had my radio telephone. Mobile phones had not yet been invented or at least had not arrived in Almaty. The radio telephones were similar to modern smartphones but were far clunkier and it naturally had no functions and no apps other than to act as a means of communication through Almaty's television tower. In a congested outdoor area of the market, I sensed that someone was trying to wrestle the bulky phone out of my pocket. My instinctive reaction was to sweep into my arms those who were close to me, instantly wondering what I was going to do with them. I had scooped up two young boys, likely underprivileged boys but pickpockets nonetheless. As I stood there with them clasped to me a young girl stepped forward and handed the phone to me, whereupon I let the boys go for lack of knowing what to do with them. I have since wondered if the young girl should have been rewarded or if she was the hand-off person, a part of the thieving group, whose job was to disappear with the loot while the others, if caught, protested their innocence.

An expatriate woman acquaintance of mine who drives a car got into trouble while driving toward a small village well away from Almaty during the spring. The snow was melting, the road was slick and she ended up deeply mired in a very muddy ditch. She was nearing the end of her wits as to what to do when a local policeman arrived at the scene and single-handedly muscled her car out of the ditch even though the spinning wheels sprayed mud all over him. He asked for no reward but was pleased to learn that a bottle of vodka would soon be on its way to him.

If you have ever been on one of those over-crowded buses where it is impossible for the ticket seller to move about, you will have observed money being handed forward in bucket brigade style. A few moments later the ticket works its way back in the same manner. Although I am told by some local residents that they are aware that ticket money sometimes disappears along the way, I have always been utterly impressed by the effectiveness of this method of payment. Normally such a bus is filled with local residents who might be thought to be somewhere near the bottom of the economic pole, to whom the bus fare for a long ride up the mountain might be a tempting prize. All I can say is that my ticket has always come home to me after sending the payment forward.

Over the years many kindnesses and courtesies have been shown to me by local residents of Almaty for which I am thankful and which persuade me that the overwhelming disposition of local residents is of basic honesty and decency, with hospitality for strangers which is particularly warm for foreigners.

40

DID THE SOVIET UNION TRIP UP ON ITS STAIRS?

The case has been argued that the Roman Empire fell because, as its borders expanded, the need for horses outstripped the ability of the Romans to produce the grain to feed them. That is another way of saying that their demand for horses outran their food supply. Another provocative view of the fall of the Roman Empire is that the Romans poisoned themselves little by little after making the technological blunder of introducing lead pipes into their otherwise remarkable plumbing systems. Coming closer to the present time, some historians take the view that various naval empires, such as that of Venice, reached their limits and then fell back because their specialized and huge need for lumber to build ships could no longer be met once the forests of Europe had been denuded of their slow-growing ancient trees.

Much as I enjoy these simplistic analyses of otherwise complex events and much as I sometimes express my own somewhat eccentric view of matters, I am not about to argue that the Soviet Union collapsed because the Soviets never mastered the fundamentals of building stairs of uniform size.

It is true that the Soviet Union came undone and it is also true that stairs in the former Soviet Union are notable for their lack of uniformity of size. But it probably goes too far to blame the collapse on the stairs. Still, the inability of the Soviet Union to supply its populace with stairs of the same size almost certainly is one of the many indications that the Soviet economy was lacking in some vital ingredient, which resulted in the production of vast amounts of shoddy goods. And if the stairs are only one outward sign of a more fundamental flaw, then at least that fundamental flaw can be assigned responsibility for the downfall of the Soviet system even if the stairs cannot take the blame.

My candidate for the worst step in Almaty is the one on the ground floor, inside the building, that you must take before entering one of the Chinese restaurants in Almaty. The architect and the workmen did not face a daunting task when they produced this monstrous error. They were called upon to produce a mere three steps and they managed to create one that is about one and a half times as high as the other two steps. That large step is not so utterly conspicuous as to give off its own warning that special care must be taken, and the hallway, as normal, is somewhat dimly lit. In the nature of things, many people come to the restaurant who are not familiar with the building and so, time after time, the restaurant goers gain an unwelcome reminder of the erratic nature of stairs in Almaty.

This botched job is in the lobby of a heavily used building and right in front of a restaurant. I doubt that there is a worse example of poor stair construction in the city of Almaty but I would be pleased to hear of candidate bad steps that may outdo this one for disproportionality and for bad location.

Approximately 87% of the steps in my apartment building are uniform in size. We have twelve floors with each of the top 11 floors being connected by 20 steps composed of two units of 10 steps each. Each unit of 10 steps contains 9 steps of equal size but the 10th step, which is the bottom step, is about half the height of the other steps. That means that 11 of the 12 floors achieve a 90% rating. However, the 2nd floor is extraordinarily high above the 1st floor, and the connecting stairs, which are the most heavily used and worst constructed in the building, bring down the overall average for uniformity.

If you look closely at your own apartment building, you might see that many of the stairs also are uniform in size. Typically, it is the bottom step or the top step, or both of them, which fail the uniformity test. The reason is that most staircases for apartments were manufactured in modular units at some factory far away from the site of the apartment buildings. These staircases are composed of steps of uniform size. The problem of non-uniformity arises when the perfectly formed steps are badly installed. I do not know the precise origin of the engineering and installation problem but it seems that the staircase units are deliberately larger than the stairwell into which they must fit. The theory seems to be that it is better to have overlarge staircases in which the bottom step must be partly embedded in the building, producing that small first step, than to have staircases that are too small which result in an open gap when installed. Alternatively, it may be that no one ever communicated to the staircase producers the exact floor to ceiling dimension of the buildings where their staircases were to be installed.

Sometimes the lack of uniformity of the stairs can be explained by the use of marble to cover the underlying cement stairs. The pre-formed cement stairs might have been quite uniform when installed but this is sometimes ruined when an owner decides to tart up the building by covering the floors and staircases with marble. I know one building, for example, where the stairs were raised so much by the marble facade that extra wood had to be fitted to the banisters so that people could grasp them without stooping.

Now, the question can be asked whether or not uniformity of stairs is important. Why are we foreigners so critical of bad steps and why, after all, do we see this as a failing? Maybe this issue of uniformity has importance only for foreigners and is not a matter of concern to the local population. What I mean is that I know that I sometimes stumble on stairs but I am also aware that, after four years in Almaty, I am getting more and more adept at taking bad stairs in stride. One day in the not too distant future, I may not even notice that the stairs are lacking in uniformity. In this regard, it might be helpful to recall the comment of one sage that 'civilization' is the ability to constantly manage more functions at the same time. From this point of view, it might be thought that the local residents of Almaty are more civilized then the expatriate community: they can carry on all of the various functions of life while not needing to give any special attention to the stairs they climb but we foreigners often must turn our full attention to the task of walking up and down stairs, making it difficult for us to do anything else or to think of anything else at the same time. Did you ever see a local resident trip on the bad stairs?

The tolerance of bad stairs by local residents of Almaty may suggest that they have a mental attitude that is closer to the British than to the Americans. When Americans confront a problem, their immediate reaction is to try to fix it. This is the "can do" society. In my experience of living in England for 25 years, when British people confront a problem, their first reaction is to find a way to live with it. We fix a leaky roof; they fetch a bucket.

Maybe I should observe more closely how well the British expatriates and other foreigners cope with the non-uniform stairs of Almaty. Can it be that only we Americans are tripping up or falling down the stairs in Almaty?

41

FEMININITY IN ALMATY

One of the delights of being a Western man in Almaty is to observe the local women who seem to be so at ease with their femininity, who play it up so well and who apparently see no reason for toning it down or denying it. I am not talking about beauty though certainly there is an abundance of that in Almaty as well. Nor am I talking about sexual allure as such though it is clear that the sheer garments and short skirts appropriate for this time of the year work their effect.

I am talking about women who seemingly enjoy being women without any pretense of also being like men or without feeling inferior by reason of being a woman. I am talking about the very young girls with earrings, with headbands and hair clasps, with outrageously large ribbons in their hair, with high heels at a surprisingly young age, and with very long heads of hair. I am talking about well-groomed teenage girls who already have a sophisticated sense of dress. I am talking about women of all ages who comfortably wear such a wide range of garments, from local costumes to Western styles that so often exude that elusive quality known as femininity.

Femininity survives in the West, let's not be in any doubt about that. But my impression about femininity in the West is that women treat it somewhat like a change of clothing. One day they don it, and another day they don't. One day they wear that little black number which makes them feel good about being a woman, and another day they climb back into the blue jeans and once again become just another one of the guys. Of course I have seen tomboyish girls in jeans in Almaty, and I know that some of the very feminine women here also take a "day off" once in a while. I have no doubt, however, that there is far less letting down of the hair or dropping of the mask by women here than I have observed among women in the West.

Among many women in the West, femininity somehow seems to be external in nature, being heavily dependent upon clothing selection and choice of makeup. Here, by contrast, I have the impression that femininity is more nearly internal in nature, and has something to do with one's concept of self. It's not so much what you wear as who you are and how you carry yourself regardless of the wrapper.

I will avoid some of the really dangerous aspects of this topic. You know, questions like - are Western women all screwed up psychologically by the impossible demands placed upon them in modern Western society? How is it that we devised a society in which Western women are forced into making that unenviable two-out-of-three choice between being a good wife, a good mother or a good careerist? Are Eastern women superior to Western women by reason of their more evident femininity, or are they in fact the totally downtrodden members of the second sex who, for their own protection and survival in a male-dominated society, are forced by prevailing circumstances to use femininity as a last resort?

These subjects are too large for me. All I know is that, after watching Western women struggle for identity and role for several decades, with its bra burning stages and the feminist movement, with its androgynous phases, with its support groups, and with its women power periods, it is a welcome treat to see and to meet women from what may be an earlier stage of the development of society where all these "modern" problems will only be encountered at some future stage of social development.

Femininity may be internal and may not be dependent upon what a woman wears, but it does, nevertheless, have its commercial aspects.

Susan Weidner, the former Commercial Officer of the American Embassy, made the astute observation that a very high proportion of the discretionary spending of families in Almaty is devoted to the women of the household. Despite low incomes and sometimes harsh living conditions, the women are generally very well turned out. They seem to have a reasonable selection of nice clothing for the varying seasons, they exhibit good dress sense, they sport quite a bit of jewelry, and they use cosmetic makeup to good effect. In sum, despite all the economic problems that may afflict them, large numbers of local women are able to achieve world standards as head turners.

I had made this same observation about the spending power of local women before I met Susan Weidner. When I lived in micro-district Samal II, I often remarked to myself while waiting for our office driver to collect me in the morning about how such a large number of women were so astonishingly fetching as they emerged from their apartment buildings into the somewhat grim reality of the outside world. The apartment steps may be crumbling, the yet-to-be-completed road was a mess, the refuse was spilling out of the large garbage bins, half the area was a construction zone vaguely resembling war-torn Sarajevo, and yet the women would have looked entirely in place if they were instead coming out onto the streets of the 16th arrondissement in Paris. How could they possibly accomplish this? Where on earth did they find the clothing when the shops seemed so empty at that time?

Susan thought she might have spotted a U.S. marketing opportunity and she arranged for a group of local clothing buyers and others from Almaty's fashion industry to attend a clothing buyers show in New York. I don't know if this one-week venture primed the pumps of commerce in a big way but I do know that some serious contract negotiations ensued and at least a few American labels made their way into the shops of Almaty.

42
THE WAY I SEE THINGS

After writing many thousands of words for the "Almaty Perspective" column of *The Almaty Herald* newspaper, I will take the opportunity to describe here what I have been trying to accomplish, and perhaps in some way to explain why. Basically, I felt that I had had a sufficient depth of experience that I had something to say that others might enjoy sharing. Also, whereas most foreigners come here on assignments of two years or less, my experience goes back five years to the beginning of 1993.

It has been my intention in writing these articles to describe my own perceptions, which naturally are personal to me and often are anecdotal in nature. It definitely has been my intention not to undertake any fresh research in order to compose a particular essay. The result, which I guess I knew from the outset, is that I basically do not express macro perceptions of anything. On the contrary, I seem to have only micro, mini-micro or, some might say, microscopic, perceptions. (How many people are really interested in reading 2,000 words about lightbulb snatching, the eating of sunflower seeds, the art of catching a taxi, the use of balconies, the size of stairs, or how to read an invitation?) I don't have a bird's eye view of this enormous country nor even of this city; I am more like a nearsighted mouse peeking out of its hole and seeing a world inhabited by strange creatures that I can only vaguely understand.

Partly I write these articles because I think foreign readers enjoy them and get some use out of them. Many foreigners come and go all too quickly, often being insulated from local life and local conditions in Almaty by being surrounded by other foreign people. Some of these articles may help them to understand more quickly a few things that it has taken me five years to figure out, and even then I acknowledge that I may be wrong in what I say.

Some comments may help people to better understand the nuances of their own experiences in Almaty. Maybe they have noticed some of the same things about which I write, but have never thought to comment on them or have not yet grasped the significance of what they have seen. One reader from Nebraska very much enjoyed the article in which I compared Kazakhstan to my home state of South Dakota, and he told me how often he has mentioned to friends and family back home that Kazakhstan is "just like Nebraska".

People who know me well understand that it is not in my nature to ridicule others, to be deliberately offensive, or to be disrespectful of their culture, religion, or style of life. When I wrote about lightbulb snatching, for example, I was worried at first that readers might think that I was inferring that everyone in Kazakhstan is a thief. For this reason, I asked quite a few local residents to read and comment on the article in draft form. Not only did they enjoy the article but they came back to me with their own jokes and stories about lightbulb snatching, and their experiences with this problem. I had not previously known that this was a heavily worked seam of humor in Kazakhstan and other parts of the former Soviet Union.

There is a great risk when a foreigner like me tries to inject humor into stories which often touch upon the way life is lived by local residents. I spent seven years in New York, the city with the largest gathering of Jewish people on the earth. It was my good fortune to have several personal friends who were Jews, to work closely with some and to have others as acquaintances and neighbors. I learned that Jews are some of the greatest tellers of jokes in which they poke fun at themselves, grotesquely depicting themselves with all of the worst stereotypes imaginable, and they seem to enjoy this immensely.

It would be a mistake, however, to think that any non-Jew can poke the same fun, even using exactly the same joke or story, and expect to receive the same hearty response. One must be careful with ethnic jokes. Told by a New York Jew, few, if any, take offense at the story. Told by a non-Jew, there immediately can be an undercurrent of worry by the Jewish listeners that there may be a sinister side to the joke, raising questions about the motives of the person who tells it.

I have tried to spice up some of my articles with a bit of humor, mainly with plays on words and (hopefully) dry wit. Nevertheless, some of the things I have said might be interpreted negatively by local readers though I hope not. As to this, I can only say that I enjoy life in Almaty and I spend time here by choice. This is an interesting place to be right now, and it is possible to have a rich and rewarding life here even if one must also acknowledge that there can be some rough edges and unpleasant surprises in this process.

Almost all of my writing for publication in *The Almaty Herald* is read in draft form by about half a dozen local residents before it is released for use. The local readers vary from article to article. All of them speak good English, understand most or all of what is being said, including the finer nuances, and know me well enough to tell me to my face that I have gone off the edge or have made a factual mistake. Frequently, their helpful suggestions (and sometimes their stinging criticisms) cause me to adapt, modify, expand or re-write what I was going to say. I am thankful to all of these critics and helpers though I will not mention them by name to spare them from possible embarrassment.

I have been aware for a long time that it is interesting to be in Almaty during the opening up of the Republic of Kazakhstan to foreigners. At first, I was somewhat agog at what I saw. Subsequently, I am sure that my perceptions have gotten less acute as I have come to adapt to life in this country. Equally, it is clear that Kazakhstan has lost some of its tang as international norms of lifestyle and living have taken root. Nevertheless, when I visit my family in the West or take business trips abroad, it remains the case that my personal experiences and anecdotes continue to be very interesting to others. Kazakhstan, to most people in the West, is still very much a new and faraway land.

I have tried to write about my experiences and perceptions honestly, fairly and accurately. Hopefully, I have done so in an interesting and sometimes entertaining way. I do not pretend to be an expert on the Republic of Kazakhstan, and I am aware that my experience is rather limited. Often I see only the surface or just a little bit beneath the surface. Nevertheless, I have often found that, reticent as I sometimes am as a conversationalist, I can inadvertently dominate conversations in the West as story after story about life in Almaty comes rolling out. If I try to clam up out of fear that people are getting bored or will start to drift out of the room, many of them will nevertheless press me to continue to make my observations.

From comments made to me by local residents, many of whom work for foreign companies, I have become aware that quite a few readers of these articles are local residents. Many have volunteered to me that they enjoy seeing themselves from someone else's perspective. Some have suggested fresh topics that I should exploit. A few have offered critical comments; perhaps more would do so if they were not inhibited by a feeling that, in my presence, they need to be polite.

One expatriate told me that his company uses articles in the "Almaty Perspective" column as a means of bridging the cultural chasm between the foreigners and the local employees of the company. Group readings of the articles occur which give rise to discussions about my observations. I wish I could be a fly on the wall on some of those occasions.

I am aware of some local residents who seem to enjoy reading these articles for the benefit this gives of reading in the English language. It seems that the English used to describe mundane aspects of their own life is of greater interest to them than reading more abstract writings in English about politics, economics or some other more intellectual topic.

It has not been my intention to deliberately write a series of "warts-and-all" articles on life in Kazakhstan but equally it has not been my intention to sanitize my writing so that all vividness and color is lost. In doing so, I bear the same risk of all those people in all walks of life who choose to put their heads above the parapet when they were entirely at liberty to remain crouched and unnoticed behind the wall.

———

The above article had the somewhat unfortunate effect of causing several readers to conclude that I was about to stop writing, which I had not been thinking about. Not at all. It then had the further unfortunate effect of planting the idea in my own mind that I could stop whenever I wanted, and which I later did though that did coincide to some extent with the ending of my residence in Kazakhstan.

43
SKIING AT CHIMBULAK

In several articles I refer to skiing, which is important to me, and I thought there ought to be some words directly about my experiences on the slopes.

My experience of skiing at Chimbulak (now called Shymbulak) goes back to a time a decade and a half before there was a gondola lift from Medeo, and even well before the installation of modern chairlifts, the development of impressive chalets, and the appearance of other amenities at or around Almaty's premier ski area.

Like a lot of other expatriates living in Almaty in 1994 – and there were not many of us at that time – I experienced a certain amount of cabin fever as the days grew shorter and winter neared. My apartment in the Three Bogaterias on Dostyk Avenue (just above Iskra Cinema and behind the statue of poet Dzhambul) was quite grand by local standards. The previous occupants included an army general whose bespoke built-in cupboards were an attractive feature of the spacious quarters. One of my associates noted to me that I had more square meters of living space, not even counting the generous balcony on two full side of the apartment, than his whole family had when he grew up in the company of two sisters and their parents. That didn't make me any happier to be spending increasing amounts of time confined in my apartment. So I investigated how to go skiing. I had skied for many years in the United States and then in Europe but hadn't a clue as to how to go about it in Almaty until I made enquiries. The urge became irresistible after seeing several people with skis walking uphill in front of my apartment toward a bus stop,

I had two vital clues. First, I learned that rental equipment was available at Chimbulak. Second, I could catch a bus across the street from the Hotel Kazakhstan and get as far as Medeo. If I could manage the last stretch of road on my own, I could go skiing.

The next Sunday morning I set off on my adventure after donning my best jeans, a longish jacket that should have kept me warm in Siberia, a cap to cover my head, and a pair of leather gloves. Either then or on the following trip to the mountains, I also wore lightweight tracksuit trousers – Nike's made in Poland – which I purchased at the Green Market after failing to find real long johns. Not the greatest kit for skiing but sufficient to get by.

I was disappointed at the bus stop not to see any other skiers. Phase 1 of my plan involved tagging along behind others who knew the way. I pressed on without the hope for guides.

We weren't long on the road before I encountered a problem. Our bus stopped at a T-junction with another road, where many passengers disembarked. Had I spoken more than "taxi Russian" I might have learned that I too needed to transfer to another bus in order to get to Medeo. Without knowing that I was doing the right thing, I dismounted from the bus, carried along, I suppose, by crowd instinct. Anyway, it was the right move and I could see from the following bus that it did go to Medeo whereas it now became obvious that my former bus had another destination.

Having arrived at the Medeo bus stop halfway to my destination, I wandered further up, past the entry to the skating stadium, to where the road resumes its course up the mountain. A gaggle of people stood there. I guessed it was an unmarked bus stop. Well, it was and it wasn't. An army truck pulled to a stop near us and everyone piled into the rear over the tailgate. We all paid a small fare. Those with skis stowed them in the middle of the floor while the passengers sat on the benches facing each other under the canvas roof.

Off we went at a snail's pace up the steep road. At the hairpin turns I was surprised to discover that the rear wheels, which drove the vehicle, did not have a differential gear. In other words, both the inside wheel making the tight turn and the outside wheel making the wide turn, had to go around at the same speed. The result was the inside wheel doing a lot of juddering, hardly moving forward at all while keeping pace with the outer wheel, while the outer wheel kept its traction and moved us forward. The whole vehicle shuddered until the road straightened out. I wondered about the useful life of rear tires on Soviet-era military vehicles.

It didn't take long to figure out where to go to rent equipment though it did take some time to complete the transaction. The boots were in varying states of disrepair and there were only a very few in my size. I finally was content with a left boot that buckled up properly and a right boot on which one of the buckles didn't work at all and the other one was in the iffy category. The skis were acceptable but the bindings were of an old style, similar to the bear traps used many years earlier in the west.

I purchased a daily ticket and quickly set off for the lifts. No one had heard about the benefits of queuing but that was tolerable since so few people skied in those days, almost all of them being locals.

One of the first persons I met while sharing the chair lift was a fighter pilot in Kazakhstan's air force. He was a very good skier and often came to Chimbulak by hitchhiking from the airbase, he told me. If I thought he was living the life of "Top Gun", he quickly disabused me. He earned a pittance, as did his wife who was also in the military. He told me about their living conditions that included an unheated apartment and no hot water. Yet he seemed happy with his lot. Bearing in mind that one could almost hear the continuing collapse of the command economy going on around us, I supposed that he was happy to even have a job.

It goes without saying that, in those days, skiing at Chimbulak was cheap, well within the budget of any working person who was inclined to take up the sport. On subsequent occasions while skiing, I looked out for the pilot and did meet up with him from time to time, but it wasn't long before prices went up and all the locals I had met, come to know or simply recognized, disappeared from the ski area. There was no single event or price rise that I can recall that brought about this transformation but, little by little, they were scythed down by the collapse of the old economic system and the birth of the open and competitive market.

I risked all during the next few weeks, relying upon the decrepit and genuinely risky rental equipment at Chimbulak. On my next occasion of returning to England I hastily purchased some boots and then, upon my return to Almaty, went to look for the ski shop at the Green Market (Zelyoni Bazaar) that I had been told about. Despite having good general directions, I nearly missed it. It was on Zhibek Zholy Street. I walked from my apartment, emerging at the Green

Market on the continuation of Pushkin Street after Panfilov Park. I should have been close but my heart begin to sink as I walked up and down the street, looking in windows, and checking out the shops. Finally, almost ready to give up, I glanced up and discovered that the shop was one flight up. They had a fair selection of skis, and I ended up with a pair that was too long for me, practically satisfying the old method of holding up an arm to see where the wrist bent. They had modern bindings but no way to affix them to the skis. I was assured that this could be done at Chimbulak.

That Sunday I went skiing with my new skis, detached bindings and boots. I searched the basement of the hotel at Chimbulak and found a workshop which, upon first glance, was not encouraging. The man in charge had some simple clamps and a table mounted electric drill. I was worried that he was going to randomly drill all the way through the skies and use nuts and bolts to attach the bindings. I shouldn't have worried. His admirable skill made up for his lack of resources and he installed the bindings so perfectly (not to mention cheaply) that I couldn't tell one ski from the other.

You didn't have to be a scientist to notice that the air quality in Almaty is often quite bad during the winter but from Chimbulak it is particularly obvious. Time after time, while looking down upon the city, one could see that the whole area was enveloped in a gas cloud that often was impenetrable. On occasion, one can see only the top of the TV tower rising above the chemical shroud.

Chimbulak offers a great opportunity to get outdoors, breathe some fresh air and get some exercise. However, the pistes are not very long or, for the most part, not very challenging. Those who frequent the ski area jest about whether to take runs A, B, and C in that order or, perhaps, for variety, C, A, and B, or C, B, and A.

There are three stages of lifts to the top of the mountain. The last leg of the journey, stage three, was the most daunting. In the 1990's, it consisted of a single seat chairlift of a primitive type I had never seen elsewhere unless it was at a county fair roundabout for two year olds. Years later I was told that this lift constituted war booty, seized from Germany after the end of World War II. No chatting up of a neighbour on this lift. Some seats had a small chain to hook in front of the rider for safety while others had a small metal bar that could be placed in front of the rider. Some had neither. Many that did didn't function. And some worked so badly that they imperilled the rider if they didn't unhooked well in advance of arriving at the top. Few people took that lift but I put that down to the fact that the top part of the mountain was not suitable for novices or even moderate skiers. As long as it had ample snow, it offered the best skiing of the area and minimal crowding in the lift queue and on the slopes.

Single seat chairlift in action at Chimbulak – war booty from Germany.

The ski area had been groomed but some hazards remained in the 1990s. On one occasion when I was skiing with the head of the Central Asian American Enterprise Fund, he abruptly came out of his left ski after it encountered the concrete base that previously held a support tower for the main cable of the lift. My companion wasn't hurt and didn't even fall over, but he also had been separated from his ski. Both of us had to dismount from our skis and sweep them back and forth like brooms in order to locate the buried ski.

The volume of skiers picked up quickly as more and more expatriates arrived in Almaty. Soon there were serious queuing problems at the main lift and management was slow to exert control. Those of us from the United Kingdom tried to join the end of the queue and patiently wait our turn only to discover that the line ahead of us continuously grew. Locals seemed to have no inhibitions about inviting friends or acquaintances to join them in the queue, often quite brazenly, while many Europeans seemed at home doing the same. My patience was being tried but I found it hard to break the habit of queuing.

Then came my lucky break. A young woman charged with keeping some semblance of order in the queue was suffering from the sunshine. Her freckles and red hair broadcast that she shouldn't have such exposure to the sun. I alone responded to her plea to the crowd for some sun blocking cream. Thereafter, whenever she spotted me she beckoned me to move to the head of the queue. I tried to do so inconspicuously but, yielding to local ways, I did learn to jump the queue.

Led by some Australian skiers, an effort was made through private finance to undertake some major improvements at Chimbulak in the 1990's. I remember seeing a financial prospectus and I believe this initiative did bring about improvements in the main lift. However, squabbles over ownership ensued and the initiative sputtered out.

Happily, in the fall of 1999, I met a driver with a 4-wheel drive Mitsubishi van that could seat seven or eight passengers and who was quite willing to take groups of people to and from Chimbulak for a reasonable daily price. Thus started a happy relationship with Giorgi that has continued to this day. I began inviting friends and colleagues from the office to join in my weekend adventures, not just for winter skiing but also for excursions outside of Almaty in the summer. As for skiing, it turned out that Giorgi was a former member of Kazakhstan's ski team and eagerly sought the chance to be paid to drive to Chimbulak where, after chatting up the lift operators, he skied all day for free. He was a whiz at skiing. Despite a bit of a limp and more girth than in his youth, he sailed non-stop down the mountain seemingly without moving a muscle. Soon he was teaching skiing to my associates and selling some of his 13 sets of used skis at knockdown prices. What a delightful life for all of us – skiing every weekend and only 30 minutes away from my apartment.

Lunch at Chimbulak was available both in the hotel at the foot of the ski slopes and in the smaller and cosier cabin a few hundred metres up on the left where a second chair lift then operated. The food was much the same as could be found in Almaty but, after a workout on the mountain and the fresh air, it seemed tastier and fresher. Certainly the lamb shashlik was very freshly cooked with a charred taste, the herring salad and the Korean salad were excellent. The soup went down a treat. I preferred to eat at the cabin during the winter, often crammed together on the benches with people with whom conversation came easily as compared to the more spacious indoor restaurant at the hotel. Later, after the outdoor platform was constructed adjacent to the hotel, I was torn between the two destinations unless the weather settled the issue: sunshine on a fair day favoured the platform; wintry conditions led me to the cabin.

Chimbulak attracted local dignitaries and ever more foreigners. An early celebrity visitor in the mid-1990s was the then Italian Ambassador to Kazakhstan, a young looking handsome man in a stylish outfit and surrounded all the time, it seemed, by several adoring young ladies. U.S. Ambassador Elizabeth Jones (1995-97) was known to disappear from the Embassy on Wednesday afternoons in order to enjoy crowd-free skiing at Chimbulak, usually in the company of friends and contacts in the diplomatic community. A few years later I noticed Viktor Khrapunov, the then Akim of Almaty (1997-2004), in a bright red outfit, displaying the skills of a very experienced skier.

I never did see President Nazarbayev on the ski slopes though I did see him mingle in the crowd at the foot of the main chairlift on one occasion. I had mixed feelings about him being at Chimbulak. On not just a few occasions all cars going up to Medeo were pulled over and kept waiting for what seemed an endless time until the presidential caravan passed at high speed on the totally cleared road. Like the cleared road, I heard that the base chairlift was emptied of people all the way to the top so that the President, accompanied only by his guards, could go up the mountain in safety. But I also heard that he and his wife skied with the general public in the 1997-99 period, standing patiently in line for the lift.

A friend recounted an event to me that happened while skiing with a visitor from Moscow. He had skied ahead and waited at the bottom for quite a long time for the visitor to catch up. When the visitor arrived, he reported that he had collided with someone, and was immediately pounced upon by some heavies. Fortunately for him, the other party to the incident quickly and graciously announced that he had been at fault for turning in front of the visitor who was promptly released. It was only later that the visitor learned from my friend that the other party to the collision was the President of Kazakhstan.

44

A DAY AT CHIMUBLAK

Yesterday (Sunday, 16 December 2001) was one of those usual days here in the winter in Almaty. I got up and checked the outside world from the balcony and almost could not see across Dostyk Avenue (formerly Lenin Avenue) due to the fog/smog/cloud. I wondered why I had chosen this day to organize a ski trip up in the mountains. I got ready and soon received a phone call from the head of our office here in Almaty. She is an excellent skier and continues to use some bear trap bindings that she inherited from her brother and the likes of which I haven't seen for 30 years or more. She wasn't feeling too well and cancelled out of this trip. Too much wine last night with her likely meeting with the woman who heads the local office of a major international accounting firm?

Phoning one of our junior local lawyers on his mobile phone at about 9:15 was no more successful. He should have been picked up at 9:00 by Giorgi, the driver I have used for the past three years for summer outings and ski trips. I found him while catching a gypsy taxi on the streets one day to go to lunch and noticed that his Mitsubishi van had 4-wheel drive. Did he go to the Chimbulak ski area, I asked. The road is challenging even in the summer, with steep climbs and hairpin turns. He replied that it was no problem for him. I later learned that he had been on Kazakhstan's national ski team, and loved to be paid to go up there where he could ski for free while waiting for his passengers to go back to Almaty.

The local lawyer still didn't pick up his phone after five or more tries. I started to check the balcony on the back side of my building to see if Giorgi had arrived. Frustrated, I eventually went down, just as he arrived with two non-skiers I had invited along to help fill up the car: These ladies work in our office, and this was their first trip to Chimbulak for perhaps 15 years. Maybe more. Although the mountains loom over Almaty and Chimbulak is easily accessible by a powerful car, these two ladies and most of the people of Almaty seem to feel that they are inaccessible due to lack of transport, lack of money, or inertia.

We started up the mountain in the gloom of the morning. Almaty is nestled in the mountains which (to most people's consternation) are to the south of the city -- mountains should be to the north! -- and this tends to trap the bad city air when the prevailing wind is from the north. I really wanted to start this day over.

About the time we reached the apple orchards on the outskirts of the city the fog was thinning and with a few kilometers to go to

Medeo – site of the world's largest ice skating rink and a favored spot for city dwellers to take a weekend stroll -- the sky was brilliantly clear though bitingly cold.

We climbed past Medeo on the road to the ski area. Last weekend the road had been a sheet of ice, with many 4-wheel drive cars unable to make it to the ski area. Now, however, with the ski season officially begun, the road was well sanded and we powered on. On arriving, I went to the storage room and checked in my ski boot bag with my street shoes and various other unneeded items and discovered that the price had gone up from 20 Tenge to 50 Tenge ($0.33) which seemed to be rather in excess of inflation. The same price hike affected the cost of parking one's skis while taking a lunch break. However, the cost of taking a pit stop in the tended and clean WC remains 20 Tenge so the polite expression of "I'm going to spend 20 Tenge" remains apt but probably not for much longer.

It isn't much fun skiing by yourself but the ladies from our office joined me on the first trip up the lift and strolled around the first lift station while I skied further up and joined them a bit later. The day was warming up all the time and by noon many people were gathering at the outside restaurant which was warm to the feel but you could still see your breath.

The three of us met for early lunch at 12:30. The queue starts to get very long as the not-so-dedicated skiers start to show up. We joke in the office about how many of them go to Chimbulak only to take one or two runs so that they can go back to town and brag about having been skiing on the weekend.

I had the usual lunch which was shared with the office ladies - "Xe" salad (the pronunciation seems to be somewhere between "he" and "hear", being translated into English as Korean fish and likely to be herring in the West; "Korean" on a menu generally means spicy), cabbage salad, and salyanka, the spicy Russian soup, with about three kinds of bread, essential for any meal in Kazakhstan.

I met various people I know. Karlygash who previously worked for USAID where the Americans all called her Carla as if they were missionaries in the Hawaiian islands or as if they could not get their mouths to pronounce a 3-syllable name. Akram and a couple of his friends. And a few people of nodding acquaintance only. Later I spotted one of Vivendi's French expatriates.

I thought of many of the other people I have known as skiers who are no longer here. There was the Kazakhstani air force jet pilot of some years ago who probably was priced out of the market. Also gone was one of my first translators and his wife, and yet another of my former lawyers and her husband who now live in England. Another local friend is studying in the United States and her sister is necessarily in Astana for the celebration of 10 year's of independence. A former senior lawyer has gone off to the bright lights of Moscow as has one of our former expatriate lawyers. The head of an investment fund still spends time in Almaty but is shifting the base of his operation to Moscow. This is a high velocity place -- foreigners come for three years or less and seem happy to move on while at the same time many locals want their chance at the modern world without having to wait for the good times to arrive here in Almaty.

While skiing I met three "Alpinists" -- mountain climbers -- from Moscow. They had been going up and over some of the mountains (in dreadfully cold weather) and decided to enjoy a day of skiing. The guy I shared the lift with checked his "watch" and I asked what time it was only to discover that it was a device showing how high we were above sea level. It was 2,800 some meters. They had been climbing at 4,000 meters or more.

There were no government officials at the ski area which was unusual for a Sunday. However, Kazakhstan is having a 4-day weekend to celebrate the country's 10th Anniversary of Independence on Monday, 17 December (being the last country of the former USSR to declare its independence), and anyone who is anyone has been invited to Astana to attend the main celebrations. Good thing too because it sometimes happens on a Sunday that private traffic is shunted off the road while waiting for government officials to zoom up the mountain.

Looking down toward Almaty, I once spotted the top of the TV tower but, like the rest of the city, it too disappeared in the gloom for most of the day. Further off down the valley one could see a white puffy ball of cloud on top of the gray mist, and I figured this must be the smokestack of Almaty Power Consolidated, our local power utility.

My small group planned to get together at about 3:00 in order to head back to town. By then I would have skied enough and I figured that the ladies would have gotten tired of sitting around and drinking tea. In fact, they were not bored with the mountains. They had gone bowling in the morning after their stroll at the first lift station and had checked out some of the new houses that belong to the elite in this country.

While waiting for them to assemble at 3:00, I sat at the outside restaurant. Eventually a policeman came toward me -- yikes, I don't need this -- but he merely asked if he could sit at my table to have his late lunch. He was what I call a very Kazakh guy -- darkened skin from being out in the elements so much, not so tall (though many of them are) and built like the proverbial brick house. He is the kind of guy one sees on the streets in Almaty menacingly pulling over cars for a shakedown or directing traffic when the major government officials are in town and speeding around on what the locals refer to as "government streets" where ordinary rights do not prevail. He had a badge on his fur hat, formerly a red star but not any more. On his chest was the larger "MAN" badge announcing that he was in the police.

His hands were very cold (as you would expect on a bitter day without gloves). I felt them as we shook hands -- something that we do a lot of in this country. He ordered a large tea and pilaf, a mainly rice dish with a few meat bits thrown in. He commented on how my beer was cold. You might think this is too obvious for comment but here in Kazakhstan locals dread anything cold, particularly in the winter, and think that the flu or death will shortly ensue. We chatted. I told him that I was from South Dakota where we also have cold weather. I mentioned that I am a lawyer and he confessed the he too is a lawyer -- one could not help but sense an enormous gulf between us though perhaps he was oblivious to it.

Eventually the ladies showed up. One was carrying ski poles. They were Giorgi's -- yet again he had found a likely candidate to buy skis from him and to take skiing lessons from him. She had switched her street boots for his ski boots, and had taken those first, infectious lessons on how to ski. That guy must love me for all the "victims" I have introduced to him. I introduced them to my new friend Marat. We chatted more and I eventually picked up the bill for our table, my beer and his cheap meal. He was very grateful but immediately asked the ladies which was our car. The three of us pointed down to the car park to the Mitsubishi. I was a bit slow on the uptake and the ladies were even slower. Marat thought I was bribing him with the free meal to protect me from being shaken down by him for driving after drinking! I am unsure if he ever figured out that we had a driver and that I was not bribing him but I kind of hoped that he somehow caught on that, contrary to one of the national past times, I was not bribing him.

Anyway, he announced that we were just starting the 3-day holiday marking the end of Ramadan, and I was invited to join him and his family for beshparmak. And beer, I said, and he was very agreeable. Did I like beshparmak? You bet. I have eaten it many times, including about seven weddings, three funerals, and one Doctor of Law graduation dinner celebration. I thanked him very much for his invitation and perhaps to his relief as well as mine I didn't ask for his address and just what time I should show up for the dinner. Hospitality is very important in this country but sometimes it is meant and sometimes it isn't. I figured he was required to return my simple hospitality and I was required to accept his offer of counter-hospitality but not really required to take him up on it. We waved goodbye and I thought that he seemed to be a nice guy living in a tough world.

We drove down the mountain and re-entered the gloom of Almaty at just about the same density as we left it some hours earlier. Giorgi told us that it had been brilliant also at Talgar, the small town where he lives near Mount Talgar.

As I said, it was a kind of "usual day" in Almaty, nothing particularly noteworthy, a day much like I would expect to repeat often during the course of the winter.

The author at the top of Chimbulak ski area.

45

A DAYTRIP TO KAPCHAGAI

Last Sunday I once again spent the day at Kapchagai. This is the large artificial lake to the northwest of Almaty that was created three decades or more ago when Soviet planners sought to harness the water to make electricity and to help avert future mudslides and other water disasters for the Almaty region.

We set out early in the day in order to get our full money's worth. To me at least an 8:00 a.m. departure on a Sunday is early even though I am a natural early riser. However, the weather was not entirely cooperative in this unusual summer – the gathering clouds at 4:00 p.m. sent us scurrying home where we eventually encountered the torrents of water cascading down the streets and sidewalks in the aftermath of one of Almaty's major rain storms of this very wet and windy July.

At the outskirts of Almaty we came across the dense settlement of kiosks that specialize in beach wear, beach implements, inflatable lifesavers, beach balls and so on. Like the diamond merchants in London and specialist businesses everywhere, I guess the individual traders decided that their prospects of making a sale were increased, not reduced, by being in such close proximity to their competitors. Seeing all of these bright articles for the beach gave comfort that we were indeed on our way to Kapchagai.

We drove the usual route, proceeding somewhat slowly along the pockmarked highway. The road condition presents a typical example of the infrastructure plight of this country. Here is a major road to one of the most important holiday destinations of Kazakhstan. In theory, the road was well laid out. It is at least four lanes wide, part of it divided. But drivers on both sides need to use both lanes in their direction in order to steer around the bumps, holes and rough spots. Sometimes cars simply drive over and along the white divider line, as if it literally shows them where to go, presumably on the basis that this is the least used and safest section of the road. Another sign of the infrastructure plight of this country is the fact that some of the worst parts of the road consist of long patches that had in fact been repaired; the repairs were of such inferior quality that they seemed to make the road worse than where it had not previously been repaired.

We passed the city of Kapchagai on the right, much of which looks like an industrial wasteland with rusting hulks of metal and derelict or semi-completed buildings. We arrived at the large bridge where the young girls sporting badges on their white t-shirts enforce the ecology law. Our driver has a multi-year ecology license and we quickly passed on our way. We carried on for quite a long time, observing several abandoned or nearly abandoned compounds of holiday cabins and huts, until our driver turned off to the right and to the beach after passing yet another control barrier. It remains unclear to me if this was a definite destination of our driver based on past experience or if he simply decided that we had arrived at one of the many suitable turning off points and took it.

Our initial reaction was that the beach at which we had arrived had not been well selected. In particular, it was strewn with litter. Clearly it was a well-used but also well-worn beach. Clearly also the money paid for the preservation of the ecology of this region was not being converted into any kind of beach patrol or beach clean-up brigade. We persuaded the driver to press on further down the beach and it seemed to become cleaner and cleaner the further we progressed away from the main road. Finally, we alit at an acceptable spot. Even here, however, the nuisance of previous visitors was visited upon us. We organized a clean-up of our part of the beach. The world may be going to hell but we were going to have a clean beach for the day. Several plastic bottles were collected. Various bits of broken glass were found, some having been smoothed down to a harmless state by their long residence in the water but many others were quite lethal. A couple of dead fish were included in the detritus of our sweep of the beach.

I was capable of being depressed by the large amount of junk we found on our relatively clean part of the beach. Local residents seem to have no discipline at all in regard to litter. Perhaps they are too soon into the age of affluence and the age of plastic to know that it is unacceptable to simply toss the stuff on the beach to the detriment of everyone who may follow them in life. I was totally amazed to find a neat pile of freshly smashed glass bottles! Who on earth would be so crass as to neatly pile up glass bottles and then pound them to pieces? We found numerous pieces of wire and metal rods of the type used in reinforcing concrete, all of which we collected up and disposed of far from the beach. Next time I will bring a large black plastic bag.

We had a very enjoyable day. We swam in the clear and quite cool water. We played badminton. We tossed the frisbee both in and out of the water. We swam again and again. We watched the minnows. We strolled along the beach. We ate our packed lunch. We drank.

Speaking of drink, I must note that this outing was made all the more successful by my purchase of a Rubbermaid cooler from Ramstore earlier in the week. Clearly, Western consumerism has washed ashore here in Almaty! I first spotted the coolers at Ramstore on Monday, May 17, and I made a mental note to buy one though it was inconvenient to do so at that time. A few days later, on Saturday, May 22, I returned to Ramstore to make my purchase only to discover that every one of their coolers of all sizes had already been sold. Quite obviously the 4-wheel drive fraternity in Almaty had quickly discovered the marvels of this particular bit of plastic and the entire supply was bought up. Fortunately, Ramstore seems responsive to consumer requirements and, before going to Kapchagai, I discovered that they now stock a very generous supply of coolers, no longer limited to a shelf but piled high in the middle of the floor.

We were entirely self-reliant on this trip. We might have been in the middle of the Sahara Desert. We brought our own food, drink and entertainment. We expected nothing to be provided for us, not even a simple table on which to eat nor a toilet to use in case the duration of our stay exceeded the capacity of one of the members of our group. In this respect, I was reminded of the primitive but enjoyable circumstances of my youth in LaBolt, South Dakota, more decades ago than I care to think about. There, in a long-ago time, we used to have summer picnic lunches down near the dam that had been built during the Depression as a WPA project. No one thought that this was primitive. No one thought that the situation called out for commercial exploitation. No one complained that we had no fast-food outlets. Of course, it might have been better with commercial exploitation, with some fast-food outlets, and other conveniences of modern life, but we were a durable people with inner resources on which to draw. So it is with modern users of Kapchagai Lake.

Near our stretch of beach as far as the eye could see I spotted several derelict buildings, huts and holiday residences, many of which looked like they had been vandalized. Probably the transition from command economy to private enterprise has not been particularly smooth at Kapchagai. Indeed, I saw little evidence of any fresh investment thought I did see some traces of efforts by new owners/occupiers to take current advantage of the Soviet-era structures.

Everywhere we looked there was evidence of the undeveloped or underdeveloped condition of tourism at this lake. Only one water skier passed our way. A small flotilla of boats remained out on the lake for much of the afternoon, most being inflatable craft or even rubber inner tubes from trucks. One ski-jet sped past our beach, a lonely figure from the future helping some entrepreneur to quickly recover his $7,000 investment in these noisy but exciting implements. I did not see a single pontoon barge or raft which continues to be

211

a popular way to recycle 55 gallon steel barrels on lakes throughout America.

I do not remember seeing any other foreigners at Kapchagai. Early in the day two cars with diplomatic license plates sped past us, heedless of the bad condition of the road, but they carried on past our turnoff point. On the way home we spotted one car with the yellow license plate indicative of a foreign investor. (Cars owned by representative offices had license plates with black letters on yellow backgrounds, diplomats had plates with red backgrounds, and locally-owned cars sported plates with white backgrounds. Owners of cars with yellow plates tended to be challenged more often than cars with local plates.)

With the storm clouds closing in on us, we packed up quickly for the return trip to Almaty. As we approached Raimbek Avenue, we came to an underpass that was very deeply flooded. Several drivers had attempted the impossible and became stranded. Others, reflecting the current casualness with the law of Almaty's drivers, simply used the sidewalks as driveways.

I slept very well that Sunday night and also on Monday night. I had had a good day. I had enjoyed some good company. I had had some good exercise. I had enjoyed some air far cleaner than that which we obtain in Almaty. Is this the height of Western consumerism? Certainly not. But is this a highly acceptable way to pass a day during the summer here in Almaty? You bet.

46

A DAYTRIP TO ILI-ALATAU NATIONAL PARK

The Greater Almaty Tourist Board was so excited about "A Daytrip to Kapchagai", published last week, that they immediately asked me to do a write-up about my next excursion. They did not even complain that I had given bad directions about the location of Lake Kapchagai. I had said that Kapchagai is to the northwest of Almaty whereas only one end of the lake is due north of Almaty and the lake itself then extends off to the east, like a long pennant or banner, not to the west.

The spokesperson for the Greater Almaty Tourist Board said that it is quite understandable that a foreigner should be confused about directions. Everyone knows that mountains are supposed to be to the north but, contrarily, here in Almaty they are to the south. Some cartographers honor the natural truth that mountains must be to the north by tipping Almaty upside down on their maps just to make everyone feel comfortable. They also avoid placing a north-pointing arrow on the map, knowing that this would disturb many people and distract from their understanding of the map.

Other mapmakers depict the city in its geographically correct orientation but this actually confuses most people so these mapmakers need to insert prominent warnings on their maps along with that north-pointing arrow. People who use these geographically correct maps usually turn them upside down in order to get the mountains back where they belong, at the top of the map. Of course it is difficult to read the street names and city names this way but at least the mountains are where they are supposed to be. Anyway, said the lady from the GATB, most foreigners do not actually do their own driving, so my giving of imprecise directions is probably irrelevant and I should not feel bad about this mistake.

This Sunday I went to Ili-Alatau National Park, this country's first national park. Having taken too much sun last weekend at Lake Kapchagai, I wanted to go somewhere closer to Almaty and to spend more time in the car.

Bearing in mind my past failings in giving directions, I will be somewhat general in saying how to get to the National Park. If you take the same road that leads to Charyn Canyon and eventually to Khan Tangri Mountain, you take a right turn when you are 43 kilometers out of Almaty. You then carry on for another 14 kilometers to a right turning that leads to the National Park. A road sign in Kazakh, Russian and English points the way.

Don't be in too much of a rush to get to the Park because there are several interesting things to see and do along the way. Shortly after taking that right turn at the 43 kilometer point, you will cross the Almaty Canal, that concrete channel that diverts water from the river at Chelek and brings it to Almaty 116 kilometers away. In the morning, the canal was empty of people. Returning in the evening, it was alive with children wading in its cool water.

As you approach the small village of Issyk, you will see mounds in the fields to the left and even more mounds to the right of the road. It is said that these are burial mounds that date back maybe 400 years, perhaps about the time the Pilgrims were arriving in America.

In the village of Issyk you will see, on the right, a monument depicting and commemorating Kazakhstan's Gold Warrior. The plaque by the side of the monument records the fact that the Gold Warrior had been found on this site and that he dates back to 400 B.C.! As I hear it, he was discovered after a dam burst caused a flood that exposed some gold to the light of day nearly two and a half millennia after it had been buried. A child found a link of a gold chain or from the gold armor and took it home to much parental excitement. One thing led to another and 30 or so years ago – somebody remembers 1968 – the Gold Warrior was discovered. If you want to know more about the Gold Warrior, check him out at the National Museum.

Monument to the Golden Man on the road from Almaty to the town on Issyk.

For Kazakhs in search of their roots and in search of a national identity, this find is important. This may have been a country of nomads, with little recorded history, but 2,400 years ago there was someone here with sufficient wealth and with enough artisans at his control to be interred with the real gold trappings of a warrior that later history would record as significant. In this regard, the Gold Warrior is similar to the endless cemetery that one sees at faraway Atyrau – Kazakhs take pride in these tangible but scarce pieces of evidence that they have been here for a very long time.

If you take the correct turning 57 kilometers out of Almaty, you will be on your way to the National Park. Before you arrive at the entrance of the Park you will come to a fish farm. If you have never seen a fish farm before, stop off and take a look. There are several long rectangular ponds where the fish live, each pond containing fish of a particular size. If you help with their feeding, you will see the water turn virtually black with their churning and dense concentration.

Trout in a feeding frenzy in one of the trout farm's ponds
just before entering Ili-Alatau National Park.

Remember this fish farm as you continue your journey up the valley. If you have brought fishing tackle with you and if you do not catch any fish in the river – as we did not – you can always return to the fish farm with the guarantee that you can catch as many as you are willing to pay for. Even the most novice of anglers can land a fish in less time than it takes to bait the hook with a piece of corn. If your children are bored with summer holidays and have tired of Fantasy World, give them a trip back to nature at the fish farm. Shortly after leaving the fish farm, one sees, on the right, an eroded cliff face that vaguely reminds one of the colorful canyon walls at Charyn Canyon.

The guards at the entrance of the Park work out of a familiar and styleless metal hut on wheels, evidence of another era, but adjacent to it is a nearly completed log cabin-style gatehouse. The route through the National Park follows the natural contours of Turgin Valley and the mountain stream that flows down it. Sometimes you are on one side of the river and sometimes you are on the other. A few kilometers further on one sees across the river the semi-completed and now derelict Pioneer camp with its pointy metal roofs.

For the most part, this is an excursion in nature in the raw. This is not an area densely populated with day trippers, unlike the lower part of the road up to Big Almaty Lake (reservoir), where many of Almaty's weekenders make their Saturday or Sunday outing without exertion. Ili-Alatau is for a somewhat more hearty and durable crowd. The drive from the entrance of the park to what seemed to me to be the heart of the Park takes about one hour. The first half hour is spent on a tarmac-surfaced road. A bit rough, yes, but quite passable even for two-wheel drive cars. After that, the nature in the raw part starts to show through. Driving constantly upwards, the car often is required to crawl in its lowest gear. Recent rock falls have rendered the road nearly impassable at several points. At one point, you pass a sheer cliff with enough fissures in it to persuade you that a rock or a boulder is likely to drop at any moment. Here, as on so many occasions, I am glad I have an intrepid driver who seems to have been everywhere in Kazakhstan at least once before.

Lunch was taken near the rushing mountain stream. Having no idea if fish could be caught here, we put out two lines and toyed with the idea of fishing. We found enough mushrooms to cook up a hot brew to serve with our otherwise cold lunch. While searching for mushrooms, during our after-lunch stroll, and on the drive we observe the large variety of wild flowers, and their jumble reminds me of a difficult 1,000-piece puzzle that I completed a long time ago which was crammed with plants of all sorts.

After all the rubbish and other debris at Lake Kapchagai, I found Ili-Alatau National Park to be quite clean but this may arise in part from its evident lower rate of use. And even then there were some of the typical signs that Soviet engineers had been here and had not cleaned up after themselves. The marks of blasters' drilling holes were prominent on a very large boulder in the river; elsewhere I spotted a large coil of metal cable in the river. It seems that no part of this country was untouched by Soviet engineers who left telltale signs wherever they went.

Although I heard some English and other foreign voices at the fish farm, it seemed like the National Park itself is relatively unknown or unused by the expatriate crowd.

We crawled up Turgin Valley and eventually arrived at the junction of two small streams. Up above we could see the white dome of an astronomical observatory standing atop a bald mountain. We exchanged opinions about how best to make use of this mountain as a ski resort. The mountain is entirely clear of trees and boulders. From afar, it seems to be immaculately manicured. I wondered if someone had tried to cultivate the mountain. Everywhere you look there are parallel rows that appear, from a distance, to be very much like the furrow marks of a plow. But no, these are sheep trails – sheep graze across the side of a mountain, not up and down, and over the decades they have left their indelible marks like the elevation lines on a map. Far up one small valley to the left, we see two yurtas, probably home to the shepherds who earlier had been seen on horseback looking after their sheep.

The author deep in Ili-Alatau National Park with an observatory on the bald mountain behind him and a clump of trees ahead of him with mushrooms.

We didn't try to go up to the observatory. Having seen three women bearing large bags of mushrooms, we turned to the right, forded the river and proceeded up the dirt trail towards the fir trees that capped this mountain. Here indeed were mushrooms – some too red, some too old but many just right for picking and eating. We spent half an hour scrambling in the thicket, working up a sweat, picking the mushrooms and also swatting country flies -- flies with no previous human contact who are too dumb to move when you try to swat them. We scared up a night owl from its daytime perch. A vole scurried out of our way.

The way in to the National Park is also the way out. That is when we returned to the fish farm to quickly land three good-sized fish for the price of Tg. 1,100 and to take several souvenir photographs to record this famous event.

By the way, modern-day driving instructions say the Park is far more accessible than it was when this article was written in 1999. It is only 36.6 kilometers from Almaty, accessible within one hour via Gornaya Street, Abay Avenue and Gornaya Street, or Ryskulov Avenue.

47
A WET WEEKEND AT ISSYK KUL

I have lived in England for many years. It does not rain there nearly as much as many foreigners think but, from long habit, English people usually have contingency plans in case it does rain. No place in the island of Great Britain is more than 80 miles from the sea and so England, Wales and Scotland tend to be cloudy and moist countries. Thus, when planning a picnic, school outing or graduation, most people have a plan in mind and the necessary raingear at hand if it rains. This nearness of the rain affects people's thinking. Some people carry umbrellas even when sunshine is virtually guaranteed. English people do not bitterly complain if they are at a county fair or outdoor birthday party and the rain comes along. They pull on their wellies (boots), open up their brollies (umbrellas), and carry on as if nothing had happened. Of course they would prefer to have a bright sunny day with a cloudless sky but they know how to cope with the other kind of weather and do not treat it as a disaster.

This past weekend I had a chance to put to the test my English weather training. Up to now my summer excursions had been blessed by very good weather. The early spring trip to Big Almaty Lake (reservoir) was terrific – the temperature was warm enough to wear shorts even though the reservoir was frozen solid and the steep slopes still had deep pockets of snow where we chilled our drinks. All around us the beautiful spring mountain flowers were in bloom. The day trip to Kapchagai involved too much sunshine. Admittedly this was followed by a real drenching but by then it was time to go home anyway. The trip to Charyn Canyon was similar. The sun blazed down for most of the day and then the skies opened up so that we had to dash the last 100 meters up the steep slope that was made treacherous by loose gravel. Even then the rain lifted long enough for us to have our meal in the open air before starting the long trip back to Almaty. The weather on the visit to Ili-Alatau National Park was exceptionally nice throughout the day.

The unfortunate hallmark of this weekend's trip to Issyk Kul in the Kyrgyz Republic was rain. It rained from about the time we crossed the border into the Kyrgyz Republic on Friday night until part of our group left in mid-day on Sunday.

I have been working in Almaty for almost seven years and, despite its fame as a resort, I have never before been able to get to Issyk Kul. I have been to Bishkek many times, but always on business and usually in the winter. So, I was looking forward very much to this trip which turned a bit sour in the damp and cold.

Some of us set off at 7:00 p.m. on Friday. This was one hour later than planned by my office comrades. They seemed to enjoy the preparations for the trip so much that the departure time slipped. We drove into the gathering dusk, eventually taking a break for our rear-of-the-car dinner. This was at a roadside eating spot where a number of vendors sell food. They were very excited to see us pull into the layby, their only visitors until a trucker from Russia arrived. They shouted to us to extol the virtues of their food but we were self-sufficient on this first leg of the trip.

The drive to and from Issyk Kul was remarkably free from interference by the police. We were on the road for about eleven hours in total but, apart from the ecology barrier to Issyk Kul, we were stopped by only one lone Kazakhstani policeman standing by the side of the highway, and he was satisfied by a perfunctory check of documents.

As dusk turned to night the rain started, slowing us down and adding to our driving time. After going south for about three hours, we turned left not far from the Kyrgyz border and carried on to a small border crossing point. The Kazakh border guards warned us that there were bandits along the road to the lake and they cautioned us to be careful. This warning was repeated by the Kirgyz border guards. It was unclear if there had been a recent incident or if they were simply passing on a rumor. Anyway, we were not disturbed by any bandits unless, that is, the ecology police who control entry to the Issyk Kul area can be so classified. We pulled up at the barrier along with several other cars.

After a brief discussion, we gained admission upon the payment of $30 in U.S. cash, $15 per car in our small cavalcade. We obtained no receipt because the official cost is higher. There was no long discussion or haggling in this transaction. The guard in question seemed to know exactly what to do and our drivers were similarly street wise. Our guard then personally escorted us past the other guards to ensure that no one checked to see if we had a special entry permit. Not having that permit could have meant difficulty in exiting from the Issyk Kul area. As it turned out, however, there was no challenge at the time of our departure.

The Kyrgyz road was in very good condition and, despite the rain, we arrived at our holiday resort at the appointed hour of 1:00 a.m. on Saturday morning. We gained admission from a surly gate guard who seemed to know nothing about our scheduled arrival. We had booked some cabins through an agent in Almaty who assured us that the relevant rooms with hot and cold water and toilets were reserved for us and that the Director of the camp would be awaiting our arrival at 1:00 a.m. As we waited at the gate for permission to enter a car departed. The gatekeeper also allowed us to enter at the same time and we saw this as a good sign. Unfortunately, it seems that the Director was leaving as we were entering, and no one at all knew about our booking and our arrival time.

The staff tried to react appropriately but quickly announced that they lacked the number of beds we required. There was an undertone of discussion in the Kyrgyz language that suggested that the lack was not of beds but of sheets. They seemed to be really trying to help us but, apart from a bit of ineffective scurrying about in the hour between 1 a.m. and 2 a.m., nothing much happened. Then they spotted foreign names on our list of guests. Suddenly, the level of activity increased. It seemed that their failure to provide suitable accommodation to a party of Western visitors was about to embarrass the entire Kyrgyz Republic in front of the rest of the world. At this point, all of us switched into English that was so convincing that the head lady of the establishment asked if we had a translator with us! They redoubled their efforts to find space/sheets for us but to no avail. In the meantime, we ate the rest of our packed lunches and checked out the disco.

Our accommodation was supposed to include hot and cold running water and our own toilets. This came as a considerable surprise to the camp personnel. Although there was an abundance of cold water, they had never had hot water in the cabins nor private toilets. In Almaty we had agreed to pay $10 per person per day. We eventually got this down to $7.50 for the shortened weekend. I suppose that someone who pays so little for room and full board should not complain too much about a few inconveniences but we had been led to believe by the agent in Almaty that all of this was possible. None of the local members of our delegation were surprised by the ineptitude or the lying by the agent in Almaty. (We later had a serious confrontation with the agent in Almaty who gave a full refund of the entirely unearned commission that had already been paid.)

We eventually found cabins at the neighboring camp. This was a Soviet-era facility that clearly was resting on its oars, deteriorating year by year through lack of new investment. The chalets seemed to have been built from kits where the end result sat on concrete supports. The walls were tacky from bad varnish that refused to set completely, and anyone who leaned on a wall or put a towel over a railing to dry might have to peel themselves or the towel away from the sticky goo. Weeds grew everywhere. Drainpipes leaked. The communal outdoor toilet was – well, a communal outdoor toilet. Blessedly, the beds were comfortable even if rather short for me.

Tacky cabin at Issyk Kul, Kyrgyzstan.

The next day, we swam in the slightly salty water during a brief lull in the rain. The water really is very clear and there was no place at which I could not see the bottom. One member of our group had brought his guitar, and we sang songs in front of one cabin during another lull in the rain. Then it was off to the yurta restaurant for a tasty dinner followed by a group sauna that we reserved for 9:00 p.m. Some of us then moved on for several hours to the disco that was lively with a weekend crowd. A couple of the local young men engaged in a kind of aggressive form of dance in which they moved through the other dancers at high speed, something I have not seen in Almaty for a few years. It might be called running but it definitely was to the rhythm of the music. The evening was topped off for some of us by a bonfire on the beach till the early morning.

On Sunday we paid the price for our exhausting Saturday night, not that this was unexpected. Indeed, it may have been wanted by those who were intent on wresting the utmost out of the weekend. Some arose early for the 9:00 a.m. breakfast; others almost missed the lunch. It had rained all night and this continued into the morning. We ate throughout the weekend from our packed food, from the restaurant and yurta, and from food bought from vendors who worked the camp. The most distinctive food was the chebachki fish. They are the size of overgrown sardines and are sold on strings of wire that have been run through their eyes. Someone said this fish grows only in Issyk Kul and in lakes in Siberia but a dictionary refers to it as "rudd" in English, which is a European fish. As we left on Sunday, we could see dozens and dozens of roadside vendors selling these chebachki fish on their rings of wire.

Just as our departure from Almaty was delayed, so it took quite a long time for five of us to take our leave of the main group. Everyone had to say goodbye to everyone, the car was checked, the route was confirmed, and so on, all as we stood in the rain and gloom of the day. Warm clothes were left behind for the others who were determined to get their full weekend holiday. Adding insult to injury, we had to pay the surly gatekeeper to open the gate for our departure. The sky cleared a bit after we drove away from our camp and the five of us in our car were jealous the next morning upon learning that our companions were rewarded with three or four hours of bright sunshine, enough to redden their skin.

On the way home we stopped off for a late lunch at a cluster of about 30 yurtas and metal trailers located up in the Kyrgyz mountains. We ate at Seagull Yurta (Ak-Chardak in Kyrgyz). If I had been driving here alone with a foreign wife and foreign children I probably would have given the place a miss. Interesting looking and something that the locals enjoy, but will I wake up dead tomorrow from eating the shashlik? However, with my local traveling companions this was nothing more than a typical shopping expedition. The vendors were all hawking their goods, flashing their identical sticks of shashlik at us as if theirs was entirely unique whereas they all probably came from a couple of sheep that were butchered that morning. Corn on the cob was available. Some washed down their food with a milk drink called Airan.

As we drove, I noticed the many new large metal underground gasoline storage tanks that were sitting at roadside sites, like beached whales, ready to be interred underground as part of new gasoline service stations. It seems that Kyrgyzstan, like Kazakhstan, is about to experience a boom in the development of gas stations. These huge tanks also litter the roadside on the way to Ili-Alatau National Park and other roads on the outskirts of Almaty.

As we entered Kazakhstan, there was a new house (restaurant?) where the upper floor consists of two concrete yurtas – space for the grandparents to feel comfortable?

My conclusion about Issyk Kul: too far away from Almaty for a comfortable weekend visit; it has a lot to offer; but you need to be far more discriminating than we were in the selection of a place to stay.

48

A TRIP TO BIG BUDDHA AND KAPCHAGAI LAKE

On a recent Sunday (11 June 2000), I started my summer program of outings. During the winter, weekly skiing at Chimbulak suppressed the cabin fever symptoms that arise from spending too much time cooped up in an apartment. But the snow is long gone, and I quickly got over the shock of re-learning how much weekend there is in two days if you don't get up before dawn on Sunday, spend the day on the mountain and come home exhausted in the dark of night. I'm not complaining about my apartment. It is very large, with at least one room that is surplus to requirements -- I'm bilingual and speak English English as well as American English -- and a wrap-around balcony that is very inviting when the sun is not directly shining on it.

So, now it is already mid-summer and the walls of the apartment are beginning to get closer. I am feeling the itch for some fresh air, some natural exercise and (dare I say it?) some sunshine and a bit of a tan.

We decided to return to Kapchagai Lake, if only to see if the ice cubes are still floating up there. Since my group was not yet prepared for a lot of sunshine, we got off to a gentle start.

It rained heavily on Saturday night -- potentially ominous -- but the sky was clear on arising and it stayed that way for much of the day with only a few puffy white clouds dotting the late afternoon sky.

Consistent with the intended soft start to the summer program, the driver picked up the first person only at 10:00 a.m. Some of us are tough individuals with lots of hiking experience but some are not, so the lunch provisions reflected our affluence and the increasing availability of take-away foods in Almaty. Outside the door of the "Russia" Shopping Center on Dostyk Avenue we bought a Tg. 600 cooked chicken that was cut to manageable pieces and placed in the heat retaining foil bag. Inside, we bought some pre-made salads and sufficient drinks to last one thirsty day.

We bantered with the driver during the ride to Kapchagai Lake, and made an impromptu decision to visit Big Buddha, maybe 30 minutes beyond Kapchagai Lake, on the Ili River. We didn't need to be in the sun for so long and, as Big Buddha was so close, we decided to kill two birds with one stone. Previous discussions about Big Buddha had wrongly led me to believe that these riverside petroglyphs were a couple of hours further away from Kapchagai Lake, way out there in the wilderness.

You may want to know how to locate Big Buddha. Many people in Almaty know a little bit about Big Buddha, and they regard that name as a geographical place as well as the thing that is there when you arrive. However, it is rare to find anyone who has actually visited Big Buddha and even rarer to find anyone who claims to know anything about Big Buddha. Anyway, you take the main road from Almaty to Kapchagai Lake, drive past the town and the lake, continue for some kilometers, and then take a left turn when you reach the sun-bleached and ancient covered wagon where khoumis (a milk product) is sold and where dusty trails proceed to the left and to the right. Hopefully that wagon will still be there when you make your trip because there are no other no road signs or any other markings to indicate that the dusty one-lane trail off to the left is the route to some of the mysteries of the ancient past. Overall, Big Buddha is about 120 kilometers from Almaty.

The road winds its way down toward the Ili River. Here there are virtually no signs of human existence. The landscape appeared to be burned up and there were none of those Kazakh cowboys who populate the open spaces on the way to Bishkek. Just when I was about to conclude that we could not be more remote from mankind than if we were on the moon, I noticed a line of telephone poles silently marching their way from the horizon on the right to the horizon on the left. Curiously, they bore no electric wires. We wondered -- are these examples of the thieving of copper wires in remote places or have these poles simply been abandoned to stand there until, many years from now, they topple over from age?

We drove on. To the left there was evidence of one or two other trails for vehicles, but less used than ours. This side of the Ili River has high bluffs or high rock formations, and the road passes through an opening in them. Some kilometers ahead we could see a small stretch of the Ili River through the opening in the bluffs. We arrived at the river and took a left turn. Soon our driver mentioned that the petroglyphs were immediately on our left. I could see flat-faced rocks and several people climbing up in the rocks, but nothing I immediately saw seemed particularly noteworthy.

We drove past the petroglyphs and parked the car above the road in a potentially breezy spot. On emerging from the car we were immediately assailed by gnats. Hundreds and hundreds of them.

They did no harm, of course, but these pesky little black insects got into eyes, ears and noses. Soon all of us were swishing handkerchiefs, hats, hands and bits of foliage to fend them off. They completely put us off the idea of eating at this spot. As one wag noted later, the gnats may have been there to protect Big Buddha. In truth, the site was not litter strewn despite the fact that there was no indication that this area has any government supervision or protection. Later, someone mentioned to me that the gnats are present on a highly seasonal basis; we had chosen the wrong time to pay a visit. We never did learn when was the right time.

Two local buses from Almaty arrived. Last summer, a member of our office staff told me that he had taken a bus to Big Buddha. It seems, therefore, that it is possible for local residents and enterprising foreigners to make an excursion to Big Buddha without making a big expedition out of it.

Having emerged from the car and having developed a certain resignation to the presence of the gnats, we discovered two prominent sets of rock carvings separated by only a few meters of loose rocks that could be scampered over with relatively ease. Of course there were no informative signs, no Park Rangers giving lectures or warning people against touching these ancient markings, and no printed handouts to give even a clue as to what these rocks were all about.

We first examined the right-most carvings. There were some primitive drawings of animals - recent prank copies of cave paintings from France? Some symbols reminded us of Zodiac symbols and there were some deeply etched lines of a design. All of this was preparation for going over to the left where the main Buddha carvings were to be found. Here, within the reach of your arm, was a large flat surface on which had been deeply scratched the ornate outline of Buddha in the classic seated posture with similar but smaller figures in the seated position on his left and on his right.

The author by Big Buddha on the Ili River.

I was more intrigued than awed. I immediately wanted to know more. Who had come here, when and why? Did the Buddhists come up the Ili River by boat determined to leave their mark? Did indigenous people live in this area at that time although it is now entirely abandoned? Did the Buddhists add their rock carvings to far more ancient carvings that were already there? And how much has the physical character of this spot changed since the rocks were scratched with Buddha's image? Clearly there is a lot of loose rubble around, the result of the continual erosion of the rock outcroppings that hang high above Big Buddha. Looking up I spotted a huge overhanging piece of cliff. An enormous chunk of that cliff had fallen away in recent times, probably tumbling down near to where we were standing. Maybe there were more petroglyphs that could be located if only these monstrous pieces of the cliff could be up-righted.

Some say that the central, main figure of Buddha belongs to the 2nd Century B.C. while the lesser figures on either side were carved there in the 16th or 17th centuries A.D. Yet a sceptic ventured that these carvings had simply been put there in modern times as part of a Russian movie. Locals seem to refer to them as tamgalytas, "stones with sacred signs".

By the way, you can see a few specimens of petroglyphs at the National Museum in Almaty on the lower level. Unfortunately, they are quite inadequately marked and you cannot determine from where they came. The floor staff at the National Museum seem to have no information about Big Buddha.

Quickly abandoning the idea of taking our lunch at Big Buddha, we retreated from the gnats and found a suitable beach at Kapchagai Lake. It reminded me of my childhood summers at the dam constructed by the WPA during the Great Depression near my home at LaBolt, South Dakota. That is to say, this was nature in the raw, there to use and share without anyone's leave but also without any amenities. Three hundred meters off to the right, a group of cows meandered down to the water for a drink. Later, while strolling along the beach, we dodged the occasional cow pies.

The fact that a few clouds were breezing over the land while the lake was cloudless overhead sparked a conversation about the ecological effects of the artificial Soviet-era Kapchagai Lake. It is accepted as a given fact by local residents in Almaty that Kapchagai Lake constitutes an ecological disaster. Not on the order of the Aral Sea (Lake) catastrophe, but bad enough to cause an immediate outpouring of bile at what the Soviet planners did. Local residents are convinced that the large volume of water trapped in Kapchagai Lake has irretrievably altered the climate of Almaty, for the worse. Years ago there were no mosquitoes in Almaty. Now they abound because of the continual presence of water. The mountains to the south of Almaty trap the moisture in the air and send it pouring down on Almaty. Not far away, the land is parched, just as Almaty used to be, but nowadays in Almaty we have rain, an abundance of snow in the winter and overall a climate that has become dissimilar to that of the surrounding area.

49

A TRIP TO THE SINGING DUNES

We had the choice of departing for the Singing Dunes at 6:00 a.m. and driving for 300 kilometers, partly through an old military firing range, or leaving at 9:00 a.m. and driving only 150 kilometers. However, the destinations were not exactly the same. The long route actually takes you to the Singing Dunes after crossing above Lake Kapchagai; the lazy bones trip takes you below the lake to the opposite side of the Ili River and, if there are no friendly boaters around -- there weren't for us -- you can only observe the dunes across the expanse of the Ili River.

The Singing Dunes are located north-east of Almaty, in the Altyn-Emel National Park on the right bank of the Ili River. They have been measured at three kilometers long though our driver said they were four kilometers in length.

We opted for the lazy bones trip. Apart from being able one day to say that we had climbed the 150 meter high dunes, there were no compelling reasons to take the more grueling trip. Anyway, I am a bit familiar with sand dunes. The main distinguishing feature is that they are sandy. After that, well, they tend to be hot and mostly they just sit there. Environmentalists and geologists can get quite excited about them but, as conversation pieces, they are rather dry.

One reason I know about sand dunes is that there are some in the State of Michigan, way off in the middle of the United States and far from any seaside. I never heard that they sing, but they do move.

You don't have to run in front of them to avoid getting covered up. You don't even have to walk fast. Probably a snail is safe so long as it moves in the right direction. But they do move eastward because of the prevailing wind from the west, and if you own a house or farm downwind from those sand dunes, you probably ought to increase your insurance coverage or put the property up for sale while it still has some value.

Since we probably were not going to set foot on the Singing Dunes themselves, our day tended to concentrate on our trip which pretty much suits my philosophy of life anyway: it's the journey in life that counts, not the arriving.

Not far out of Almaty we stopped at a roadside nan kiln (tandyr). Maybe you have seen one of these on your own excursions. These are little brick and stucco kilns about one meter high with a large round opening at the top. The friendly baker at this kiln happily demonstrated his skills for us. His wife brought out some bread dough on plate-size platters, ready to be inserted into the kiln. He donned a long 'oven glove' of a type I have never seen before. It was heavily padded and reached up to his armpit. The hand was shaped something like a giant baseball mitten, with a great big padded round thing the size of a large pizza. He plopped one of the flat doughs on to the pad, wiped the exposed side with some water, and then reached down into the kiln to stick the bread on the side of the wall. After inserting a few of these, he removed the great big mitten and used long metal tongs to detach and retrieve some cooked tandyrnans. His wife glazed the fresh loaves. The sights were good, the smell delicious, and we soon found ourselves buying three tandyrnans to see us through the day. In fact, we devoured the first tandyrnan as soon as we returned to our car and resumed our way to the Singing Dunes.

The tandyrnan man and family at roadside kiln bakery.

Imposing Mount Talgar was shrouded in clouds as we drove on our way to the east. Much later, as we returned home with the sun setting in the west, Mount Talgar was still obscured from our view.

We arrived at the village of Malovodnoye which local residents know as a horse-trading town. Off to the right we could see a large number of horses and ponies on display in a yard that was dedicated to this purpose. We wondered if the horses were for riding or eating. We didn't stop to inspect the horses but we did stop at a waterspout on the left of the road where we filled our bottles with tasty fresh water.

Later we passed through a village where they concentrate on raising chickens and, predictably, many roadside vendors were proudly displaying their live chickens in wire cages. We didn't check the prices but imagined that they were much cheaper than buying chicken pieces from the local supermarket in Almaty.

The roadside vendors in the next village concentrated on watermelons, a huge number of them. I was going to count them but I gave up after two million.

As we neared Chilik, where Philip Morris operates tobacco fields for its large factory at Energetichesky village, we could see tobacco fields as well as occasional fields of ripening sunflowers. The road-straddling town of Ucheasy is dominated by tobacco growing. Every house sports its own neat draping lines of tobacco leaves drying in the open. Unlike the poultry town, here there were no roadside samples of the local produce for sale. At the fork in the road in Chilik we turned to the right.

Eventually we arrived at a turning off point. A tiny blue sign on a tall pole marks the way to the river. The words were so small that you would have to stop the car completely in order to read them. We now left the main road for the last leg of our trip on 20 or 30 kilometers of unimproved, bone jarring washboard roads.

Warning signs told us that it was necessary to pay a fee to the groundskeeper who had placed nails in the neighboring roads for those who tried to avoid payment. This budding capitalist landowner really preferred petrol for his vehicles but accepted a small cash donation from us to gain access to his hinterland.

We followed the primitive road as best we could in what we hoped was a straight line to the river bank. This was difficult, however, because there were many forks in the road and many cross roads, all of which had been recently used even though we saw no traffic out there. The thought crossed my mind that learners may come out here to practice driving their cars. It also occurred to me that dune buggies might be out here chewing up the countryside as they do in America's far West but, as we know full well, the affluent few have not yet gone so far as to take their wild driving off the streets of Almaty.

We reached the river. Across it we could see the full length of the closest Singing Dune and the tops of others behind it. They stand there like four long rectangular haystacks, a few kilometers long, with little clearance between them, and with the nearest one coming close to the edge of the river. During the course of the day not one person was spotted on that side of the river.

Our group, driver and car with Singing Dunes across the Ili River.

The dunes are located in a gap between the hills that are found on that side of the river. Probably the wind channels through that little valley and builds up the dunes. It occurred to me, however, that these dunes might be manmade. Soviet planners constructed Lake Kapchagai and they obviously were aware that a leisure lake required sandy beaches. So, they parked a large amount of beach sand nearby, ready to be distributed when the lake filled up. In the meantime, however, the Soviet Union fell apart, stranding this enormous warehouse of sand a few kilometers upstream from the intended beaches which, to this day, are mainly strewn with sharp rocks.

The Ili River was quite dirty. It may be fed by mountain streams of clear water but by now it was carrying a lot of gray grit, some of which had washed up on our shore as a thin layer of mud. The whole river moves by quickly but there was a very rapid channel of water about 20 meters offshore which carries lots of tree trunks, branches and other flotsam possibly coming down from China. I watched for 20 minutes or so while we ate our lunch, and it seemed that a large tree or branch went by every few seconds, spaced out by about 100 meter intervals. Presumably all of this junk ends Up in Lake Kapchagai.

Catfish thrive in murky waters, and these can be caught near the Singing Dunes. One of our riverside neighbors pulled in a four kilo catfish while we watched.

The author with a big fish from the Ili River near the Singing Dunes.

We found a small sand dune to explore on our side of the river. It didn't sing but it had a nice hum as the constant wind swept through the shrubs, bushes, and grasses that clung to the sand. The sand was exceedingly fine, the type that is used in hour glasses. If you walked near the ridge of sand, you could send a bunch of it cascading down the side of the dune much like a fluid. The dune supports some vegetation that survives only by having very long roots. Some of these had become exposed to light and it took some time before we realized what they were. Here were tufts of grass and little bushes with roots extending for five or six meters or more across the dune. You quickly realize why such plants are used to stop desertification in parts of Africa.

We started the long trip back to Almaty by taking a slight diversion to an abandoned collective dairy farm where the tall water standpipe is rusting in the hot sun. A long pipe ran from the standpipe over to an artesian well but was no longer connected to the well. Instead, the pipe coming out of the ground now gushes out its hot and slightly salty water into a shallow pond. We didn't realize at first that the water was hot and we looked forward to getting into our swimsuits and taking a refreshing splash.

The pond was already populated by an extended family of local residents who seemed to be associated with the nearby pickup truck. Most of them were seated on a tractor tire on the bottom of the pond but they took turns standing under the water as it came out of the pipe. The group included a young lady who for lack of a swimsuit was sitting there in her underwear. Upon our arrival modesty required her to turn slightly away from us but not for long and soon she too was taking her turn under the spouting water.

We wondered about these people. Was this their weekly bath because they lacked hot water where they live? Or did they come here for the beneficial effects of the spa-like water? Was this a popular rural banya? A couple of other cars filled with people arrived as we were leaving. Was there some social protocol among the users that allowed one family exclusive use so long as they didn't hog the water for too long? Did they book their places at the pond?

We stood by the pond gawking like tourists, wondering about all of these things. Then one of the women in our party slipped on her swimsuit and broke the social ice by wading out into the water. One by one the rest of us joined the party. There was much laughing and joking in our group, to the amusement of the local residents, as we discovered how very hot that water was. If you imagine the hottest shower you have ever taken and then think of it as a few degrees hotter, that is how hot this water was. According to one of the local residents, the water was 48 to 50 degrees C. After standing in the pond for 15 minutes, your lower legs were raw red showing exactly where the waterline was.

Having left the pond and having donned her rural costume, the young lady tied a colorful ribbon to the top of the water pipe, joining several other faded strips of cloth. All over this part of Kazakhstan one can see 'wishing trees' near natural springs where people have tied strips of cloth, and this artesian well qualified for the same treatment.

Now it was our turn to be gawked at. As the extended family dried themselves and put on their clothes, they stared at us in much the same way as we had stared at them, but it was all in good nature with increasing banter between us. They smiled easily and probably thought we were a bunch of city slickers just as we may have thought of them as a bunch of country bumpkins. It didn't take long before we all felt the bonding of the pond experience, and we happily waved goodbye to them when they left and again when we caught up with them further up the road where they were filling bottles from a source of cold water.

Earlier, our driver started to wash his car with water from the pond but the head of the extended family yelled at him to stop in a commanding voice. I immediately thought that our driver had broken one of the many local taboos that constantly surprise us foreigners. Was this sacred water to be used only for the cleansing of human bodies and was something awful about to happen to our driver? No, this was a matter of technology. The local man knew that the salt content of the water was damaging to metal.

The abandoned collective farm has become a nature reserve through lack of human exploitation. As we drove toward the main road we spotted some antelopes (jeyrun) off to the left. They were difficult to see because they were the same color as the tall drying grass, but when they moved they were a delight to behold. Off to the right a large bird was spooked by our car and it soared away, landing in the top of one of the few trees that dotted this floodplain. I guess it was an ibis (tsaplya). Later we spotted two of them enjoying some formation flying. There was more wildlife in this area than I recalled seeing on many other trips throughout Kazakhstan.

Shortly after reaching the main road we again came across the two large burial mounds off the left side of the road. They looked so neat and clear of vegetation, and we wondered how many people must have been involved in their construction, a thought inspired in part by the fact that this area now seems bereft of people.

The trip back to Almaty was an extended shopping excursion. I think it is a worldwide phenomenon that agricultural producers like to cut out the middlemen while earning some undeclared cash income. So, we bought a bucket full of ripe tomatoes for KTZ 100, a large plastic bag of red apples (which I dislike for their mushy consistency), and another large plastic bag of pale green apples (a real delight and only KTZ 90). We skipped the ham in the Russian town where this is a specialty and also the fish at the bus stop near Almaty (too many dried fish and not enough fresh fish at this late hour of the day). The chickens in the poultry town had gone home for the night but the watermelon vendors looked like they were going to sit with their heavy produce through the long night ahead of them.

50

A TRIP TO ISSYK LAKE

Last week's trip to the Singing Dunes was a heavy outing, making for a long day. All that fresh air, sunshine and exercise required a few days to get back on to an even keel. So our plans for the following Sunday were trimmed down to less taxing proportions. We decided to go once more to the east, past Talgar, up to the village of Issyk and then, this time, over to Lake Issyk, about 80 kilometers from Almaty.

On the way we again stopped at the roadside tandyrnan baker near Panfilov farm. I had brought along my recent photos and gave him the one showing him at work. It was not such a good photo, revealing only the left side of his face, but he and his family seemed tickled pink by it. This was a reminder, perhaps, of how shallow are the inroads of Western/international life and lifestyle in this country. In Almaty, many local residents have their own cameras and no longer anxiously ask to have a copy of every snap in which they appear. In this regard and many others, life in the countryside may take some years to catch up with developments in the 'Southern Capital'. Anyway, I was soon presented with a hot tandyrnan straight from the oven as my special thank you for the photo.

Still wanting to capture this bread baking business on film, I asked if I could do some re-takes. No problem with that, and soon the baker's entire family had lined themselves up for a photo, no doubt hoping that I will pass this way again very soon.

We ignored the many roadside watermelon sellers on the surmise that their produce from neighboring countries contains too many nitrates. Further down the road we bought a beauty that was certified by the vendor to be from the adjacent field.

Eventually, we turned right and immediately crossed over Almaty's Great Canal. We continued past the dozens of ancient burial mounds on both sides of the road. We alit again at the monument to the Golden Man, a familiar sight to some of us but new to others in our group. In the middle of Issyk, we took a turn up the valley to the right. Had we continued straight, we would have returned to the fish farm, Ili Alatau national park, and the water falls.

The road follows the river, most of the time gaining altitude but never crossing the river as the valley deepens. We encountered a gigantic painting of Lenin's bust on the side of an enormous rock outcrop. It looked surprisingly fresh. As we neared the lake, I noticed that several concrete structures were in a state of semi-demolition. One house was gone entirely except for its tiled floor. Evidence of a Soviet-era resort?

We eventually arrived at a parking lot that looks down on the manmade lake below. There were too many people for our comfort within easy walking distance of the parking lot so we followed the restricted-access road to the right. This required the use of some local know-how. The guard was supposed to open the gate only to holders of special permits. However, he informed us that we could enter for 500 Tenge as soon as his boss left. (As the saying goes, "Everything is possible in Kazakhstan.") We crossed some small streams, and gained access to a flat plain of gravel that contains a few trees. Presumably this is the former bed of the much larger lake that burst the dam in 1963. Most of the trees had already been claimed by early bird visitors seeking shade from the hot sun. Our watermelon and our supply of drinks were quickly submerged in an icy stream. Our car too was parked in the shallow stream, in the shade of two trees.

The lake seems to be quite deep and there are only a couple of areas where the sandy beach allows you to gently enter the very cold water at your own pace. Unfortunately, we did not discover this until later. We jumped into the lake at a point where there was no shelf. Worse yet, the bank tended to collapse into the water exactly when you got to the point when you were ready to decide whether or not to go into the water. During my second swim of the day I had the unpleasant experience of the sandy bank collapsing into the water with each step that I took to try to get out of the lake! The solution was to run up the embankment faster than it was disappearing into the deep.

The lake is posted with "No Swimming" signs. Probably these are connected with the fact that there are fast-flowing outlets for the water through tall concrete sluices with metal grates. Moreover, the water is cold, the lake is deep, it is difficult merely to wade due to the collapsing sandbanks, and the water streaming into the lake definitely has a strong current. Despite the many deterrents, quite a few people braved the water for brief swims.

The water has a milky green tone, nothing like the dirty appearance of the Ili River at the Singing Dunes that discouraged us from taking a dip there.

We were talking about leaving just when our driver mentioned that we had better go. The water level rises in the afternoon due to accelerating melting of snow in the mountains, and there was a risk that our car could not negotiate the streams. We drove up to the lookout area above the car park where a tall Orthodox Christian cross can be found. This gives a pleasant view of the lake below, the main stream that feeds the lake, the dam at the site of the 1963 washout and flood, and the beginning of the river that escapes from the sluice gates.

The author standing by the Orthodox cross
on a bluff overlooking Issyk Lake.

I was pleased when our driver, on his own initiative, started collecting up the unsightly empty bottles and other rubbish left by thoughtless visitors. On all of my travels it has been my intention to leave our site in better condition than we found it. Upon arrival, we police up the area for our own comfort, particularly broken bottles, and then take our own refuse with us when we leave. Here, however, we had stopped for only a few moments, and could easily have walked away from the mess. Everyone joined in the cleanup.

A better view by far was found after leaving the vicinity of the lake. There is a spot that overlooks the river and the valley below which extends downstream for many kilometers. We took our view at a spot where I thought someone had been buried, the site being marked by a flat round red granite memorial. The view is excellent. One can understand why someone who knew this area might want to be buried overlooking the gorgeous view. The reality, however, is more prosaic. This particular individual, like too many others in this country, had died in a car accident, probably in a horrible death after going over the cliff.

The viewing spot is high above the river. Far below the river now looks like a miniature version of reality. Off to the right, downstream, the river flows on as if endlessly, with steep valley walls on both sides. "Awesome" may be too strong a word. "Spectacular" probably should be reserved for America's Grand Canyon and a few other genuinely magnificent wonders of nature. However, I really doubt if anyone can look over the steep edge of this roadside spot and not immediately be filled with thoughts of the beauty and wonder of the world in which we live.

Further down the road we pulled off the road to pick some rather tart but tasty green apples. Half a kilometer more and we were filling up plastic shopping bags with wild apricots and a few wild raspberries. Someone mentioned that a British expert has claimed that apricots and apples originated in this part of the world. They have been found growing so high up in the mountains that they cannot have been introduced fruits. People from afar came to this part of the world and took the apricots and apples away for cultivation. The apricot trees were clinging to the steep mountainside, and we risked sliding down the embankment while gathering up our fruit.

The editor of The Almaty Herald never told me there was a word limit on the articles I was writing. Nevertheless, I had my own time constraints and an article of around 1,500 words seemed as much as most readers could put up with. This may be the reason why, in the above article, I did not write about our encounter with the archaeologist who oversaw the excavation of Kazakhstan's famous "Golden Man" (who equally likely was a Golden Princess).

The road we took to Issyk Lake passed by a large number of burial mounds, some on the left side of the road and far more on the right side. I had seen them on previous trips and had gained some information about them but there never was any evidence of a dig going on that would have inspired me to dig further as to what was going on.

Well, on this trip there was something going on at the mound closest to our destination. A yurta was standing on the site, as was an outhouse, and the yurta seemed to be open. Thus, on the way back from our visit to the lake and our picnic, I made an abrupt change of plans and asked the driver to turn on to the property so we could enquire. We then had the pleasure of meeting Dr. Kemel Akishev, now retired but formerly of the Kazakhstan Institute of Archeology.

The former dam had burst, so we were told, sending huge volumes of water cascading down the mountain and eventually unearthing one or more burial mounds. When a farmer told the police that his plow had turned up a gold item, the archeologists had been called in, the tomb excavated, and more than 4,000 pieces of gold were uncovered along with bones and remnants of clothing that were first declared to be those of a warrior but which, on further reflection, seem equally or more strongly consistent with having belonged to a female, likely a princess. The excavation we saw was of some other mound but it was exciting nevertheless. I have always wanted to participate in a "dig", with spade or dusting brush in hand, and this may have been the closest I will ever get to realizing that ambition.

The old archeologist was welcoming and all too easily recounted his part in the dramatic story of the finding of the Golden Man. Within the yurta he had spread out a display of many artifacts as well as a rather old photograph of himself with President Nazarbayev.

It being a Sunday and he being in retirement, we asked what propelled him to be on the site. It was not entirely dedication to his profession. With a smile on his face, he told us without a pause that it was his way of getting away from his wife.

We had purchased some watermelons on our way to Lake Issyk with the idea of perhaps eating one there and taking the other back to Almaty to round off a meal during the week. We were having such animated conversation, however, and Dr. Akishev was so amiable and eager to talk that we invited him to join us at the picnic table near the doorway of the yurta. It was a thoroughly enjoyable way to end what had been a very enjoyable day at Lake Issyk.

51
A TRIP TO ENGLAND

I had been planning to return to England anyway so I jumped at the chance to buy a cheap British Airways ticket when they celebrated the commencement of their new Sunday flight to Gatwick Airport. I strongly prefer Heathrow Airport, near to my home on the western outskirts of London but, well, money is money. The flight was about two-thirds filled, mostly with local residents including quite a few teenagers and younger children. They were not obvious 'New Kazakhs', and they were not obvious government people. They seemed quite ordinary. One of the signs of the times perhaps.

The flight also had many smokers some of whom violated the conditions of the flight by lighting up in the toilets. Near the end of the flight, when the smokers were getting increasingly desperate for a fag, the captain gave a stern warning that sounded as if arrests might follow at Gatwick if the problem persisted. There were even more violators on the return trip to Almaty but the warning was toned down, probably because the captain did not expect to be backed up by local law enforcement officers. The warnings, in English only, seemed ineffective. For most of the passengers on these flights, the captains might as well have been talking about the next movie for our entertainment. It would have been better, though perhaps still futile, to post notices in Russian and Kazakh in the toilets.

During part of my stay in England I was joined by friends from Kazakhstan. I took them to Windsor Castle for my umpteenth visit and then, for a change of pace, I took them to Windsor's leisure center. In addition to the usual swimming pool, it has a fun area with two very tall water slides, some water spouts and sprinklers, and other features including a wave-making machine. It helps to be young to be in this activity swimming pool but that is not necessary.

Ah, what was that which we overheard in our vicinity? The Russian language? Yes. And not only that, it was being spoken by Asians who turned out to be Kazakhs from Almaty! We quickly made the easy acquaintance that arises among strangers who find themselves in a foreign country but which might be so difficult in Almaty. The husband and wife were studying in England with two teenage daughters and a toddler. We avoided potentially awkward questions, such as how a mature family of five found themselves spending months in expensive England, but our curiosity was there all the time, looking for clues, for evidence of something interesting or damning.

In London, we engaged in many of those touring activities that are compulsory for people from this part of the world. We went to Madame Tussauds, the Tower of London, Harrods, and many other places. One of the newest compulsory activities is to take a ride on the London Eye, the big wheel with futuristic pods located across the River Thames from Parliament. It opened to the public on 9 March 2000, and was still a new and attractive tourist destination. It towers over much of London. We arrived at 5:00 p.m. and joined the long queue to purchase our tickets. After buying our tickets we needed to join the massive queue of those waiting to board the London Eye. This inspired one of my Kazakh friends to scout around to see how to beat the system. Queue beating -- really 'system beating' -- was part of the Soviet way of life and it persists in post-Soviet Kazakhstan.

Soon my friend returned to the ticket buying queue to report that she had found some Russians from Moscow who were well advanced in the main queue. They were very happily holding 'our places' for us. System beating survives in Russia too, and I guess that membership in the CIS brings with it the rights of international brotherhood and queue jumping. My friend was proud of her achievement; I was appalled. We were going to jump a large queue in England in broad daylight?

Having bought our tickets, we conversed with the Russians. My friends were about to jump the barrier but we then discovered that our tickets were for the 8:00 p.m. "flight" whereas the Russians held tickets for 6:00 o'clock. The Russians had the solution for us. They too had initially purchased 8 o'clock tickets but then gave the ticket seller a hard luck story about having a previous commitment for the evening. Like us, they did not want to idle away a couple of hours while waiting to board the London Eye. No sooner said then done -- off shot one of our Kazakhs to the ticket seller and, within five minutes, returned with our new 6 o'clock tickets.

The moment was nearly at hand for me to face my Waterloo. Could I bring myself to jump the queue to join the Russians or would I separate from my criminal friends and go to the end of the queue by myself? We now encountered another clever anti-queue-jumping measure of the London Eye people. Valid ticket holders still cannot board the London Eye if their tickets have not been manually marked by the queue minders at the very end of the queue. So, now we had to race to the end of the queue for this validation function before we could even consider jumping the queue. Fortunately for me, while we accomplished this task the Russians had boarded their pod and we had no choice but to go to the end of the queue. About an hour later we were soaring above London.

A few days later we returned to Almaty. The young girl who sat behind us on the plane had lived with an English family for two months while studying the English language at Chelmsford. I guessed she was about 14 or 15. She complained, in good humor, that the young children in the family didn't let her sleep as much as she wanted. They seemed to think of her both as a temporary member of the family and as a special guest. They served her breakfast in bed and constantly talked to her in English, which, of course, is exactly what had been intended by her intensive course in English. To me she seemed surprisingly mature. She spoke to her American neighbor on the flight, a consultant on a special mission to Kazakhstan, as a young adult, virtually his equal. She was so happy to be returning to Kazakhstan that her pleasure exuded from her. At the same time, she was already anxious to return to England. "Everything is so easy" she mentioned to us, the unspoken negative implication being that "everything" is still not so easy in Kazakhstan.

It was amazing to me how many Kazakhstani people were on the airplane. Not so long ago, it was exceptional to find more than a few non-foreigners on an international flight to or from the West, and most of these were government officials of the male gender. Now, we foreigners are the exceptions. There were around 220 people on the flight to Almaty of which about 20 were foreigners.

The Kazakhstanis on the airplane were in good humor, easily smiling at each other and engaging in conversation with strangers. On the bus to the airplane at Gatwick Airport, some ethnic Kazakhs -- strangers until that moment -- were questioning each other, trying to identify a common relative in Uralsk. One of my companions had one year ago made the observation that Kazakhstani citizens, while travelling abroad, take on a slightly different personality. Those who spend some time outside the country start to smile more broadly and more easily, to converse with strangers, and generally to drop their guard. But as soon as the plane lands in Almaty they resume a more tight-lipped composure. It was possible to drop one's guard and relax on a foreign trip. Here, back at home, these traits seem not to be rewarded. Suspicion and threat are seen to be everywhere. Abroad, life must have seemed so uncomplicated.

On the return flight we were joined by a 16-strong Kazakh band plus eight dancers who had participated in a folk music festival in Freiburg, Switzerland. This was the Karaganda National Orchestra Named after Tatteambet (a famous balladeer). They had performed three times a day for 10 days, apparently to high praise. It seems that Kazakh music and performances are much appreciated in Switzerland. This is easy to imagine. How many other countries can still mount a musical program with authentic local costumes, with strange musical instruments that yield more music per string than most people can imagine, and with such enthusiastic dancing. These musicians were very happy. They had achieved international acclaim. They had seen something of the West, and they were proud to be Kazakhs.

When the airplane touched down in Almaty, the musicians led the excited applause in which many others participated. This was a happy landing and a happy homecoming. Here were local people who were proud to have represented their country abroad, and who were happy to be returning to their own country.

The victorious return to Kazakhstan soon soured, however. As the members of the band gathered outside the arrival reception hall at Almaty Airport some local official roughly ordered them to move inside. One member of the band was overheard to mutter under his breath: "It's beginning again." We imagined that the 200 or so citizens of Kazakhstan who had briefly enjoyed their time in the West were in course of a quick transformation back into their former selves -- undemonstrative in public and incapable of being easily read. Welcome home!

52
A TRIP TO BUTAKOVKA WATERFALL

On May 9, 2001, Victory Day (which used to be Victory over Germany Day but time and commercial interests heal many wounds), I finally made it to what some people call Butakovka Waterfall. I am not sure it has its own proper name but the village close to the entrance of the park where the waterfall is located is Butakovka so at least this name gives it a geographical locale.

I first tried to go to the waterfall in the summer of 1993. A small group of us took the road out of town in the direction of Medeo but turned off to the left toward Butakovka village. We continued on to the end of the road, passing some Soviet era structures that looked like abandoned dormitories. The road stops a little further on at a stream that our cars could not ford, and we crossed over a rustic/crude footbridge similar to the one now in place. From there we hiked along the path of the river until we came upon a strange young woman with a high squeaky voice and her hair done up in dreadlocks who sold simple pancakes and homemade juices to hikers who passed her way. She informed us that she had abandoned society and preferred to live in her large 2-room army tent in which one room was given over to a large table and about a dozen seats for the visitors. Outside some upturned logs provided extra seating. Every so often she ran out of kerosene for her fire. She then hiked to the village and carried back the heavy can with any other supplies she needed.

Welcoming Tent in the region of Budaovka Falls.

I believe that this woman was situated at the spot just below which, on a level stretch closer to the river, there is now to be found a picnic table and two fixed benches for about 10 people. In 1993 our group did not progress far beyond this spot. Some Western hikers on their way down from the waterfall reported that it would take at least 45 minutes more to reach the waterfall, and that didn't leave sufficient time for two members of our group to catch their flight to Moscow. In the intervening years I have taken many other excursions and sight-seeing expeditions but somehow I never made it back to the waterfall.

We encountered snow on a few occasions and it was worth remembering that we were getting higher even than the Chimbulak ski area. When we were in sight of the waterfall there was a snowfield perhaps 20 meters wide that we had to slip and slide across.

It takes a quite hearty type of person to make it up to the waterfall. Our group of 14 people soon became a scattered line of people, with the stragglers falling further and further behind. However, everyone made it to the top.

Being somewhat difficult to reach, the waterfall had only a few visitors on this moderately warm day. However, one group was completing their visit when we arrived, and another group showed up about an hour later to find that yet another group was already in occupation but the latter soon started their descent.

In 1993, access to Butakovka waterfall was unrestricted. Now, the waterfall is part of Ili-Alatau National Park and a small hut with a road gate needs to be passed in order to enter the park. The charge is Tg. 300 per car or Tg. 100 per person. Since we had four people in the back seat and me in the front with the driver, this was a no brainer issue, and we asked the driver to continue on for a few more kilometers. Later we had reason to regret that our drivers halted only four kilometers into the park. This left us with a very substantial hike on the paved road just to get into the wilderness whereas we could have driven much further. We also made the mistake of not asking to be picked up by the same taxi drivers at a designated time. These radio taxis charged us only Tg. 400 per car for the one-way trip, and there were some among us who, hours later, while on the long trek back to the main Medeo-Almaty road, would have paid Tg. 4,000 for a taxi.

We took many precautions to avoid ticks that can transmit encephalitis. This is a horrible diseased that has claimed several lives already this summer in Kazakhstan but mainly in areas close to Russia. Opinions varied as to whether the ticks lurk in the grass or fall out of the trees. The prevailing opinion was that we should avoid sitting on the grass. Most of us had long-legged trousers which we tucked into our socks, long-sleeved shirts with turned-up collars to protect the upper body, and hats to cover the head, all of which served to protect us from the sun as well. Even so, there were frequent body checks and quite a few of us felt totally persuaded at increasingly frequent intervals that a dreaded tick had landed on them. I have the benefit of being vaccinated against encephalitis, but that is no reason to be careless.

The waterfall is high, not very wide and its water is quite cold. We had empty drinking bottles which we held up for refills. At the base, there is a splash area where we stood to admire the falls and the view. Looking back to the trail, we could see the snow that has survived the increasing heat of the summer and the lengthening of the days.

Budakovka Waterfalls.

Having taken our safety precautions, we were appalled as we retraced our way down the mountain to see so many local residents and foreigners playing on the grass with bare feet and exposing plenty of skin to the sun and to the ticks.

A sign of modern affluent times and the change from 1993 is that we encountered five or more motorcycles during our hike. These were lightweight, all-terrain vehicles and the aim of their operators seemed to be to find the steepest slopes up which they could charge. This entailed a fair amount of fumes, a lot of noise, and quite a bit of dust and dirt thrown up in the air. One of bikers eyed our picnic site for a long time and then, while some of us were eating, proceeded to zip up the slope immediately behind us, leaving us in his dust and wondering angrily where he learned his manners.

On our homeward journey, while we rested at the entry gate to await the stragglers and some taxis, the women guards in the hut were obviously having a very happy time celebrating Victory Day. They spotted us drinking from our plastic water bottles. They became quite animated and I thought they were saying that we shouldn't be drinking that water. However, they were trying to shame us for not drinking vodka to celebrate victory in the Patriotic War. We guessed that, like many local residents, they celebrate more than the end of the war during the course of a year.

Rather spontaneously, I invited everyone to come to my apartment where we could order up some pizzas. All of us were hungry from our exertion and no one dissented at the proposal. So about a dozen of us sat on the floor of my apartment's large balcony, relaxed, and refreshed ourselves after an exhilarating and memorable day in the mountains.

Victory Day Parade, 9 May 1995,
fifty years after the end of the war in Europe.

53
THE ALMATY METRO

I was never very good at collecting stamps or coins, not that I didn't try. It was just that my older brother always seemed to be so far ahead of me that it was discouraging. There was one occasion, however, when I took some comfort in his discomfort. Our great-uncle Aaron possessed a single gold coin, having failed to turn it in after President Roosevelt required gold coins to be exchanged for paper money in 1933. Knowing my brother's prowess in collecting coins, our great-uncle gave it to Charles. Was I green! But there was only one coin. So where was my comfort? Turned out that treasured and illegal gold coin was a virtually worthless counterfeit.

In any event, I later in life discovered that my forte is in accumulation, not collecting. I have stacks, boxes, and piles of all sorts of things. As a matter of fact, I eventually had to have a second garden shed installed just to store some of my lifetime accumulations. Treasures of my youth. Things that were once integral to the daily lives of my now grown up children. Notes, newspaper clippings and writings for projects that may yet turn into an activity for me, maybe even profit. Army uniform and duffle bag that I was told to keep after being discharged from the army in the 1960s "just in case you are called up again". My first metal skis (Head 360s). A child's antique homemade wooden crutch picked up years ago in Vermont.

When pressed to disclose a collection, my automatic response for some years has been to reply "urban rapid transit systems" – Metros, subways, elevated trains.

I can't be entirely sure when I first went on a tube but it may have been that of Boston's Metropolitan Transit Authority, the MTA made famous by the 1959 hit recording by the Kingston Trio, you know the one, where a guy named Charlie is trapped in the system. "Did he every return? No, he never returned." Boston has the oldest underground transportation system in North America, having placed its first streetcars under the ground in 1897.

A year-long stay in Europe after graduating from law school did wonders for my collection. I took a French language course in Paris and naturally made extensive use of its Métro, which included some old carriages whose doors slammed abruptly shut but also the new rubber-wheeled, non-squeaky line under the Avenue Champs Elysées which seemed so utterly modern.

An Easter holiday in Spain brought me the subways in Madrid and Barcelona. I don't have many memories of the Metro de Madrid but Barcelona's was unforgettable. The carriages on the Barcelona Metro looked like they had been designed by manufacturers of stately horse-drawn carriages such as those used by the Queen of England on state occasions. I can't remember now if those lines that swept down from each end of the carriage were functional as straps that held the carriages and acted as shock absorbers or if they were simply glued-on excess baggage that the designer added for effect.

At the end of the school year in Paris, while awaiting exam results, I hitch hiked to Berlin for a first visit, crossing over into East Berlin on an elevated portion of the S-Bahn (over ground railway) but also taking the U-Bahn (the underground metro) while touring the city.

Upon my return to Paris, I joined two colleagues for a camping trip in a Volkswagen Beetle through the Iron Curtain countries and deep into the Soviet Union. This gave me the famous Moscow Metro with its deep stations, long escalators, heavy use of marble and lots of artwork. I also picked up the Saint Petersburg Metro (then

Leningrad Metro), the deepest in the world, as we exited the USSR via Finland.

Shortly after Europe, I collected the New York subway while working as a lawyer in Manhattan for seven years. During the workweek I regularly rode on the Lexington Avenue line to Wall Street. That was before the advent of air conditioning. Summers could be horrible standing there in the heat and the aroma of the great unwashed, with sweat trickling down the back and collecting at the belt line. Somehow it never occurred to people back then to ride in the comfort of shorts and then change into a suit in the office.

I have had relatives in the Washington, D.C. area for years and so, not long after that city's Metro became operational in 1975, I had a ride on it, being duly impressed with the stations' high ceilings and set back, anti-graffiti walls. It hasn't fared well over the years, however, and it is the butt of many jokes, abusive remarks and political cartoons.

I might have added the London underground to my collection in 1965 because I wanted to join throngs of others crossing from Paris to London for Winston Churchill's funeral. However, my passport was tied up with Iron Curtain countries and I had to weigh the possibility of sacrificing weeks of exciting travel in strange places against a couple of days in England for a one-time funeral. London had to wait until a 1968 trip.

A few years ago I paid a visit to some relatives in San Francisco and took the chance to ride on all the forms of public transport, including BART as well as the famous cable cars.

Finally, the Almaty Metro. I first learned about the Almaty Metro in 1993 while staying at the Alma-Ata Hotel, close to the Opera. It was summer and, in the absence of air conditioning, it was necessary to keep the windows open. That was unfortunate because throughout the night my sleep was disturbed by almighty crashing and banging as loads of rubble emerged from the depths and dumped into a metal storage hopper. Further crashing and banging then occurred when a truck arrived to be filled with rubble tumbling down a metal chute.

I later learned that there already was a very long history of construction of the project, and I might then have been told for the first time that, during Soviet times, the object of labor was not to complete a project but to keep a job. This came home to me later when I moved into an apartment up in Samal II and could see and hear the construction activity at the Lenin Museum. Lenin Museum? Yes, the purpose eventually changed and you probably know the building by its current name, the Presidential Palace. On a Sunday morning, one could see welders high up on the girders endlessly welding. Eventually, the City Architect called for help from the foreign construction engineers over at the Marco Polo Hotel (for which read Hyatt, then read Rahat), and after that it seemed as though much more of the activity was end-result oriented.

Anyway, I missed the subway's opening in Almaty but in July 2012, I finally got my rides. Great subway. Clean, well managed, and not too expensive. Compares well with some of the best in the world.

I was quite proud of my collection until I recently learned that there are more than 160 major metropolitan transit systems in the world, many of them with underground portions. Yikes, too many rapid transit systems, not enough time!

54

CHARYN CANYON AND
A HAPPY MOMENT

It is a bit difficult to select the single happiest moment in a long lifetime of what has been a pretty good and pleasing life with lots of ups and not so many downs. I suppose, therefore, at the outset that it is well to be a bit specific about what I mean by the happiest moment. What I have in mind is a really joyful experience that stands out which, just to think about it, brings back a smile of delight. In other words, I am mainly not talking about a day-long experience and not even an experience with long-lasting consequences but, rather, about some moment or some duration of moments during which one was really transported out of oneself and was thrilled.

That occasion for me was in the spring of 1999. I had been working in Almaty, Kazakhstan, for most of the past seven years and, like many other expatriates, I sometimes felt rather trapped in the city. During the winter months, it was possible to avoid cabin fever by going up into the mountains for skiing, and for the lunch and society that accompanied it. And I had exploited that to the full. But during non-skiing months, one really felt confined in Almaty. I didn't drive a car while in Almaty, having the use of the company car during the business week and for work-related activities on the weekends. I rarely imposed on our drivers on the weekends out of respect for their need and desire to be with their families and/or to do their own personal things.

Lots of expatriates felt a keen need to get away from Almaty but for them this usually meant getting to the West or at least to Moscow (four hours away by air). I tried to break out of this mould by organizing trips into the countryside using my personal driver, Giorgi. He seemed to have been everywhere in Kazakhstan and was well acquainted with all the touristic spots.

On one occasion, we organized a day outing which included seven of us plus Giorgi. Two of us were expatriates, me and a German fellow, being the boyfriend of one of the ladies in our group. This was in May of 1999.

Our destination was Charyn Canyon – the local Grand Canyon – which, being located 200 kilometres east of Almaty, close to the Chinese border, had caused us to start our day rather early. We rode for a long time and then Giorgi pulled the car off the road at a certain point. I don't recall that it was marked and it seemed that there was no road for us to follow. Eventually, however, we came to a stop at the rim of the canyon. I noticed for the first time that Giorgi had brought along a pistol. It had been hidden under some clothing on top of the divider unit between the two front seats. Did he know something that we didn't about the dangers of roaming around the countryside?

We dismounted and proceeded to clamber far down into the canyon. We then hiked past toppled pillars of stone that had been carved away from the cliffs by erosion, and came to the fast-flowing river. It was clear that this was a popular destination for sightseers. Some government agency had installed wooden tables with benches plus two outhouses. Civilization encroached! Off to the right we spotted a couple of pup tents.

The river was not only fast running, it was cascading and it was cold. This was melt off snow from the mountains. That didn't stop the most trepid of our group from getting in the water. But they had to cling on to low hanging tree branches for dear life out of fear of being swept away.

To our left was a simple device for transporting people across the wide river. It consisted of a thick cable holding a tray plus a second cable that the rider used to pull himself or herself across the river. The device sagged the further out the rider went until it nearly dipped into the raging water. I didn't see any warning signs or instructions for use, and I didn't spot any safety net downstream to catch anyone unlucky enough to fall off the contraception. Needless to say, we didn't cross the river though we did see daredevils taking the ride.

Our trip was cut a bit short when it started to rain. We raced up the cliff to get to our car. Fortunately, the rain paused long enough for us to eat our picnic lunch. The rain resumed and we set off for home.

Just as the rain stopped again, we came upon several local people – "peasants" would not be inaccurate as a description but I don't know if they regarded themselves as such. They had darkened skin, the dark, leathery tan of people who spend much of their lives in the open air. They were standing by the side of the road with large plastic trays on the ground in front of them containing all kinds of fish – some small and some rather large, all sorted out.

Initially we drove past them but then the conversation started within our car that it would be nice to buy some freshly caught fish. And so, at our request, Giorgi turned the car around and we drove back to the roadside vendors. As we stepped out of the car, the strong wind caught us and we sensed that the rain would soon start again. Our spirits were high. The vendors were ecstatic and so were we. Their very high spirits as they sought to hawk their wares to us were infectious and we soon found ourselves grinning. Maybe we were the only customers they had that day. I couldn't stop beaming and I could see that all the others in our group were in the same condition, and so were the vendors.

The enthusiastic roadside fish sellers.

One of the local ladies, however, was a bit sour, and came up to me and asked in the Kazakh language in a demanding way how it was that I knew Kazakh people. I guess she couldn't believe that an obvious foreigner would be out in the countryside with ethnic Kazakhs and having a nice day with them. Anyway, a reply was given to her by one of my friends and she retreated back into the crowd.

Well, that was it – one of the happiest moments of my life. I felt entirely transported out of myself and fully given over to a rapturous feeling of joy. And I was not alone. All of us had this silly grin on our faces, much as if we had encountered aliens who had made us giddy from the experience.

That wasn't the end of the story. We all bought fish, including Giorgi, and happily returned to Almaty.

ACKNOWLEDGEMENTS

When I was 17 or perhaps 18 years old and in high school in Watertown, South Dakota, I was required to write a rather long -- or so it seemed at the time -- research paper on a topic of my choice. Likely this was for history class. I chose to write about Marco Polo and his travels to China, and I enjoyed very much reading everything about him that I could locate. However, when it came to writing my own paper, I quickly realized that I had nothing to say that was authentically from me. I could copy or rephrase material out of books, encyclopedias, and magazines. I could change the order and mix the materials up so that it would be more difficult for others to find the source of my plagiarism. I could try to impose my own organization on what other people had written but there still was no "me" in what I was trying to write.

I procrastinated, delayed, stalled, and made excuses for not starting my paper, the due date for which was rapidly approaching. Finally, I could wait no longer and I got out the typewriter and put in the paper. Nothing happened. Time passed and more nothing happened. I ruined several sheets of paper with false starts. Still nothing happened. An overwhelming sense of failure started to envelop me. I wondered how it was possible that other students had something to say while I, having done all my research and having prepared so well, still had nothing to say of my own. I have never felt so defeated in all my life as when I tried to write that paper. Nearly in tears, I turned to my mother for guidance. While I remember my dilemma very well, I do not remember exactly my mother's words. But I think she got me past my writer's cramp by persuading me to skip the first paragraph of the paper and to just starting writing somewhere, anywhere, in the paper. With her guidance, I learned a ploy that has been of service to me ever since, and the words have been spewing out in abundance. Don't worry about a perfect first sentence. Just start writing somewhere, making up the building blocks of whatever it is you are writing. Eventually the opening paragraph and the conclusion will fall into place as will the body of the document.

So, although it has been a long time in coming and although I still do not regard myself as a "natural" writer, I would like to take this opportunity to acknowledge the help of my mother a long time ago to develop my writing skills and for helping me to find the "me" to put into whatever it is that I am writing.

Finally, I wish to thank my sisters, Peg O'Hara and Audrey Zimmerle, for their thoughtful suggestions for improving the book and for their very thorough proofreading of it, proving, as Peg said, that "Every writer needs a proofreader."

Most of the articles in this book were originally published in the long-defunct *The Almaty Herald* weekly, English-language newspaper. The following table identifies when those articles were published.

1	Hey, Where Am I?	30 January 1997
2	The Condor Has Landed!	6 November 1997
3	The American Embassy Business Roundtable	4 December 1996
4	Hard Times in Kazakhstan	First publication
5	The Market Economy	29 May 1997
6	Direct Marketing	29 May 1997
7	How to Read an Invitation	22 May 1997
8	Bank Accounts	29 May 1997
9	Our Plastic Friend	3 July 1997
10	Much Ado Versus Nothing	14 August 1997
11	A Day of Sledding	29 May 1997
12	Eating Out in Times Past	Updated 5 February 1999
13	Telephone Manners	15 January 1998
14	Take the Load Off Your Feet	9 January 1997
15	Hellos, Goodbyes and Congratulations	13 February 1997
16	Strange Strangers	6 February 1997
17	Fringe Advertising	18 May 1999
18	Kazakhstan's National Pastime	26 December 1996
19	The Universal History of Paper	10 April 1997
20	East Meets West Over the Dinner Table	24 April 1997
21	English Penetration	18 September 1997
22	English as She is Spoken	12 February 1998
23	The Perils of the Open Road	27 November 1997
24	Consumerism in Kazakhstan	First publication
25	Cranes, Taxis and Expensive Cars	27 January 1999
26	Paper Weight	24 July 1997
27	Take in a Wedding	7 May 1998
28	The Dangers of Drink	26 February 1998

29	Spotlight on Light Bulbs	12 December 1996
30	Rules of the Road	17 April 1997
31	Tripping the Light Fantastic	16 October 1997
32	Taxi! Taxi!	20 March 1997
33	Upside Down, Inside Out, and Back to Front	8 October 1998
34	In Praise of Apartment Balconies	6 March 1997
35	Lucky Tickets	20 April 1999
36	Close Scrapes	25 February 1999
37	The Expatriate Community	22 January 1998
38	The Goodbye Party	15 May 1997
39	Good News Report	8 May 1997
40	Did the Soviet Union Trip on its Stairs?	13 March 1997
41	Femininity in Almaty	13 June 1997
42	The Way I See Things	21 August 1997
43	Skiing at Chimbulak	First publication
44	A Day at Chimbulak	First publication
45	A Daytrip to Kapchagai	22 July 1999
46	A Daytrip to Ili-Alatau National Park	29 July 1999
47	A Wet Weekend at Issyk Kul	12 August 1999
48	A Trip to Big Buddha and Kapchagai	22 June 2000
49	A Trip to the Singing Dunes	3 August 2000
50	A Trip to Issyk Lake	10 August 2000
51	A Trip to England	September 2000
52	A trip to Butakova WaterFall	17-24 May 2001
53	The Almaty Metro	First publication
54	Charyn Canyon and a Happy Moment	First publication

Printed in the United States
By Bookmasters